MAMA'S BLACK CHILD

A Veteran's Memoir

By J. Paul Montgomery

MAMA'S BLACK CHILD
A Veteran's Memoir

Copyright 2022 by Julius Paul Montgomery

All rights reserved

Printed in the United States

Printed and distributed by: 3 Plus Creative Media

Montgomery, Julius Paul. 1941 - MAMA'S BLACK CHILD
A Veteran's Memoir / J. Paul Montgomery

ISBN: 979-8-218-05464-9

PREFACE

At the tender age of eleven years, I knew that I was not compatible with my community or my family. The available careers dangles before this impressionable black boy were construction worker, schoolteacher, or maybe working in the orange grove. My qualms about becoming a construction worker centered on working for my older brother. I had misgivings about going to college to become a schoolteacher (which was my mother's wish). If I became a grove worker, I would have to work for a white man with an education probably inferior to my own.

At that age, if I could have selected a career for myself, I would have been an airplane pilot. However, when I was eleven, little black boys were not allowed to become airplane pilots. In my community, I knew only a few people who could be called successful; that is, if success is defined as succeeding fully or in accordance with one's own desires. That is how I determine success. However, with the black mentality usually subordinate to the white man's wishes, sometimes blacks were confused about their "success.' If they were in their so-called station in life, perhaps kept there by subtle or not-so-subtle force, they mistakenly thought they were successful. Using my definition of success, those men in my community who were successful have left an indelible mark on my life.

One such man was my father. Not wanting to work for my older brother and not being able to accept any of the other careers available to me, I enlisted in the U.S. Army. In the army, everyone started on the same foot, and the same authority governed everybody. In other words, I felt that with everybody marching to the same music, I could become a success, and if for some reason I failed, I had no one to blame but myself. I knew there were some prejudices in the army, and I also knew that if I were given half a chance to succeed, I would. In this country, one should never have to say, "For lack of a chance, I was not successful." But when we are truly honest, we all know there are still communities in this country that offer little or no chance. Possibly, there are communities with lesser chance than what my community offered some thirty-two years ago.

This book is about experiences and people that framed my life and the lives of others who are black and lived in similar communities over the years. It is about those things that we did in order to make our lives better. I will talk about life prior to my army career, and about those who were not as lucky as me.

I feel that after you have read this book, you will agree that if our experiences have not made life better for ourselves, our communities or our race, then our efforts can be rendered useless when compared to the greater form of a more progressive and productive culture, community, or society. That is, if progressiveness is defined as to not be bound by authoritarianism or orthodoxy or traditional forms.

This book will let you be the judge, if you can draw from events as the take place in our lives over these years as to what purpose the greater society says we have served. Whatever society says our purpose has been, there are those moments of our past, and I am sure in our future, that society will not be able to judge, for they can only be experienced. They encompass fear, devastation, anger, rage, paralysis, and slaughter.

Table of Contents

PREFACE iii
Chapter 1: What Will I Be When I Grow Up? 1
Chapter 2: Mama's Black Child 11
Chapter 3: No Angels 17
Chapter 4: An Escape 23
Chapter 5: Jackson, A New Beginning 32
Chapter 6: A Transformation 38
Chapter 7: Doing Manly Things 45
Chapter 8: Christmas Of 1959 49
Chapter 9: Expectations & Pain 72
Chapter 10: Limitations 89
Chapter 11: My Knee And Ankle 96
Chapter 12: Oahu, Hawaii 114
Chapter 13: The Big Island, Hawaii 123
Chapter 14: Thailand 127
Chapter 15: Home 131
Chapter 16: Germany 139
Chapter 17: Home Again 147
Chapter 18: Vietnam 151
Chapter 19: Fort Meade, Maryland 160
Chapter 20: Korea 162
Chapter 21: Fort Hood, Texas 169
Chapter 22: Recruiting Duties 176
Chapter 23: Germany Again 185
Chapter 24: Retirement 189
Chapter 25: Civilian Recruiter (GS7 Recruiting Specialist) 194
Chapter 26: Churches Organized To Assist (Cota) 199

Chapter 27:Hospitalization 203
APPENDIX 206
HERO'S IN SCHOOLS 211
ABOUT THE AUTHOR 222

Chapter 1

What Will I Be When I Grow Up?

It was an afternoon in early June 1952. School was turning out for the summer and our community of Clermont, Florida, was experiencing an exciting first. My older sister Deloris and several other students from our community were graduating from high school. On this afternoon, my mother, my five brothers, my baby sister, and I waited eagerly on the front porch to congratulate my sister. As we waited, our conversation was about careers.

My mother spoke of one of the boy's new opportunities. "Tom can be a foreman in the groves, now that he has his diploma. "I strongly objected to my mother's aspirations for Tom and said, "Once I am out of high school, I am going to become an airplane pilot. "My mother countered with, "Boy, you know you are colored" and began to explain to me that the United States of America had not yet made a room to train black boys to become airplane pilots. I found this unacceptable. It made me feel as if I was being physically raped. My mother continued, "You will have to work in the orange groves, just like every other colored person, or not eat!"

Deep down I knew I would not work in the groves for any extended period, possibly for weekend spending money or during Christmas break to buy presents, but for the time I had enough talk about careers. I mentally left my mother to play a mind game with myself.

Mind games were my greatest pastime, and at eleven years old, I seldom played with any of my five brothers or anyone else for that matter because questions always came up, and I found most answers unacceptable. My older brother James (13) and I were totally incompatible. His greatest concern was accepted. I wanted to be respected. In my mind, I was able to any barrier with all the rights answers and could even become an airplane pilot.

However, on the day that gave our community it first graduating class, I needed a real answer as to why little black boys could not grow up to be airplane pilots, and the only method I had was through the mind games I played with myself.

My first question to myself was, *who had airplanes?* My answers was the U.S. Army did. *Who did I know that was in U.S. Army?* No one, but I knew Arthur. Arthur was one of my classmates. Some say he was the smartest in the class; however, I knew better and would one day prove different. In any case, Arthur was my only hope for an answer to my question. Arthur's father, Mr. Henry Dean, was a sergeant in the army, and I had to get an answer from him or through him. *Could blacks be airplane pilots in the U.S. Army?*

Arthur would be playing in the big field across from his house or playing basketball at the school the next day, now that school was out. The only problem I had at this point was mustering enough nerve to talk to Arthur. After all, he was the smart kid, and I was the kid who stayed to himself all the time. Arthur was an exceptional athlete, but I had two left feet. We had nothing in common; however, I felt I was just as smart. To accomplish my objective, I would use a third person who was also an athlete. Aaron was a super athlete but was slow academically. I had often helped Aaron with his homework, and he was one of the few kids in my community I played with. My strategy was to start an argument with Aaron about Mr. Dean and ask Arthur to verify my point. My argument would be that Mr. Dean was an air-plane pilot. Aaron would have to disagree, and we would call Arthur to verify. It would make little difference as to how the argument would be verified; the following question would be, did he know any other blacks who were airplane pilots? The following day, I put my game to the test and was successful. Mr. Dean was not an airplane pilot but rather a radio repairman; however, Arthur knew of Colonel Davis, who was an airplane pilot, and in command of a squadron with all colored pilots assigned to him. These pilots had received their training from an all-black school in Alabama. This was good enough for me. Blacks could fly airplanes, and the army was the place where this was a reality. For sure, I would join the U.S. Army. By this time in our nation's history, the air force was being born. However, to me there was no other branch of the armed forces except the army because it was my understanding that the army gave black men the opportunity to fly airplanes. I would enlist as soon as I became of age.

After making the decision to enlist, though it would be six years before I would be old enough, life began to change for me. I knew what I would do in life, and for this reason, I felt that someday I too would be somebody respected. I think because I knew what I would do, and talked about it most of the time, or because my father had already started a family home-building business, my mother, father, and older brothers and sisters became somewhat repressive. They would make statements such as, "How is it possible for you to become a soldier when you can't take orders?" or "You said you could not work in the groves. How would you be able to make it in the army, where everybody ordered you around?

"I think my family failed to understand my objective in life, and at the age of eleven, I was not prepared to explain. Nor could I accept that my father's business could one day be successful enough to employ my five brothers and me. Besides, I didn't think I could have ever worked under my older brother, which I am sure I would have had to do if I had not planned for an army enlistment upon my coming of age. At the time, my father's business barely kept him in work.

My mother was working in the orange groves on a daily basis, and my brother James worked in a kitchen at the local white folk's hotel. During the summer months, we all worked in the groves with my mother.

My summer experiences are some I will never forget. The days would start about 5 a.m., gathering firewood for the old wood-burning stove so my mother or older sister could cook biscuits for breakfast and also for lunch in the orange grove. After breakfast, we would all catch the crew truck for the grove. Normally, our ride on the crew truck would be about an hour, and after arriving, we would wait for the dew to dry off the trees.

It was somewhat hazardous to pick oranges while the trees were still wet; one could catch a death of a cold. Or, the poisons that were used to spray the trees to keep the fruit flies down would stick to your skin and cause irritation, or even death. My cousin Edroy was poisoned, and to this day, he is unable to walk. Nor can he support his family on his workmen's compensation insurance.

I hated the groves and the white bosses who were in charge. It was hard for me to understand why my mother could not accept my feelings. I was willing to take orders, but I could not accept a dead-end career. I was also willing to work, but not under these bad and hazardous conditions. I could even get used to working for a white man, but only if white men would agree to work for black men. To me, it was easy enough to understand wanting to be respected; however, for the blacks within my community, respect was a one-way street that belonged to whites only!

After several summers of working in the groves, I began to work for my father during the months after school closed for the summer. Possibly, this was because my father's business was growing, or possibly it was because my mother knew I did not respect white men.

My father had several maintenance contracts. One such contract was the upkeep of an all-white apartment complex. My job was spot painting. In doing my job, I had very close contact with the white tenants and with one family in particular: Mr. and Mrs. Mims from South Georgia. My father was also of South Georgia descent. Mr. Mims and my father seemed to have a lot in common.

Both Mr. and Mrs. Mims quizzed me almost daily, whenever they got the chance. Most questions concerned the bible; however, we did discuss other subject matters. One day, Mrs. Mims asked: "Paul, how did you get to be so smart, being a colored boy? You are too smart to be colored. Not that I don't think coloreds could be smart."

I came to resent those statements after I learned her meaning; however, at that time I considered her statements a compliment. Mr. and Mrs. Mims became a good part of my life while I was growing up in the little town of Clermont, and even after I was in the U.S. Army. After a while, though, I think I outgrew them and stopped visiting.

The other whites that I remember having an effect on my childhood life were the county nurse, the icemen, the grove foremen, the building supply deliverymen, and salesmen from the building supply. In most cases, Mr. and Mrs. Mims being an exception, I could never leave the presence of white persons soon enough. I felt there was so little I could do to protect myself if one wanted to hurt me. It was almost as if I was the prey, and they were the predators, even with those who I felt were good persons; I did not trust them.

My school nurse came to our school only during immunization time; however, she seemed to give a complete physical and always a note to take home to my mother. Once, Mrs. O'Brian examined me and gave me a subsequent note for my mother that included instructions on the care of ground itch. My mother refused to respond to the <note, which led to my principal, Mr. Whitehurst, making a visit to our home.

At this particular visit, we were enjoying beans and rice for supper, and for whatever reason he dared to make a comment concerning an unbalanced diet and the possibility that this was the reason for the condition of my foot. My mother asked the principal to leave and blamed me for him coming into our home. My foot healed from this very common Florida fungus with little or no outside help except the coming of winter. The following year, the process would repeat itself, and life would go on in this small colored community of central Florida.

The most lasting experience having to deal with white folk was with the icemen, Troy and Red. It was Red who frightened me the most. Red was about six feet four inches tall, with freckles and red hair. I always thought him to be a Klansman, and still think possibly he was. Whenever I saw him, I ran for the nearest hiding place, but I think he always saw me. He would have his ice tool in his hand and would shake it toward my hiding place. The ice tool had sharp hooks at each end, and was bent in a way to hook into a block of ice to be carried for short distances. I just knew, for sure, one day he would catch me, hook me like he would fifty pounds of ice, and carry me away.

Whenever I was in the house and saw any white man, I would hide under the bed. It had only been a few years before, when I was about seven, that the local Sheriff had killed two of our neighbors. The KKK had also burned several crosses in our community. The sheriff and Klansman claimed four colored men had raped a young white woman from the Bay Lake community, twelve miles west of Clermont. During those times, the National Guard was called. I was told they were there to protect the colored community, but for me it was a terrifying experience. They had real guns, and they were all white. I did not feel protected.

This whole incident was called the Greenlee case, named after the youngest of the four colored men accused of raping the Bay Lake white woman. The Greenlee case became a statement to the young black men of central Florida and was heard loud and clear. My question was, *why did the National Guard not have black men? After all, was this not the same army that allowed black men to become airplane pilots?* It was explained to me, yes, this was the same army; however, black men were not permitted to serve with white men, even in the army where black men could become airplane pilots. This caused me some problems, but I still wanted to become a pilot. I accepted the explanation. My mother had always protected my five brothers and me in her own way. I was instructed to stay away from white women and to always say "sir" to white men, and to not to look any white folk in the eye when they were talking to me. Those were the rules we lived by when dealing with the problem, or our mother would whip us for disrespect.

Troy, the second iceman, had several daughters who helped on his route from time to time. The girls were very beautiful and flirtatious. Occasionally, I would see one of Troy's girls in the woods near our house with various white men, and they were not picking berries. Due to my mother's continuing counseling, whenever the girls accompanied their father on his ice delivery, I would hide and admire the girls from a distance to protect myself, mostly from the penalty that my mother would inflict on me. Troy himself seemed to be an okay man trying to make a living for his family.

From as long as I could remember, my mother was up at 5 a.m. making biscuits and grits, with bacon and sausage from the smokehouse. By the time I was ready to go to school, my mother would have already caught the crew truck for the orange grove.

The crew truck was a rolling death trap. Several of our neighbors had already been killed while riding a crew truck to the picking field and groves, including my mother's younger sister. But during those times, this seemed to be the only way for black folk to maintain an adequate lifestyle, especially when there were twelve mouths to feed. However, it was not for me, and I was sure I would beat this system.

In one way, the system was not all bad. During the late 1940s and early 1950s, few if any banks made loans to the black community. Yet, we had needs for extra money: at the beginning of the school year to buy school clothing; at Christmas time; and to buy big ticket items such as stoves, ice boxes, and other furnishings for the household. When these needs arose, my mother would take the entire family to the grove (with the exception of my father, who had started his own home-repair business but was not making enough money to take care of our family).

Through these means, we were able to double our income and buy whatever we needed, including a family car. In most cases, the car would be bought from a private owner, possibly the boss man or someone the boss man knew. Sometimes, we would even triple our income.

My older sisters and brothers were hard workers and accepted this way of life. In most cases, I was just along for the ride, and the extra whippings I got were for not doing my part and not doing all the little things that little black children did to gain the respect of the white boss.

Times were hard, but we could not have been considered poor; my father made fair money from his business. And with my mother's income, we had almost anything, and everything the white folk had, if not more. We owned a large home with several acres, a 1949 Chevrolet, a pickup truck for my dad's business, and a television and record player. We had inside plumbing and electric lights and always, hot food on our table. I guess one could say we were doing well.

For the most part, my family accepted this life. They felt we were doing great. They saw no reason why my sisters, brothers, and I could not go to an all-black college and become schoolteachers or something that a black educated person was allowed to do in the 1950s.

Well, life was not great, and I saw no reason why blacks could not compete with the whites in all facets of the American society.

Why was there a water fountain for whites and a water fountain for blacks, a school for whites and a school for blacks? And most of all, why were whites less learned than blacks permitted to direct the lives and the communities of blacks?

The most outstanding memory of my young life had to do with the white foreman who was poorly educated, yet he controlled and manipulated black men who were physically more powerful and also more intellectually sound. This indelible period of my life caused a profound separation between my older brother and me, and does even to this day. At this time, I was fourteen and my older brother was seventeen. For several years, my older brother had told me about his boss, Willie, and how he would take half of his crew's money every payday. For whatever reason, my brother thought this made Willie clever, and he felt it necessary to give me fair warning not to bet with Willie now that I was old enough to work in the groves on my own.

It was June 1955. My first day's experience is one I would rather not remember but sense I must. The hot Florida sun shone down on our bare backs with a temperature index of about 110 degrees. The Florida sand under our feet at mid-day was like a fully fired furnace, and the only protection I had on my feet was cloth sneakers, which were little or no protection at all. For the most part, the sneakers stayed full of hot sand that the chop hoe kicked up when I pulled it down to cut the weeds from around the newly planted orange trees.

Our foreman, Mr. Willie, as we were required to call him, sat in his jeep pick up some distant away, with his eyes glued to me. On occasion, he would holler, "Catch it up, Paul. If you don't, you will have to work through the lunch hour." The lunch hour was the hour most embedded in my mind; an "hour" that was really only thirty minutes. Within those thirty minutes, I would be able to empty the hot sand from my shoes, eat, and get a cool drink. But more important, I would ask my older brother to slow the pace down.

Mr. Willie's crew had eight black men: several older men, James, "Sleepy," Lester, and me. As I looked up the row of small orange trees, the seven of them were far ahead of me, with my older brother James in the lead. When lunchtime came, James was some twenty trees out front, and the others were scattered in-between.

The rule was, all rows must be caught up before lunch and quitting time. When the boss blew his jeep horn for lunch, the others would double back and help me finish my row. The older men would always make remarks such as, "Boy, if you are too lazy to keep up, you need to stay home with your mommy," or something to that effect. My older brother James would also counsel me on the subject of keeping up during the lunch period.

My personal thoughts were how dumb it was to work in 100-degreeplus weather while one man sat in the shade making all the rules. Moreover, why would one of the eight of us compete with the rest of us in hoeing an orange tree? It was all so crazy to me because chances were we would never be rewarded for our extra efforts anyway.

It was some two weeks after I had been on the job that I had my first and last confrontation with an orange grove foreman. On this day, about 3 in the afternoon, the other field workers and I were working in the tree nursery under the dose supervision of our boss. I asked Mr. Willie for permission to go take a crap, and was given permission to do so.

Upon my return, Mr. Willie began setting me up for my first bet. The other field workers were busy pruning trees with their pruning knives. I knelt within my own assigned row, opened my pruning knife, and began to try and catch up with the others, who were far ahead of me. Then Mr. Willie said, 'Paul, I bet you five dollars, payable payday, that you pissed before you took a shit when you took your crap.

"I accepted the bet. "Okay. All of you know everybody pisses before they shit, right?" All the other field workers agreed with Mr. Willie, including James.

I became very irate, I think mostly because all the blacks supported the white foreman, but especially when my own brother was not on my side. I stood up in my row, with my knife to my side. "Mr. Willie," I said, "You cannot prove I pissed before I took a shit unless you go and find the pile of shit, and I will not give you five dollars until the bet is proven."

Mr. Willie checked the reaction of the other workers, who at about this time, had all gone back to work, with all eyes toward the ground.

I am sure it was the workers' negative reaction that inspired Mr. Willie to make his next move. He charged me saying, "Nigger, I am going to kill you, even if I have to kill every nigger in Clermont." I stood my ground, ready for him, but he stopped just before reaching me.

All the other workers continued to work without looking up. I was very scared because I knew the penalty for standing up to a white man could have very well been death—about as quick as making an advance toward a white woman, as our neighbor boys had been accused of doing and had met death at the hand of the local sheriff. But still, I was feeling very good about my actions as we stood there looking one another in the eye for several seconds. Finally, he gave in.

His demeanor at this time was not what I expected. It seemed that he became almost human and recognized me for the first time for what I was— a fourteen-year-old boy.

For this, I gained a little respect for Mr. Willie and lost all respect for my fellow black workers, including my brother James, who I had once looked up to. I thought this would soon be in my past and I would be a pilot, flying airplanes in the U.S. Army.

Chapter 2

Mama's Black Child

My older sisters and brother were what colored folk called yellow niggers. Being of a darker complexion, I was called a darkie and was not accepted by my mother's eleven sisters and extended family. The color of their skin ranged from being yellow to very fair skinned. Blacks born during the 1940s to a family of lighter complexioned colored persons faced a serious dilemma. Skin color within the black community established a very defined stratification. During my early childhood, a darkie wishing to establish him- or herself would have to develop enormous skills and a quick savvy.

Arguments could be made that such skills developed by self-conscious blacks could and did account for the success of our earlier athletes and entertainers. Some achieved monumental success. I am speaking of such greats as Jackie Robinson, Nat King Cole, Jesse Owens, and James Brown, just to name a few. They may have faced the same dilemmas as I did during the 1940s and early 1950s.

My older brother James was everything I wanted to be. He was muscular, tall, lighter skinned, and had lots of friends. He also had the love of our nuclear and extended family. By my own self-analysis, I could never measure up to him.

However, after the incident in the orange grove with our boss man, Mr. Willie, I felt better about myself. I had an inner feeling and power that I felt exceeded that of James's. Knew that now. But what I did not know was where this inner strength and power would lead me. *Was it a power that could be properly honest? Or was it one to lead me to destruction within this uncertain world?*

My grandmother was a strong-willed, self-educated woman. She would be the winner at any cost. She lost her husband early on in life, but not before he had fathered 14 children for her to raise. I would say her origin was American Indian, Scottish Irish, and African American. All losers, as far as the greater American society was concerned. But within our community because of her complexion and beauty, she was one notch up in the winner column. Now the question was, *Where does this leave me?* The answer was, not very well off.

During those years, the only true thing we had was our family — with the extended family being just as important as the nuclear one. Big Mama, as we all called her, was very much in charge. There was no doubt about that. Big Mama's income was derived from the farm and timber properties she had left in Georgia after the death of my grandfather. Some 300 acres gave her a manageable income to take care of her large family, with the assistance of all family members doing their part in the orange groves.

But can you imagine what it must have been like being a member of a family of about 50 when you were the only black face? Well, for me, it was almost as bad as being a member of the KKK when everyone had a sheet but me.

Life was not easy under these conditions. All times, it seemed I had nothing to look forward to. Big Mama's house sat beside Highway 50, running east and west through the black quarters of Clermont. It was a big two-story house, with lots of flowers and fruit trees. About one mile west of our house, two blocks off the highway in Lincoln Park, Highway 50 crossed Highway 27, two miles east of Big Mama's house. These were the only two highways I knew of in the whole world. I did know from conversation between my uncles and aunts that Highway 27 ran north toward Georgia and south to Miami, where Big Mama's sister, Aunt Mitt, lived. Highway 50 ran east to Orlando, about 25 miles away, and west to Tampa, about 70 miles, 'where I had never been.

However, I knew where Big Mama's house was. The place where everyone went for guidance and to have new dresses made for the girls and women of our family. Where everyone was considered, except me, or so it seemed. I am sure my mother and father loved me, but with all the other pressures from the greater part of this big family, that love was lost somewhere between our house and Big Mama's. 'We went to Big Mama's house for everything. For entertainment, that mostly meant playing with my yellow cousins. Older folks, except my mom and dad, getting a drink of corn liquor sent from Georgia was reason enough to visit. Of all the fuss made over Big Mama's house, my only satisfaction was to know that I too was part of this family that, possibly from the outside, looked to be nigger rich.

I also got some satisfaction to be seen playing with the lighter skinned children until I figured out I was not accepted as their equal. After making this discovery, I learned to play by myself.

There were also other lessons: Black nigger kids got what yellow nigger kids did not want. When candy was being passed around, I got only what was left after everyone else had theirs. When dinnertime came at Big Mama's house, I never got to sit in a chair at the table, but rather on the floor, with a tin plate and no spoon.

The time would come during these early years of my life when the only person I identified with would be my father. It was not because he was black, like me because I never thought of him like that. Rather, it was because he talked with me as well as to me. He gave me candy without it being picked over, and I could select the piece of my choice. In his presence, I did get to sit at the dining table, and sometimes, sit on his lap and eat from his plate. Of all my childhood memories, one of my greatest enjoyments was sitting on my dad's lap and eating from his plate.

Even at that, it seemed when my older brother was present, I came in second place, even with my dad. I would like to think it was not because of my older brother's lighter complexion that he was closer to my father but rather because he was the older son. I think I am correct in this assumption. In any case, I hope so. But many problems did stem from what I saw as difference in treatment. Maybe it was just in my head in my father's case, but with my mother, I got about the same treatment at home as I got at Big
Mama's house.

There was an exception. Whenever I made a comment about the difference in treatment, I got a killing of a whipping. Literally, from the top of my head to the bottom of my feet, and I mean literally. Whippings did not stop me from feeling the way I felt; they only made me want to leave home. I knew I would as soon as I got that opportunity.

I was about 10 years old when I heard my mother talking to my father early in the morning. The conversation went something like this: "James Lewis (my older brother) can work at the hotel after school. Paul . . . I don't think he can. I feel you will have to take him to work with you when you need help."

I will always resent the fact that my dad took me out of school day after day to work while James went to school. During my sixth grade year, I missed more than 90 days of a 270-day school year while working with my father. I repeated the sixth grade.

I always felt I should have been the one in school because I felt that I was almost twice as smart as my brother in my schoolwork. I am also sure my parents were aware of this fact. However, I am also sure my parents knew that being a smart black boy had little or nothing to do with success. But one's complexion did. After all, were not white men always in charge of black men, regardless of the degree of intelligence?

But to me, success was not just putting food on the table or having your own place. To me, success was standing up for what you believed in and standing on one's own two feet. In our neighborhood, only a few dared to try, one of whom was my father.

Another was Uncle Joe, who was not my uncle; we just called him Uncle Joe. He was a black man. I should say a proud black man. I guess you can say Uncle Joe was my idea of what black men should have been. He was also my classmate Arthur's grandfather. To me, Uncle Joe was a success.

I think when one fails to stand on his own two feet, it makes little difference how much money he makes. Life will always find a way to take it away. I think my older brother falls into this category. For the most part, he never stood on his own two feet, figuratively speaking. He always followed others' ideas, like thumping my head, would almost always be Abraham Jones idea, and James and Pop Hodges would always follow suit. If I told my mother about the thumping, for one reason or another, I almost always ended up getting the whipping.

Let's talk about Uncle Joe. Uncle Joe was about five foot seven. He wore bib overalls, a long-sleeve shirt, and an old felt hat, even during the hottest days of summer. In his right hand, he would have a long stick reminiscent of the shepherds of Jesus's days who watched their flock by night.

You know the story of the three wise men. To me, Uncle Joe could very well have been one of the wise men in every sense of the word. At times, I would watch him for hours from a distant hiding place because he would not let anyone get close to his livestock. He had hundreds of turkeys, cows, and one hell of a bull.

Uncle Joe's homestead was a two-story house made of old fieldstone. It is very beautiful, and it still stands today. In his driveway was a new Lincoln car, and the yard had several adorable flower gardens that were kept to perfection. An assortment of fruit trees: peaches, oranges, pears, grapefruit, and other citrus fruits common to the Florida environment also surrounded his homestead. He never had to catch the crew truck to the orange groves. All he did was watch his own place and stand his ground as a black man. To me, he was what a man should be—a protector of what was his.

The only person I could think of to give you a real account of the impression he made upon my childhood would be William Beckworth, the black cowboy who led wagon trains west to California along Beckworth Trail during the days of the early west. Uncle Joe's stick would have to be traded for a Colt 45, and his sitting place for a saddled mustang, but other than that, he had all of the qualifications. His face was old, with many lines that showed he had endured 70 years or more, and I am sure he had.

Once a year, there would be a community barbecue. Uncle Joe was one of the men in charge of cooking the meat. A deep hole would be dug, and old bedsprings would be supported over the fire within the hole. Preparing for the May 20 picnic celebrating the day in 1865 when slaves were freed in Florida, Uncle Joe and several other older men from the community would place sides of hogs on the springs.

These were great times for me. The men allowed me to sit by the fire and listen to Uncle Joe's tall tales. He talked about times when he had chased eleven white men from stealing his livestock, with a shotgun. How he had owned three homesteads in his lifetime. In all my days, I had never heard of a black man running off a white man with a shotgun. To me, this alone made him one of the most outstanding black men of our community. Standing up to a white man, boy!

Maybe it was Uncle Joe I was thinking of when, later in life, I stood up to Mr. Willie in the orange grove. I would watch the hog sizzling over the fire, hoping for a piece and listening to Uncle Joe's tall tales until I remembered I would get another whipping for missing supper. I would run home prepared for my whipping but feeling that my evening of entertainment would more than make up for it.

If I may borrow an excerpt from *Clermont Gem of the Hills*, I will tell also of a successful black woman of my young childhood— Aunt Sally, as we all called her. Within the population of Clermont, lived a modest, unassuming Seoul who for thirty years and more had been one of the most important characters in the community. She was called from her bed at all hours of the night, away from her family more than she was with them. Frequently, she went for many hours without sleep, always a comfort and solace and genuine ministering angel wherever she was. Mothers of the community and grown men and women with families of their own called Sally Townsend blessed.

For three decades, Sally had been the nurse attendant for practically every mother and newborn baby in this entire community, both black and white. No matter how strenuous her duties or how tedious they were, she appeared to be happy in her work. Never a cross word passed through her lips, and gentleness was in her every act. If the angel Gabriel marks down the record of mortals for a reward in heaven, her book must be a great one. And when she was measured for flowing robes, wings of white, and harps of gold, surely Sally Townsend was fitted with the greatest in the heavenly wardrobe. Sally Townsend was the midwife who delivered me from my mother's womb. She was indeed a success, for she was pleased with her place in life. I am sure she received many rewards.

Chapter 3

No Angels

The house that my father built sat off a dirt road one-half mile north of Florida's Highway 50 on an acre and a half of land. To our southeast was Uncle Joe's homestead, and to our west Big Mama's house. Within these grounds, we had a patch of sugar cane for making homemade syrup. This would be accomplished seven miles north of our place at the Isom's, who had a cane press pulled by a mule. I know little or nothing about making syrup; however, we would cut the cane and deliver it to the Isom's, and several days later, we would pick up gallons of syrup for morning breakfast.

We also had hogs that required feeding in the morning before going to school and also in the evening after school. Wood would have to be gathered from the wood yard, and our single milk cow, Ida, had to be staked out. We raised an assortment of greens, peas, corn, peanuts, Irish and sweet potatoes, also other foods our family needed, except dried beans, peas, and flour, which we bought from the white folks' grocery store, with occasional candy and other goodies to satisfy a sweet tooth.

Our house had three bedrooms, a living and dining room, a bathroom, a kitchen, and a front porch, with a swing that hung from the ceiling. In 1955, Daddy added a garage for our brand new 1955 Chevrolet.

My dad, James Wallace Montgomery, stood five foot seven inches tall; however, for the most of my life that would be about ten feet to me. I thought there was nothing he could not do. When I look back on those early days of my life, he did do almost everything necessary or required to keep a large family fed and reasonably comfortable. If he had any fault, it would have been giving in to my mother.

The one thing that stands out most in my mind about him is seeing him pushing a homemade wheelbarrow that I am sure he used until he bought his first car. He transported any and everything that had to be moved within our homestead, including groceries from the white folks' grocery store, some two miles across the colored quarters. The wheelbarrow was also used early in my father's business to transport his tools.

My father almost single-handedly, with only the help he got from me after I came of age, built almost every black person's home within our community that, over the years, had grown to a respectable size.

From as early as I can remember, I have never seen him smoke, drink, use a profane word, or miss church unless he was sick. I can recall only two times that my father was sick. Both times were from poison ivy he came in contact with while on a fishing trip. Fishing and hunting were about his only form of entertainment.

My father was not much of a disciplinarian. This department was usually left to my mother, which possibly could have been another fault on his part.

If working hard kills, my father would have died at an early age. However, I can recall only a few times his labor was supervised by another man—black or white—and this was after he had entertained every other option. However, he never seemed to mind other family members working in the orange grove. I think possibly he did but found it necessary to move ahead in life, so he permitted it.

It was many years later that I lost some respect for my dad. It was during trying times for all of us. My mother was in the hospital at the point of death, and I had flown down from my job in Greenville, South Carolina, to be with the family. We had taken my father's Lincoln from Clermont to Orlando, where my mother was hospitalized. In the lobby, I saw a very poor black girl who was pregnant and did not have a way back to her camp, where migrant workers were housed outside of the city. I had asked my father to let me use his car to take her home and he refused. He said no and gave no excuse as to why.

I remembered my father as being kind, compassionate, giving, and willing to help others. *Was it possible that success had hardened hint to the degree that he had forgotten what it was like to be poor or in need? Or, did he feel like it was not his responsibility and that he should stay out of other people's business? Or maybe he felt others should make it the same as he did, through hard work and planning for the future.* It was not until several years later that I got somewhat of an understanding as to how my father felt.

I had given up my job as a recruiter counselor with the U.S. government. I felt I could do freelance counseling and thought I could get some help from him and my old community in Clermont. Together, we would help one of the poorest areas in the U.S.A. to begin standing on its own two feet, and off the roll of welfare.

My objective was to build a learning center for the elementary and middle school kids and do job counseling for parents of poor families in Clermont. The center would be named after one of my heroes, Mrs. Sally Townsend.

My father was not willing to help. His primary reason was the inability to communicate with his peers—those who had struggled along with him and made good. In fact, most older blacks who had made good during an early era refused to join hands with another black who had also made good during that same era, even for the betterment of their own community.

However, I found my younger brothers, who were of a different era than James and were in a position to help with the project, were willing to assist.

Was it possible that, for a period of time, my father and other near the same age were looked over after reaching a degree of prominence within the black communities? Did this happen because of the new days of integration? And is it not possible that they were saying you have looked to the white man all of this time, why come to ne now? Can I say and be correct that, for a time, even their own sons and daughters had rendered my father and his successful peers useless?

Now I wonder if an apology could be made to them, should we as sons and daughters be given a reprieve. I would like that very much, for at 92, my dad and other seniors still had a lot to offer. We still need their help in making America a better place for those who cannot help themselves.

My mother, Julia Mal Montgomery, was hard as nails. She stood about six feet. In her youth, she could use an axe, hoe, ladder, and fruit sack, and also a whipping switch, as well or better than the average man. Her cooking was outstanding. As long as I can remember, my mother was up at 5:-00 in the morning, and this you could set your watch by.

If my mother had any weakness, it would be fear of or too much respect for the white race. I think this fear goes back to her childhood and the power whites had over blacks. I was never willing to show the respect to whites that my mother demanded. In fact, I would rather not be bothered by them at all. I tried always to stay out of their way at any cost.

Because of this, my mother and I were not very close. I think she thought I was lazy and disrespectful. It was because of my feelings toward whites that I knew I had to leave home as soon as I became of age. I am sure my brothers and sisters accepted my mother reasoning —that for a black to keep employment in Clermont, he or she had to show respect unless self-employed. All bosses were white, and we all had to eat.

My father was a very lucky man to find a woman like my mother. I have yet to know another like her. She worked day and night to help push my father. She also knew where to put a dollar to make a better life for the family. I am sure she made the best decisions on behalf of the family when she encouraged my father to allow my older brother to at-tend school and work in the white folks' kitchen and for me to be kept out of school to work in my father's business.

The fact that my mother was partial to lighter-complexion blacks was simply because there were no dark-skinned blacks in her nuclear family. From a perspective of preparing me to live and survive in a world that did not allow black men to make real meaningful decisions, the whippings I got almost daily were justified. However, for me to leave home to escape the pressures because of my personality was also the right decision.

All things considered, my mother was a very good mother and a good wife to my father. I think my mother's need to have the better things of life also inspired my father and made for a better life for us all.

If there was one thing in life that I hold against my mother, it would be her refusal to give me the assistance I needed when I called her from Vietnam, after I had been involved in destroying a Vietnamese village with many women and children. I had been relieved of my duty and was under flagging action with instruction to be court-martialed. Again, I think she could have been rolling with the flow of things.

The war was an unpopular war, so none of us who fought it got much help or assistance from home when we needed it. I am still looking for the inner strength to forgive my mother and others for the support we did not get from home.

In any case, the charges were dropped some six months after I was assigned to my new unit in the states. I was allowed to finish my military career and retire. My nightmares, however, have not gone away. I still see the mangled bodies cut to pieces from the 90-millimeter main gun of our M48A3 tanks. (I pray for forgiveness, and that I too might forgive.)

My eldest sister Gloria was a passionate and compassionate young lady. At one time or another, she fell in and out of love with every teenage boy in our community, or so it seemed. Finally, she married an eighteen-year-old migrant worker who lived over a juke joint. She was seventeen and pregnant. From as early as I can remember, she had been like a mother to me. With my mother working in the orange grove or busy having another baby, I looked to Gloria for most of my needs. She was seven years my senior and had looked after me from as early as birth—doing everything from changing my diapers to fighting my fights for me.

My second sister, Deloris, had a totally different personality. I wanted nothing to do with her, and the only reason I can come up with is, Gloria had a somewhat lighter complexion than Deloris. I had been taught that fair was beautiful and dark was ugly.

In any case, my sister Gloria saw me through some pretty rough times. I almost resented her getting married. As it turned out, Gloria getting married was like getting an older brother. For me, this was good. My older brother James and I had nothing in common, and with Speedy, as we all called Gloria's husband, maybe I would get some positive responses from an older brother figure.

Speedy was not all I thought he would be because if my brother James was a hard worker, Speedy was a super hard worker. The two of them had everything in common, and in a way, this too was good because now James gave most of his attention to Speedy as opposed to his other crazy friends who use to thump me on my head. Now I was allowed to tag along once in a while. I think Gloria might have had something to do with that, but even then, I was an outsider.

It was not long before my father's business grew to the point that both Speedy and James started to work with my dad and me. At first, this was good because I knew more about the work that we were doing, and for a short time, we were all equals. But as we soon took on more work, both James and Speedy pulled ahead, and it was not long before both moved out on their own as block masons.

About this time, my dad pulled me out of school. He said it would be only for one year, but it had been two, and I was getting closer and closer to enlistment age. At this point in my life, I faced a dilemma: If I went into the army, it would seem that I deserted my father when he needed me the most. However, if I stayed to help him, I am sure I would have lived to regret it.

My brother James now had a family of his own to look out for. My sister Deloris was still in college, and it looked to me that I pretty much had the load of assisting my father and my family all by myself.

I had four other brothers at home. Alexander had always been the infantile type. Willie was only ten, Wilbert, six, and Lawrence, four. Two other sisters, Marshanell was eight, and Maryon two.

I knew my dad needed all the help I could give. But I was now eighteen and had been out of school since my sixteenth birthday, trying to help my father make it to a point that he could pull the load by himself. Deep inside, I knew that would be several years coming. I made a decision. If my dad would buy me a car, I would stay and help. If not, I would join the army. I did not feel right about this decision, but then too, my dad was not paying me a salary, and at this age, I felt I needed something for myself.

Chapter 4

An Escape

We were all sitting on the front breezeway of our new house that we were all so proud of. My dad had built it in 1957. For some, it was the grandest house within the black community, exceeding even Uncle Joe's house—or for that matter, most houses, including those in the white community. I had discussed with my father the possibility of buying a 1951 Ford that I had looked at parked on Highway 50. It was at the station down from Big Mama's house. My dad had told me he would have to discuss it with my mother. In this setting, I thought it would be a good time to bring the subject up, if there ever would be a good time.

I had a hard time with this—the car and the possibility of leaving home. I knew the load the family already had. The loan from the bank to build our new house, my sister Deloris still in college, and five younger sisters and brothers still in elementary or high school. I had thought I should not buy that car from that cracker anyway. He would not even let black folk get a drink from his water cooler or use the bathroom. But I wanted the car!

I thought it was only fair to have something of my own. After all, I had worked two years without pay. Did that not deserve something? I approached the subject slowly, "I am now eighteen, and I think I should be paid for working. "My mother replied, "Your Daddy can't afford to pay you, boy. We have a house note, and your sister is still in college."

"Well, Daddy, how about that car that I showed you at the service station? Eddie Bass has a car, and he only works in the orange groves on weekends." It was my mother's turn again. "You are not Eddie Bass, and we can't afford to buy you a car, let alone insurance, and that is the end of the matter." I think the next statement hit my dad pretty hard. "Well," I said, "I will be enlisting in the army on Monday."

The following day (Sunday), I missed church to say my good-byes. Eddie picked me up in the early afternoon, and we made our way north about eight miles to High-Way-In-The-Hills, an all-white resort area where we could buy beer after 1 p.m. Blacks were allowed to drive through the drive-through package store for carry outs. We hit the drive-through, bought a six-pack, and headed back to Clermont.

For the next few hours, we drove through the colored quarters, making several runs back to the package store for beer. Eddie had lots of girls to see. I was mostly along for the ride. I had dropped out of school at sixteen and had lost almost total contact with my age group.

I was beginning to get pretty drunk, and I am sure Eddie was too. We were now speeding through the colored quarters, finally stopping at the local juke joint. The music was good and loud, and for a few dollars or a pint of liquor, we could have had any of the women that hung around the joint. For that matter, being young and pretty good looking, if we had played our cards right, we could have had them for nothing.

However, our objective was to let everyone know that this was our last day in Clermont. So, we just danced and acted the fool. We told everyone, come Tuesday afternoon, we both would be soldiers in a man's army. We hung around until past midnight and agreed if we were going to make it to Jacksonville on Monday, we best call it a day.

Eddie dropped me off at my parents' house, and with some effort, I made it to the back door of the downstairs. I managed to get the door opened. My four younger brothers were sound asleep. I fell on the couch in the downstairs living area and was awakened by the noises of my brothers getting ready for school the following morning. By the time I made it upstairs, my mother and dad had already left for work. That was just fine with me, after the night I had had.

It was about ten o'clock when Eddie pulled up outside in his '51 Mercury. I put a few things in a paper bag, and we were ready for our trip to the recruiting main station in Jacksonville, after a quick stop at the local recruiting station in Leesburg. Then we would receive our instructions and meal and lodging tickets.

The Mercury had loud pipes, and Eddie made it a point to make sure everyone knew we were leaving. We took off from my parents' house like a bat out of hell. A cloud of dust from the dirt road let everyone know we were heading toward Highway 27 North. About 20 miles, and we would be in Leesburg. After getting lodging, food tickets, and instructions from the local recruiter, we were north-bound again.

As we headed north, I could not help but think of my dad. He was a good man, and I began to have second thoughts about leaving him with the heavy load that he and my mother would have to carry. I remembered the first time I had come this far north. My father's sister had died, and my mother and father had agreed that I would be the one to accompany my father to Georgia to attend the funeral.

First, Thad to have a suit, so I had also had the opportunity to visit Orlando for the first time. We shopped on Church Street, at a department store run by Jews. I remember the price of the suit my dad bought. The Jew started at $30, and my dad's final offer was $19. The Jewish gentleman accepted the offer, and I had my first lesson in dealing with Jewish merchants.

We had been on the road about an hour and were passing through Ocala, Florida, a town known for breeding racehorses. There was also the Florida National Forest. Both the horses and the forest were a sight to see. There were long white-rail fences stretching as far as the eye could see. Occasionally, along the fences, were horses so pretty it should have been a sin to ride one.

The national forest was abundant in deer and wild boar. Hunting was allowed by permit only, which only rich white folk could obtain. The forest and the pastures were so green, they looked as if they were in a picture.

Eddie's conversation since the time we had left Clermont was about a single subject matter—the most effective approach of getting into a girl's panties, about which I believed he was an expert. One reason Eddie wanted to join the army was to get away from several girls who said he was the father of their baby. One of the pregnant girls was my first cousin.

I wished he would change the subject. I had made several attempts by bringing up basic training and what careers would be offered to blacks in the army. I also wondered how soon it would be before I could attend flight school after basic training. No matter how the subject started, it always ended up on some little sweet thing in Clermont, Leesburg, or Groveland —all areas of the Lake County community, whose students attended a single high school in Leesburg.

I had attended Leesburg's Carver Heights High School for two years. I had finished only the tenth grade. Eddie had his diploma. I was somewhat worried about my chances in the army without a diploma. As far as the girl department, I had never been serious about one. My mother and Sunday school teachers constantly reminded me about the responsibilities that went along with getting a girl pregnant. Eddie attended the same Sunday school class, but this was also his main topic in Sunday school, even to the point of trying to set me up with his sister.

The next city after Ocala was Gainesville, Florida, home of the University of Florida. The most exciting thing happening in Gainesville was the black law student, Mr. Hawkings. He was the first black to be enrolled at the university — with the help of the Florida National Guard, the NAACP, news media, and whatever other forces to keep the KKK or local law enforcement from bringing Mr. Hawkings's educational aspirations to an abrupt end at the end of a rope or in a Florida swamp with a hole in his head.

Mrs. Hawkins, Mr. Hawkings's wife, had been my tenth grade algebra teacher. Mr. Hawkings's younger brother was the star running back on the Carver Heights champion football team. Lake County had a whole host of Hawkings. They all had reasons to be concerned about their health. The same sheriff (McCall) was the local Sheriff who took the credit for the death of my neighbors in the Greenlee case.

It was now getting close to lunch hour. We would soon need to make a decision about what and where we would eat. Public restaurants were not open to blacks, and it was somewhat difficult to find the black community in an unfamiliar city. The normal thing for traveling blacks was to hit the closest grocery store and buy whatever groceries needed to put together a simple lunch. Mostly pressed ham, bologna, a loaf of white bread, soda water, and a spread of some type.

We elected to do the normal thing and had lunch outside of a small convenience store. It wasn't smart for two young blacks to have lunch along the public highway unless they were working for the highway department— and then only with their white boss in close proximity. From this point, our next stop was the big city of Jacksonville, Florida.

Highway 27 turned into Highway 301 just outside of Ocala, and now we were past Gainesville. I thought how close I was to my father's birthplace, a small Southern Georgia, turpentine community—the town of Moultrie. That had been 52 years ago. I wondered what life must have been like for him, or if there had been any improvement during the past 52 years. The answer had to be yes because for sure, there were no black airplane pilots 52 years ago.

Highway 301 would take us past the Florida State Penitentiary. I was told it was at some point between the state penitentiary and the Lake County Prison that the sheriff's department had killed several of the six from my community involved in the Greenlee case.

My hopes grew higher that I would meet all the requirements to be accepted into the army. If enlisted, I would be able to leave my childhood memories buried somewhere in the past that had brought me this far.

However, I could never forget my father and his workload. I thought how strong he had to have been to obtain the success he had in life. I thought how he had made his truck and his lawn mower available to me on Saturdays so I could have spending money. Wasn't that enough? But, again, I knew I was making the right decision to leave Clermont and Lake County. I could never be like my older brother or sisters. And the next time I stood up to a white man, he might not be as understanding as Mr. Willie, four years past.

We made it into Jacksonville about 3:30 p.m. on October 13, 1959. Our first objective was to find the motel we were instructed to check into, which was on the black side of town. It was against the law for blacks to be housed in the Holiday Inn or any other major motel chain in the South. After hitting the black side of town, it was easy to find the right motel. There was only one that side of town, or in the city for that matter, that the U.S. government housed young black men in for subsequent enlistment into the armed services.

Once we found the motel, Eddie suggested we blow the dull joint and find some women and get some pussy. The closest thing we found to women who were willing to give up some pussy, as Eddie had put it, was hookers. The going price was ten and two: Ten dollars for the girl and two dollars for the room. For this sum, one would probably get a dose of clap that the army would have to eradicate, that is, if we were lucky enough to get in.

After talking with several girls and not being able to get to first base without money up front, we decided to buy a fifth of liquor and take in an X-rated movie. The place was very dark. We had to feel our way to our seats, bumping into an occasional old man or some pervert playing with himself. After several minutes, we managed to find a seat and to focus in on the action on the screen.

This was a first time for me. I was not so sure if I was enjoying myself. I did find it somewhat erotic, but I was not so sure I would enjoy some woman sucking me off and then kissing me with that stuff still running from the side of her mouth.

We sat and passed the bottle with our eyes glued to the action on the screen. This was getting pretty intense, to say the least. I had to ask Eddie where the guy was putting his dick in her butt hole or her pussy. The answer was both. It was truly amazing to see a women being pumped from behind by one guy while she sucked off another. I continued to watch in amazement. I asked Eddie about those things I could not accept or understand. Always getting answers from the more experienced eighteen-year-old.

As we sat through two showings of this erotic free-for-all, we finished off the fifth between us. By the time the second showing was over, we were very drunk. Eddie assured me he would get us back to our motel.

It was after midnight when we knocked on the door of the motel. We were told the motel was closed for the night. We had no choice but to sleep in the car and hope for the best.

It was about 6:30 a.m. when we were awoken by a constant rumbling of voices passing the car. We assessed that it was time for breakfast, and if we were going to survive the morning, we best make this event. We made it to the closest washroom in the motel, washed some of the terrible taste of the night from our mouths, and joined the crowd for breakfast.

Breakfast was at an all-black cafe next to the motel. The place was so small that we had to wait in line to be served. The menu was grits, bacon or sausage, eggs, and biscuits. Possibly because I was so hungry, the food was the best I had ever tasted. I asked for seconds, and a very sweet old lady loaded me up with a good-sized second serving. I felt almost fully recovered from the experience of the night.

Just a few minutes after I had finished breakfast, a very impressive black army sergeant entered the cafe and announced that the bus for the recruiting main station was being loaded out front. As I stepped up on the bus, I was surprised to find it half full of white boys. The black sergeant who I had been so impressed by was very clear in his instruction. "On this bus the state of Florida laws do not apply; you colored boys sit anywhere you can find a seat."

For me, this was somewhat uncomfortable, and I found myself making it to the back of the bus. Eddie and I found a seat together. I already felt that I was in a different world. In fact, I think all of us—both white and black— were totally uncomfortable. One could hear a pin drop from the time the bus departed the cafe until we reached the recruiting main station.

Upon arriving, we were placed in a single file and were ordered to file through the double doors and follow the yellow line that directed us to an open bay. I was very unprepared for the next order: We were ordered to disrobe. I could not help but look around the room, mostly to see who was looking at me. I saw all sizes, black and white. I quickly confirmed that not all men were created equal.

The next order was even more unacceptable than the first. We were ordered to bend over, reach back, and spread our cheeks, and would you believe that men in white coats armed with flashlights inspected our assholes with the lights. They rammed their middle finger as far as they could straight up our butt holes. Afterward, they came around in front and gave all a short arms inspection and some, really short. We were told that we could put our underwear back on. From this point on, the physical was not so bad: chest x-rays, a look at our ears and eyes, a deep breath here and there, a few pricks in the finger, and we were allowed to get dressed.

We then were seated in a classroom and given number-two lead pencils and a booklet. The proctor instructed us not to open the booklets until we were told to do so. The first test concerned reading, word definition, and arithmetic. At this point, I wished I had gotten a good night's sleep.

I looked around the room for Eddie, to see if he was having any problems. He was just sitting there looking into space. After several tests, Eddie was still just sitting there. I did the best I could with the test and hoped I had passed. After the testing, we were all sent to a waiting room to learn if we would soon be soldiers.

The roll call was several hours later. The sergeant informed us that if he said to fall in to the left, we would be getting a one-way ticket home. If he said to fall in to the right, we would be getting a one-way ticket to Fort Jackson, South Carolina. I was told to fall in to the right. I felt good about myself. I would be a soldier—possibly an airplane pilot.

Eddie was told to fall in to the left. He would be driving the Mercury back to Clermont alone. Back to the orange groves and dead-end jobs. To the signs that read "White Only!" To the world where black men were always "Boy" when talking to the white boss. To a world where there was little or no justice for black men. Where black men were being slaughtered in the name of justice. Where, for most black men, education was more of a dream than a reality. Back to little hope and great disparity. But, men have made it, even with these odds. My father was one such man. However, I didn't think Eddie fit that category.

My group was being briefed for our swearing-in ceremony and our subsequent train ride to Fort Jackson. It was somewhat funny. I was not afraid anymore. I knew I would be a good soldier. I was sure I would not leave the army until retirement because my short life had already shown me the hardships of a black head of household in an environment where whites were always right and blacks had little to say about their career, education, public facilities, or in general, those things that controlled their lives.

On the train from Jacksonville to Fort Jackson, I was in a vacuum, somewhere between two worlds. The world that I was leaving behind contained many things that were precious and dear to me, but it was a world where I could never have control over those very things. The world ahead was something I had dreamed of for more than seven years. A world that allowed black men to fly airplanes and to be placed in charge of men, both black and white. The world ahead would be the better world for me. I was a person who needed to control, even if that control was over just a few men.

I thought of Colonel Davis, who Arthur told me was in charge of a squadron of black pilots. It would be one of the greatest honors for me if I could meet this black colonel. I would ask him how it felt to be in command of a group of intelligent black men. I had heard of men in the army working their way up through the ranks. Maybe if I was a really good soldier I too could have a command one day. That would really be something.

I also thought of Eddie. I wished I had asked him if black people did the things we saw in the X-rated movies. I am sure he would have had an answer for me. I also wondered why he had not tried to pass the army test. *Did he think he did not have a chance? Had the night of booze and X-rated films been too much for him? Maybe he got cold feet and didn't want to leave the world that he felt he knew so much about.* I have often wondered how black men could be so comfortable in that world which Eddie had elected to return to.

I was so caught up in myself, I almost missed dinner. It was the tall black prior-service soldier who had been placed in charge and reminded me it was time to eat and directed me to the dining car. Just yesterday, I had been unable to eat at the same cafe or sleep in the same motel with anyone who was white. Now I was being encouraged to sit and eat with them in the dining car, and with a black man in charge. Why were things the way they were?

Could these things that were happening on the train that was still on southern soil in America not have been accepted outside of the train? From the train, I could see black men, women, and children, making out the best that they could in rundown, unpainted shacks, waving as we passed. When would the time come that those who waived could also enjoy a better living standard? *When would they have a more productive way of life—or would that time ever come?*

Chapter 5

Jackson, A New Beginning

It was past midnight when the train pulled into the station at Columbia, South Carolina, and the army was out in force to meet us. There were four sergeants, an American Indian, a Puerto Rican, and two whites. A civilian drove the army bus that they loaded us on. Upon arriving on base, the sergeants were the first off the bus, and fixed themselves an equal distance apart in front of the bus.

The Indian identified himself as the first platoon sergeant; the two white sergeants were the second and third platoon; and the Puerto Rican, the fourth platoon. A fifth sergeant with seemingly more strips than I could count met the bus as it pulled up in front of the building that he had exited to give us orders. If we were 5' to 5'6" inches tall, we were to fall in front of the first platoon sergeant. If we were 5'7" to 5'8" inches, we were to fall in front of the second platoon sergeant. If we were 59" to 5'11", we were to fall in front of the third platoon sergeant. And, if we were six feet or over, we were to fall in front of the fourth platoon sergeant.

I was an even six feet, according to the physical I had just had in Jacksonville, but I knew I was six foot one inch. In any case, it looked like I was in the fourth platoon.

It took forever getting everyone in the right place. The temperature was about 36 degrees, and I still had on Florida clothing; I was freezing. Finally, everyone was in place, and the sergeant with all the stripes told the other sergeants to take charge of their men and file them into the mess hall for chow.

It took some effort to get Uncle Sam's newest recruits to respond to army drill commands. After several attempts on the part of the four platoon sergeants, though, we formed a single line, facing what looked to also be new army assessments standing behind the serving line, ready to serve us our very first army chow. We were now armed with medal trays fixed in position to receive our midnight meal. The menu was steak and potatoes, and coffee if you wanted it.

I found it very odd to be sitting in a big dining area past midnight, with some hundred or more men eating steak and potatoes. However, this was a new beginning, and I am sure I would come to know and do many other odd things before seeing home again. The steak was tough as shoe leather, and I had some trouble cutting it with my knife. If I were at home, I would have used my hands, but I ended up giving up on the steak and ate the potatoes.

No sooner I had finished the potatoes, than the sergeant with all the stripes stood in the middle of the dining area and, at the top of his voice, shouted, "First platoon! Second platoon! Third platoon! Fourth platoon! Fall outside on your platoon sergeant." Scared me almost to death. The new recruits were knocking over tables and chairs. Then the command was, "Pick up those chairs and straighten those tables! Fall out! Fall out!"

After we were all outside, it was left to us to find the position we had been in prior to going into the mess hall. At this point of my army career, I was about ready to throw in the towel, and I had been on an army post less than one hour.

The recruit I had stood next to was Robert LeCorne, Jr.—a black boy out of north Florida. It was LeCorne who found me and helped me get into place because I was hopelessly lost in a sea of new faces that had little or no meaning to me. Through this experience, I learned my first military lesson: When in a military formation, you are always responsible for the man to your right.

After everyone found their places, we were marched to our quarters, a wood frame two-story building. Words in black with a white background just to the right of the entrance let you know this was the fourth platoon quarters. The top floor of the same building was the second platoon.

As we approached the building, our Puerto Rican platoon sergeant made his way to the front of the group, holding a very impressive instrument that looked like a foot-long bullet between the thumb and forefinger of both hands. He marched in a backward manner, and when he was just a few feet away from the building, he made a fancy foot movement and commanded the group to halt.

In broken English, he introduced himself as Sergeant First Class Quinnones and welcomed us to the U.S. Army and the fourth platoon. About this time, I was so cold I just knew if I touched my ears, they would have fallen off. Finally, he instructed us how we would file into the building. The first single line to the right, which included me, was between six feet and six foot one inch tall. The smallest of the fourth platoon made up the first squad. The second squad, all about six foot two inches to six three, the third squad about six foot three to six four, and the fourth, six foot four and above.

The first squad was instructed to file into the building, march to the end of the building, do a column left at the last bunk beds to the far side, do a column left at the first bunk bed, and stop at the last bunk bed that was not occupied. There were ten men in each squad and ten sets of bunk beds on each side of the building. This put me at the very first or last set of bunks as you entered the front entrance of the fourth platoon on the left side of the building. The second squad was instructed to file in and occupy the bunks on the right side of the building. The third squad marched in and was instructed to take a position behind each man of the first squad. The fourth squad was instructed to march in and take a position behind each man of the second.

Now that we were all in the building, SFC Quinnones took the center of the room, faced the first and third quad, and commanded them to do a left face. Then he made an about-face, and commanded the second and fourth squads to do a right-face. Now that the first and third were facing the second and fourth squads, bunk assignments were made. The first squad was assigned the bottom bunks, with foot and wall lockers to the left. The third squad was assigned the top bunks, with foot and wall lockers to the right. SFC Quinnones then did another an about-face, and made bunk assignments to the second and forth squads.

I was really impressed. I had been on an army post for less than two hours and had had a meal with more than a hundred men. I had learned how to execute military facing movements, how to fall in and out of a military formation, and had been assigned sleeping quarters.

The next order that SFC Quinnones gave was not an easy one: "Now that you have your assigned areas, each of you will get to know your bunk buddy." My bunk buddy was a six-foot four-inch Mississippian and a bigot. Sergeant Quinnones'’s final instruction to the platoon for the night was to know who falls in to your right. I was the last man in the first squad, so no one fell in to my right. Robert LeCorne, Jr., was to my left. The bigot from Mississippi was somewhere in the fourth platoon, and that was too close.

That night while lying on the first bottom bunk on the left side of the hall of the fourth platoon, with a white bigot occupying the top bunk over me, I tried to assess my position in my short life of eighteen years. I began by back-tracking the events as they had occurred just hours prior. I was concerned as to what part the sergeant with all the stripes would play in my life in the next few weeks. For sure, he was in full control; even SFC Quinnones snapped to whenever he spoke. I had never seen anyone who could shake up so many, simply by his presence.

The mess hall scene was unprecedented in my short life-time, not even Big Mama could have gotten so many to move so fast. But an even a greater fear was in the forefront of my mind: It stood about six foot six inches, and I was able to look up and see the effects of its two hundred-plus pounds as the top bunk swayed to and fro whenever the big bigot from Mississippi rolled from one side of his bunk to the other.

I don't think I would have been so afraid of the bigot if I thought all things were equal. But through my past experiences, all things were far from being equal. To begin with, he was white and I was black. The most powerful man I had seen within my short army career was also white. He was the sergeant with all the stripes. And there was SFC Quinnones, my Puerto Rican platoon sergeant. Even if Sergeant Quinnones was on my side, how would a Puerto Rican and a black boy fair against a bigot from Mississippi and the tough white sergeant with all the stripes? My experience had proven time and time again that black could not win against white. I was also sure this rule included Puerto Ricans.

As I lay there on my bunk with the night approaching morning, I wondered why I had not thought of this type of dilemma before. It had been more than seven years past that I had made up my mind to become a soldier. From the very beginning, my thought was, once I was a soldier, I would have for the most part escaped bigotry.

The morning arrived with me getting very little sleep. I was up before the big Mississippian, and had already showered and was half dressed when he began to complain about having to sleep with niggers. He dragged himself slowly out of bed and made no attempt to give me room to finish dressing as his lengthy body reached the floor directly in front of me. If I had been on familiar ground, and if I had thought things were almost equal, I would have kicked him in the nuts. He positioned his body directly in front of me as I attempted to tie my shoes. I yielded to him because I was scared.

The morning reveille formation was much improved over the formation outside of the mess hall the previous night. Everyone had found his place, including me. We were off to the mess hall for breakfast.

Army breakfast was a new experience for me, but one I could get use to with little or no trouble. The menu included bacon, eggs, grits, potatoes, toast, milk, juices, and coffee. I found it hard to accept that the army fed so well after all the talk I had heard about missing home cooking. After breakfast, it was formation time all over again, and I had begun to learn how one could hate a sergeant with all the hollering and yelling and going on.

The rest of the day was devoted to receiving our full army issue, including an M-1 rifle. I had never seen so many clothes in all my life, let alone two pair of good boots and lots of underwear. Both regular and long johns for the terrible cold that I had already had more of than I could stand. Life had improved for me. I was willing to acknowledge that. However, by midday, I was wishing I was back home helping my dad paint houses. The duffle bag full of my army issue was almost too much for me to bear, but I knew it was a small price to pay for the feelings I felt growing inside me.

I felt, just from an observation of the past few days, that I too had the capacity to become a man. This was new to me. I had never experienced anything close to it back in Clermont, where if you were black and under sixty-five years of age, you were still called "Boy." Over sixty-five, you became "Uncle" whether you had nieces or nephews or not.

It was now clear that I could be whatever I wanted to be in life. The black sergeant who had met the bus in Jacksonville had demonstrated every trait of being his own man. So had the Puerto Rican, SFC Quinnones, and also the Indian sergeant who was assigned as the first platoon sergeant.

It was rewarding to know that I had made the right decision by enlisting in the army, even though I knew I had to deal with my bunk buddy, the big Mississippi bigot.

Chapter 6

A Transformation

I was still somewhat troubled by how blacks, Puerto Ricans, and Indians could be in charge of white men. And I had my doubts about confronting the tall Mississippian and living to write home about it. This was simply because, where I came from, it was not acceptable for blacks to even question white men.

I still remembered losing my job in the grove at the age of fourteen, when I had confronted Mr. Willie. When I ever did find the nerve to confront this bigot, I would never have written home, for it would only have caused more pain, worrying, and prayer for my safety. In my parents' world, there was only one defense when there was disagreement between blacks and whites, and that defense was "putting the matter in the hands of the Lord." One would think that I too would have shared my parents' faith in the Lord taking care of my needs. However, I found my needs were to kick some butt. Even today when I look back over my life, it becomes very physical for me. The hurt is almost unbearable.

It still seems like I live in two worlds. First, a world where I revere my parents' standard and wish it was so simple. This world leaves me with loneliness, fear, anger, and even rage because I know it is not so simple as that. In my other world, I have a great need to kick some butt; however, I am so often reminded how defenseless I really am, being a black man who has been reared under my parents' standards. With the greater black community having these same standards, again I am outraged. I wish I could have at least had support from the black church.

So my question is, what use was the transformation that I explain in the next few pages of this chapter? Could I use the leadership that the army would teach me and others like me? My parents' world, where white rule was totally accepted as supreme? In my parents' world, where I would someday return to establish a life for my sons, my daughter, and myself? Would I be able to control myself so as not to use this training against the very system that trained me?

Perhaps the army's objective was a real effort to bring black men and other minorities up to an equal footing with white men. However, I don't think one would ever get the greater part of the black community to accept this reasoning. I think that blacks, as a community would say the effort of the army was simply to use the American human resources to its best advantage in the defense of America. I, along with other black boys, just happened to be individuals who were available to be used for this purpose.

In any case, I had begun to accept that the efforts on the part of the United States Army were for real, and without recourse, and that its training objective was for each man to be able to stand on his own two feet. How else could a soldier be effective, be he black or white? From this perspective, I knew it was just a matter of time before I would kick the Mississippi bigot's ass and move closer to finding that self-respect I felt to be missing from the black communities of America.

But it was also clear that the only rights in our training environment were earned rights. For me to earn the right to kick my bunk buddy's butt would come through the rest of the platoon's approval. I had to earn that approval through demonstrated ability. It would seem that demonstrated ability would be something that could not be taken away. Ever. However, over the chapters of this book, you will learn that social acceptance or the lack of it has a way of destroying even ability once demonstrated.

After we had been issued our full field equipment, which included an M-1 Springfield semiautomatic rifle, basic training began. The first week was called zero week, or going through the motions. It was simply an observation week so the platoon sergeants could assess the strengths and weaknesses of the personnel assigned to each platoon. After zero week, the platoon sergeants assigned leadership positions, which included an acting platoon sergeant per each platoon and four squad leaders who were subordinate to the acting platoon sergeants and leaders of the platoon's four assigned squads.

I was not assigned to any of the leadership positions. But neither was the bigot. So, we were still starting out even, and I knew I would out-soldier him. It was my plan not to give him any reason to think I was anything more than the Southern nigger he had taken me to be.

All southern niggers were afraid of white men, right? I wanted him to know it was a scared southern nigger who kicked his white Mississippi ass. And I wanted him to know I had done it with most of the fourth platoon looking on. And I wanted that platoon to be on my side. I knew that this was something I would have to work at very hard. Not because I could not kick his butt, but rather because I needed the support of the platoon when the time came.

My full field gear was almost too much for me to compete with—all the straps that were designed to secure some 45 pounds on one's back. It was scary, just looking at it heaped there on the floor in front of my footlocker. Then, too, I was always just a few inches from the one person who I felt could cause my entire life to be a failure if I did not deal with him in the right manner.

The full field gear was something I soon came to realize had all of the new recruits in a puzzling dilemma. Possibly, there was just one person in the entire platoon who may have had the experience to deal with our dilemma: Private Knox, the assigned acting platoon sergeant who had one year of college reserve officer training under his belt. I had found him to be a great asset to all of us. So, I called upon him for assistance, and found myself waiting in line because almost everyone else needed his assistance as well.

The hardest thing for me to accept in trying to secure my full field gear was that, once it was properly secured, I would be able to march 20 miles with it on my back—with an additional nine pounds that came in the form of an M-1 rifle. It was finally agreed that Private Knox would help each of the four assigned acting squad leaders to assemble their full field gear. Then it would be the squad leader's responsibility to help the people assigned to his squad.

Of the five blacks assigned to the fourth platoon of forty new recruits, my assigned squad leader was the only black picked for a leadership position. Private Whiteside was an almost typical southern nigger, with one exception: he had a college education. Even though he had a quick savvy about himself, he had one trait I just could not stand.

Every time Private Whiteside gave another black instructions, he spoke so loud that everyone in the squad bay could hear him. When he was helping one of the white recruits, no one knew he was around.

However, I was sure Private Whiteside would soon after basic training become Sergeant Whiteside. He just had all the right things going for him, including knowing his place. He had often told me not to make trouble with the white boys, and life would be much easier for me, even in the army. I am sure that was good advice because life was not very easy for me, especially in the army with this one white boy anyway —the big bigot from Mississippi, who continued to call me nigger and get in my way every morning that I had been assigned as his bunk buddy. And that was from day one.

After Private Whiteside had helped me assemble my backpack, I tested it and was even more convinced that neither the backpack nor I could make the 20 miles that I was told we would have to do on a regular basis—soon. I was still sweating mastering the full field pack when the next block of instruction started: the M-1 rifle, under the supervision of SFC Quinnones.

We were marched to the arms room for the issuing of our weapons. For me, this was a special time and the real beginning of being transformed from civilian to soldier. But even with my understanding the magic of this event, I did not really understand the far-reaching effects of this magic. I did not realize the pressures this instrument would have on my life, from the first time I felt the weight and balance of it in my untrained hands until this day.

On our return to the fourth platoon barracks, now armed with the one item that truly made us different from the average Joe Blow, Sergeant Quinnones began our introduction to this very special block of instruction. He told us we would become more familiar with this item than we were with the palms of our own hands. That it would be closer to us than our own mothers. That it would become an extension of our own bodies, and at times, we would feel more naked without our weapon than we would without our trousers. Over the next 21 years of my life, I found all of what SFC Quinnones said to be true, much to my own chagrin. However, at the moment of his introduction, I found it exciting and was very eager to learn more about this almost intoxicating machine.

One week was devoted to the M-1 rifle. During this time, we learned this weapon piece by piece. First, we learned the four major groups, or the field scripting of the weapon: the trigger housing group, the bolt, the barrel group, and the stock. We were required to break the rifle down into the four major groups and reassemble the weapon while blind-folded. The idea was to be able to take the rifle apart during darkness for quick cleaning during enemy engagement. The time to accomplish this task was one minute.

Our next block of instruction was detailing the weapon, which required breaking down the major groups, which were scattered about on a table, and subsequently identifying each part and what part it played in the major group. After learning the physical structure of the M-1 rifle, the next step was to know the weapon's characteristics, i.e., its range, velocity, rate of fire per minute, effective killing range, and weight. It was not until this killing machine had intruded the most inner part of my mind that we were required to pick up our weapons before or after physical training.

Some mornings we were required to take physical training with weapons, and other mornings, we took physical training without them. However, before drills we were required to secure our weapons from the arms room. Drilling with the weapon is in most cases the most colorful and memorable part of basic combat training, but I also think it was the final step of ramming this machine right up our asses until it became part of our guts. At one time in life, I thought the right shoulder armed, and left shoulder armed, present arms, armed salute, and so on tidbit was simply to learn how to handle a rifle. Now I know there was more to it. It really was a form of indoctrination.

The final act with this killing machine was to fire it. During the last few weeks of basic combat training, M-1 rifle became an extension of our body. We were up at 0500 hours (5 a.m.), had a quick breakfast, and rushed back to the barracks. There, we strapped on the forty-five-pound field pack, hustled to the arms room to pick up the nine and a half pound rifle, and at 6 a.m., we were in formation—sixty pounds heavier than what we were when we got out of the bunk.

Over and above all this, I was still putting up with the bigot from Mississippi. From the very beginning, I found it hard to accept marching twenty miles with fifty-nine pounds strapped to my back. I found that I was not too far off base. For a great number of the new recruits, the twenty-mile march to the rifle range was a bit too much, even after four weeks of physical training and drills.

The hills of Fort Jackson were of loose, sandy soil and made marching even for a short distance tiresome. Those who had problems with the earlier physical training found themselves dropping out after five miles of hard marching and occasional double-timing. My friend the bigot, though, seemed to take it in stride.

For the most part, the two weeks of going to the range and firing the M-1 rifle was a rewarding experience. It was the first phase of our training where our results could be recorded. I fired no better than my bunk buddy. In fact, at this stage of our training, I found myself hustling just to keep up with this guy. But I made sure my boots and lockers were the best they could be. I was sure I had won more friends than he had, simply because I had tried harder to win them.

We were more than halfway through training, and I was still putting up with the abuse from the big guy from Mississippi. I knew I would soon have to take care of this business or it would be too late. I figured I had to do it in time to overcome the whole matter in time for graduation. I had to plan the best time.

Saturday was a training day, and on Sunday, most of us went to church. So, the most optimum time for the job would be Thanksgiving morning, which was the next holiday prior to graduation. I began to think the whole thing out. It would have to be early in the morning, before anyone was out of bed. Otherwise, I felt there would be too many distractions. I felt, at this stage of the game, I needed all the help I could get. Already, I knew this guy was not going to be a pushover. My final plan was to attack from the bottom.

Early on Thanksgiving morning, I would lie on the bottom bunk and kick upward, kicking him out of the top bunk, and be ready for him when he hit the floor. Then a kick in the nuts. I felt that, about that time, most of the rest of the platoon would be out of their bunks to see me finish him off. It was only a week before I would have to make good on this plan. If it did not work, well, I could kiss my future good-bye.

The week before Thanksgiving, 1959, was the longest week of my young life. I had had only one previous encounter with a white man, and from that experience, I had lost credibility with my mother because I had lost my job. If this plan didn't work, I could lose it all, including a chance at a career I had waited on since my eleventh birthday—my dream of becoming a pilot and the opportunity to win the respect I always wanted from my family and community. It *had* to work.

I don't know how others saw my performance from the time I made up my mind to take care of this bigot, but I am sure it was down one or two notches from the previous week's because I was scared as hell just thinking about what was ahead. This guy had me by a good twenty pounds. What if I did not kick hard enough to kick him out of the top bunk? What if he caught me still in my bunk after my kick? Well, I had made up my mind, and I had a good plan.

On Thanksgiving, about 0600, it was still dark in the fourth platoon building. I laid on my back, looking up at the bulge in the top bunk over me, knowing that bulge represented about 210 pounds of tough bigot that soon would have the shock of his life— possibly something he would never forget. I was sure I would never forget. I knew I had to do it. But that did not help the knots that had developed in my stomach.

I took one last deep breath and kicked upward as hard as I could. The big Mississippi bigot hit the floor with a shout, "You nigger!" By that time, I had kicked him right in the balls and pushed him to the floor. I landed on top and punched him out. With every blow, I reminded him that it was a nigger kicking his ass. To my surprise, the whole barracks was cheering me on, including the acting platoon sergeant, Private Knox. I threw some final blows and reassured myself that I had done the right thing. I felt I had a future with the U.S. Army.

Several days later, and very much to my surprise, my bunk buddy spoke to me in a kinder, gentler manner. Believe it or not, we became friends before graduation and taking Christmas leave. I felt I had become a man.

Chapter 7

Doing Manly Things

This was my second trip into Columbia, South Carolina. My first had been with a white friend, Private King, who had been the leader of my cheering squad when I kicked the Mississippi bigot's ass. For the most part, my first visit to the capital city of South Carolina had been one with mixed emotions and questions. *Why had King and I not been allowed to go into the picture show together? Why did King, after agreeing to go into the white section, climb the rails to the balcony of the picture show, where blacks were designated to sit? And why did two big white guys come up and escort both King and me to the door? Moreover, why after leaving the show, did King want to become an instant captain? Why did the military police not believe that he was an army captain taking a stroll on the black side of town with a black army private?*

I learned several lessons on my first trip to Columbia: 1) Black policemen did arrest white men, as long as both were military. 2) There are really some dumb white men. 3) Life could be great if white folk would not interfere.

For the greater part, I did not have anything against good white folk; however, to this point in my life they had caused me more pain than I cared to remember, especially when I was in the presence of seemingly every black beauty in South Carolina.

At this time in my life, I was not proficient at the art of perusal or seducing young lovely things. And in my state of mind, I had little time for lessons. I wondered if the United States government had planned the setting I was presently experiencing, and if so, where were the technical manuals to explain how to operate the system? The answer to my question was just a block away, in the form of the USO.

I quickly learned that the purpose of the USO was to serve the service man. If you could not get what you wanted from the front desk, just wait in place. It would come to you. My answer was in the form of a young coed from one of the institutions of higher learning that sat just across the street, one facing the other. Both institutions came highly recommended by the black community, and who was I to say the product was not quality.

The young lady had a very presentable package: big brown eyes, light tan complexion, black hair, and I would guess about a 34-24-36. The only thing she said to me was ten and two. And, recalling being approached by a working girl when Eddie and I were first in Jacksonville, Florida, I knew just what she was talking about.

Jacksonville seemed to be another lifetime away. Maybe it was. But that lifetime was less than two months past. As I recall from my first trip to Columbia, Allen University, sat was in the next block, on Harden and Blanding. The USO was just down the street, on Harden.

The young lady had taken me just around the corner to a rooming house to a room with a single bed and a night-stand. The bed had no covering but a single clean white sheet that was perfectly pressed. The room was simple but very clean. Again, I thought the U.S. government must supervise this whole thing. Possibly, the U.S. Government was looking at the operation from the corner of its eye.

Once the coed and I were in the room, she disrobed with the light on, and to this day, I have not seen a more beautiful picture, including all of the Playboy magazines I have viewed over the years. I am sure the lovely young thing was putting on a show for me, and I was enjoying every minute of it. She could have not been a day over 20; however, Iam sure from the very beginning she knew I had never been with a real woman.

She wanted to make it easy for me. After disrobing, she took my hand and guided me to the bed, and together we sat on the edge and made small talk until I regained my composure. She taught me the art of lovemaking, and afterward, made a show of putting on her clothing the same as she had when she disrobed. Together, we walked the short distant back to the USO.

On this the second trip to this exotic city of the Deep South, I was again seeking the company of the only real woman I had ever known in such an intimate manner. But much to my displeasure, I was unable to find her. On the campus of Benedict College, there was a battle of the bands concert taking place. Among them was the Rattler's band of Florida A&M University.

Several of my classmates were part of the Rattler's band, one of whom was a boy by the name of Harry Roundtree. We had started the eleventh grade together, and it was good to see him. But I felt, at the time, he had one step up on me, just being a part of all the excitement of the college campus. Poor me. I never even made it through the eleventh grade.

After about an hour with Harry and the excitement of the band competition, I decided to look for female companionship outside of the college environment and headed for Taylor Street. Taylor Street was lined with nightclubs, with live bands in each of the better clubs. My strategy was to find the club with the loudest music and the biggest crowd. There was a two-dollar cover at the door, and more GIs, all black, than you could shake a stick at. It was a BYOB joint.

The setup was ideal for an army training center type operation. Persons who were 21 or older could bring their booze and get a setup at a table for an additional five-dollar charge. All of us who were less than 21, would be left to stand around the wall.

Standing around the wall was like being ducks in a shooting gallery. The working girls could almost take their pick, and they did. The routine was always the same, as if these girls had their own union. They would select from a distance, using eye contact. After an approving nod from the prospective client, the working girl would walk to the spot where the client stood and whisper, 10 and 2. The rooms normally would be in a boarding house, but often were located in the back room of a family residence. I am sure the army accepted this arrangement as long as the GI was not taken the advantage of.

On this night, on my second go-around on the merry-go-round of pleasure, I learned that not all working girls were honest, even in what seemed to be the best working relationship between the army and this thriving black business community. While doing my thing in the back room, my trousers hung on the back of a chair.

Once the action was over and I went to put on my trousers, there was no wallet. I made some fuss and refused to leave. The wallet was returned, with an apology on my return to the club. For what? You be the judge. After all, I was just eighteen! But in any case, I learned my second lesson about women of the evening. This working girl had an admirer or lover who wanted her to give him some attention. It was apparent she had not wanted to be bothered; however, he continued to follow her as she tried to do her business. Seemingly, with little or no effort at all, she took a straight razor from her bag and cut off his nose with one sweep of the instrument. Blood was everywhere, and with-in a matter of minutes, so were city policemen and military police. The city policemen took the man and woman away, and business went on as nothing ever happened.

I had one week to go before graduation, and then I could be home for Christmas. This meant one more weekend in Columbia before I would go into my advanced military training. But I had learned some valuable lessons! 1) Make sure you know who you are fooling with. 2) Don't bother a working girl when she is trying to take care of business. 3) Don't lay your wallet around, when catting around. 4) It is a lot safer at the USO and on college campuses than on the streets of Columbia.

Chapter 8

Christmas Of 1959

Eight weeks prior, I would have never bet that I could accomplish all the things I would soon be able to boast about when I took my Christmas leave, which was just a week or so away. In this time I had mastered the M-1 rifle, marched twenty miles with more than sixty pounds strapped to my back, and had taken on and kicked the butt of a Mississippi bigot. I had had my first orgasm with a lovely thing from an institution of higher learning. I really felt like a man. However, there were several things I still wished for.

I wished that I had received more mail from home. For eight weeks, I had made mail call every day and had received only two letters. There were four other coloreds in my platoon, and with the exception of one, it seemed they got mail every day from their family, including boxes with homemade cookies and whatnot's.

I also wished my family could be present for my graduation. But even with my strongest prayer, I knew there was not a chance. Eight weeks had been a lifetime. We had only one final test—record firing of the M-1. All other tests, including the physical fitness test, were history. I had scored 450 of a possible 600 and had also qualified for airborne training, where you had to score 1,000 of a possible 1,200, which had included a six-mile run. After record fire, the rest of the week would be devoted to taking pictures and parade practice, getting ready for graduation day.

The morning of record fire, wakeup was as usual: 0500 hours, breakfast 0530, picking up my rifle on return from breakfast, and being in morning formation at the sound of reveille, which was always 0600 sharp.

On this morning, SFC Quinnones gave a right-face command instead of his usual left-face command that was in the direction of the rifle range, some twenty miles away. We marched about the length of a football field and did a column left, and there in the dawn of the morning were the outlines of three tractors and trailers that were referred to as cattle cars.

Starting with the first platoon, we were herded like cattle onto the trucks. The seating arrangements were a bench on each side of the trailer and one bench down the middle of the trailer, allowing the platoon sergeant to seat about sixty recruits to each of the three tractors and trailers. I think I would rather have walked.

It was a tight fit, twenty per row, with full field and M-1 rifles. By the time we reached the rifle range, my backside was numb from the hard wooden seats. But there was the consolation of knowing, if we qualified, this would be our very last trip to a rifle range with full field pack unless we were assigned to a combat unit as a permanent duty.

Of the five coloreds, Private Green, from West Virginia, was the only one who would be assigned to an infantry unit after receiving advanced infantry training, meaning eight more weeks of the same. Private LeCorne and I would be assigned as communications specialists. Private Whiteside was assigned to transportation. Private Gains, who had prior service, would not need advanced training and would be assigned to an overseas organization. I learned later that the cattle cars had been called in to speed up training so we could be finished before Christmas break.

Our cycle had started on October 22, 1959, and Christmas break was set to start December 23. The cattle car ride to the rifle range was on a Monday, as I recall, December 17. Graduation would be Friday. Saturday, December 23 I could redo Columbia and have my first Greyhound bus ride along the highways of the great south. After we were herded off the cattle cars and assembled by platoons, we were each assigned a partner from one of the other platoons. With partner and rifle in the port arm position, we were marched to the ready line of the qualifying range.

This range was not anything like the practice ranges had been. In fact, it took on the form of a jungle or forest. I saw no way one would be able to see a target from where we stood. My partner was a short black kid from the first platoon who was as puzzled as I was.

The range noncommissioned officer in charge was a six-foot-plus black guy with stripes that covered the greater part of his arms as well as his yellow helmet. He introduced himself as Master Sergeant Jackson. He explained in no uncertain terms that he was in charge. His safety lecture was, "Keep your weapon up and down range! No running on the range, but walk at a quick step pace, and only when you are told to do so."

Scorecards with number two pencils were passed to my partner, who was now standing behind me. I stood with my rifle barrel up at 60 degrees on the spot marked ready line, pointed down range as I had been instructed. Master Sergeant Jackson's next command was, "This is a walk-through drill. When you are told, you will walk to your first firing position and take a prone position, and engage your target scorers. You will help the firers locate their targets. Move to the first firing position on the firing line."

The first firing position was ten yards straight ahead of the ready line. It was marked by a path and a clearing in the bush where many other recruits had gone before us. My scorer and I walked to the first position and took up a prone position by the number: 1) Knees make contact with the ground, 2) Rifle butt makes contact with ground, and 3) Slide the rifle alongside as you take prone position, as we had been taught to do over the past weeks at the training fire range.

As we looked down range, our target popped up only ten feet or so in front of us. "That was your ten-meter target, [hope you all saw it. The next time you see it will be for record. Move to your next firing position." Just another ten meters or so we could see the foxhole, and moved to take our position, with me in the hole and my scorer taking the prone position to the side of the hole, I engaged the target with the help of my scorer. "That was your 150-meter target. Move to your next firing position." The next position was behind a post and was listed as the kneeling position. We moved to the kneeling position spot, and were getting pretty good at finding the targets that popped up in various places throughout our lane of fire in the density of the vast forest that now engulfed us. The last position was the squatting. That was some 50 meters into the thickets of the forest—mostly pines with undergrowth in the sandy hills of South Carolina. We were ordered to move to the last position and to engage our target, which was another 10-meter target. After the last target, the command was about-face.

As we walked through the forest back to the ready line, we were reminded of safety, and to keep the weapon up, and down range, and that our next run would be with live ammo and for record. We were reminded that failing to qualify could mean not graduating. By the time I reached the ready line, the palm of my hand was wet, and the temperature was about 36 degrees. Upon returning to the ready line, we were again reminded to keep the weapon up and down range. We were given a bandolier of 96 rounds—eight per clip—and were told to go for it. Each target would stay up for ten seconds, with ten seconds allowed between each position.

Standing on the ready line, rifle up and down range, and bandolier with twelve eight round clips slung across my chest, I waited for the next command. I wondered if the targets had faces, what they would look like. The last war had been the faces of the Koreans. What would the next face be? I very well could have fixed the face of our old iceman, Red. Maybe Sheriff McCall, who had killed my neighbors. But my upbringing would not have allowed that. My parents had taught me to love those who despitefully use you and abuse you. So, like almost everyone else, the faces I would see on the target would be Japs. Why Japs? I think because the Japanese were the easiest for Americans to hate. And was not I an American?

The command came: "Ready on the right." The assistants to the tall master sergeant signaled that the right side of the range was ready. "Ready on the left." The signal from the left was ready. "Ready on the firing line. Firers, watch your lane, lock and load one eight-round clip and move to the first firing position. Keep those weapons up and down range, and fire when ready."

From the first firing position, I fired three rounds to kill the target. Then I moved to the next firing position, and from the foxhole, I got the target with the first shot. Next was the kneeling position, and with two shots, I knock off the envisioned Jap. The command to move to the next target was given by an assistant who walked between firing lanes and maintained safety on the range. After firing 96 rounds, I had 68 kills, just two short of qualifying "expert."

Basic training for all practical purposes was over on the afternoon of Monday, December 17, 1959. The rest of the week would be in preparation for graduation and passing out awards. Finally, we would have the parade that would be the grand finale. As I guessed, my parents would not be present. The only black parents were Private Green's. I recall his father to have been retired from the U.S Army.

The theater where our graduation was held was nearly full. The four platoons were seated in the middle of the theater, in reverse order, starting at the front of the theater: 4th, 3rd, 2nd, and 1st platoon. This created the illusion that everyone was the same height when seated because of the slanted theater floor. We were all dressed in our army greens, and our overseas caps, better known within the ranks of GIs as the "cunt cap" because it was said to take on the form of the female genitalia when it was opened to be placed on one's head. My first planned stop after this—the last official act of basic combat training —was to visit and view a real-life cunt. However, I had no plans of putting my head into it!

Seated to our right were visitors, parents, and friends of the graduating class of Company a 19th Battalion 5th Training Regiment of the United States Army. The left was reserved for visiting commanders and flag-ranked officers. Seated on stage where the company commanders and platoon sergeants of the graduating cycle.

I had never been more impressed by anything in all of my eighteen years, and passing review was yet to come. The formal ceremony was very extensive and informative.

The regiment commander was the first to speak. He had entered the building like a king, and when he was announced, everyone in the theater came to their feet, including visitors. His speech centered on the history of the 5th regiment, who had seen action in Normandy, Korea, France, Germany, and many other places with names I couldn't pronounce. Then the company commander took the podium, and called his command to attention, as the regiment commander and his aide departed the theater.

By this time, I was so proud that I was almost in tears because nobody from my little hometown of Clermont was there to see me becoming a part of something that already had given me a sense of pride I had never thought possible. *Why was I so proud? Would that condition change? With my new uniform, and having passed the test into manhood, would I now be permitted to sit on the main floor of the picture show in Columbia?* I did not have an answer for any of these questions. However, I knew I never wanted to loose what I felt.

The company commander told us all why we should feel proud, and especially those who had performed exemplarily. There were three awards given for exemplary performance: 1) Physical Fitness, 2) Weapon Qualification, and 3) Best All-Around Trainee. There was one black to receive an award —Private Lee, from the third platoon.

The next event would be the last of the day and the last most of us would see of one another. The commander announced from the podium, "Prepare for passing review. Platoon sergeants, take charge of your platoon."

Sergeant Quinnones, our Puerto Rican platoon sergeant, came down from the stage, and I am sure I saw a tear on his cheek. He gave the command: "Left face and right file, column right, March!" As we filed out of the theater, other companies all around were filing out, and we could hear the 5th regiment band from the parade field playing military marching music. That day's events will be frozen in my mind forever. Damn! That was something.

The coming together of one platoon after another, just through perfect commands from the platoon sergeants, given in a timely manner, was something for the eye to see. One would have said that this was not possible had they seen us just eight weeks prior. The companies continued to file out of the 5th regiment theaters until it was a full regiment marching in perfect timing to army-band marching music. As we took our positions, one company after another, the commanders, parents, and friends of the graduating 5th Training Regiment were mounting the reviewing stand.

I felt that ice was going through my veins. Surely, it couldn't get any better than this. Soon the regiment parade ground was full from left to right with perfect aligned columns of young men—black and white, standing tall side by side, and feeling good about it. It was only a few days before Christmas, and for sure, one could not have a greater Christmas present than this.

The regiment commander, now standing tall in the center of the reviewing stand, gave next command: "Take charge of your companies." All of the company commanders moved at their own pace without music by the most direct route to take charge of their respective company. This part of the parade too was special because it showed a sense of ownership. Upon reaching his company, the company commander was greeted with a hand salute by the platoon sergeant, "Sir, the company is formed." The company commander then responded, "Sergeant, take your post."

A loud single bugle sounded from the band, and the regiment commander gave another command: "Adjutant Post." This sent a quickstepping captain from the reviewing stand until he reached the very center of the parade field, twenty yards or so directly in front of the viewing stand. Once there, he came to attention with a snappy move and did an about-face. Now he was facing the regiment commander. He looked back over his right shoulder, and at the top of his voice, commanded: "G-G-G-Guides Post," then looked back to the regiment commander, "Sir, the regiment is formed."

One award was given at the regiment formation: the winning recruit for Trainee of the Regiment. He and his commander marched to the center of the field, and faced the regiment commander. This time, the regiment commander came down from the stand and marched to the center of the field, with his aide carrying the award—an Army Commendation Medal. The commander and his aide stood directly in front of the company commander and the winning trainee, and a citation was read saying that the trainee (who was from another battalion) had brought great credit upon himself, his unit, and the United States Army.

Afterwards, the regiment commander marched back to the reviewing stand, took his position, and made some comments to the effect that only the best of the best were awarded commendation medals so early in an army career, and some would have a twenty-year career without such an award. Then he gave the last command of an event that will be forever etched in my memory: "Passing Review!"

The band began to play. My company was positioned almost in the middle of the regiment, with about eight other companies to our right, and eight or so to our left. The individual company commanders gave the next command. That took the effect of a chain reaction: "Company, right-face," echoing from one company to the other, until the entire regiment was facing one way in perfect alignment. Followed by the next command: "Left turn march," as the guide arm (a flag carried by a select soldier called the guide arm barer, who identifies the unit and signals when the preparatory command is given by the commander), went up and came down passing review was on its way.

As each company reached the left-turn spot marked on the parade field, one could see the guide arm lifted high. And as the command was given, the troops made the left turn staying in perfect alignment, and the guide arm came down again as each soldier keep perfect timing to the beat of the drum, one thirty-inch military step after the other.

Some ten yards or so from the reviewing stand, the command was, "Eyes right." The guide arm was dropped and held straight out in front of the barrier so the unit designation could be read from the reviewing stand, and all persons, with the exception of the right file, looked to the right. The commander surrendered a hand salute.

These moments are the pride of any soldier's life, for the command is saying to him, "You have met my approval." It's equal to the walk across the stage at a high school or college graduation.

At this point, I had nothing else to do. I knew that home would not be any more than a family affair. I had no girl. I did not even want a girl. However, at this point, I was thinking as soon as we marched past that reviewing stand, I would be Columbia bound and would again meet one of the working girls from the institution of higher learning for lessons in sex education. My duffle bag was packed and lying on my bunk. I already had my roundtrip bus ticket to home and back to Fort Jackson. I would also be receiving my advanced training as a communications specialist here.

LeCorne, Beardin, and Jackson, of the 3rd platoon, and I had already pooled our money for the cab to Columbia. An extra ten dollars to pay the cabbie to pick up the girls off Taylor Street, close to Allen and Benedict colleges. It was almost routine for the cab driver to ask trainees if extra services would be required, and one could almost always depend on the delivery. The business of prostitution in Columbia in the black community was big business. Nobody wanted the word passed around that the GI was getting a bad deal.

I was not so sure I wanted to visit Columbia; I was still on a high after passing the reviewing stand, with eyeball-to-eyeball contact with the regiment commander, who I perceived to say directly to me, "Well done, son."

But I guessed I had to go along with LeCorne and the others, now that the plans were made. As we marched into our company area, the cabs were already lined up to receive their fair for our exit wherever we wanted to go. It took about five minutes for the four of us to go in, grab our bags, and select a cab with a driver who we thought could fulfill our request.

The cab was from the Yellow Cab Company. The driver was a well-built black gentleman with a friendly face. There were no words spoken between us; he simply popped his trunk and began trying to fit our bags inside it. All bags except one fit into the trunk. That one was placed into the back seat with Jackson and Bearden. Still, no words were spoken by any of the four.

The cab driver broke the silence. "I know you boys want some action."

"Yes, but we want some of them college girls." Bearden had placed our order.

Now it was the cabbie's turn. "You know that will cost you an extra ten. Pay in advance."

Bearden passed him the ten dollars, all in the dollar bills that we had given him. The cabbie instructed us how to register at the hotel where he would drop us to wait for the girls.

"You guys will have to give me your names on a piece of paper, and when you get to the hotel you can get a room for two dollars each for one hour. The person at the front desk will direct the girls to your room when I drop them off."

The hotel was an old red-brick construction with double wooden doors and peeled paint. The lighting on the inside was dim, and a young woman signed us in at the front desk. Her only question was, "Will you be expecting company?" We told her we would, and she replied, "Make sure you print your name plain."

Business was very clearly good, for not a minute passed without a door being open and slammed. From looking at the register, we were lucky to get four rooms. There were no keys; all of the doors had sliding latches on the inside. We were instructed to only open the door if the girl who knocked knew our name.

I went to my room, latched the door behind me, and waited for the knock that came about twenty minutes after I laid down on the iron frame bed, fitted with only a sheet. The girl who knocked called me by my last name, Montgomery. I got up and opened the door. I felt cheated. The girl at the door must have been 25, and for sure not a college girl.

I asked her, "Are you going to college?" She answered, "Why? Ain't I good enough for you?"

I wanted to tell her she was not what I had ordered; however, I let her in. She was out of her clothes before I could pull off my shoes, and lying naked on the bed.

"Come on, baby. I don't got all day."

I felt like walking out of the room, but she was not half bad, lying there on the bed with no covers. She had a slender build, long hair, and a tan complexion.

I took my time. I looked at her, which she seemed to enjoy, so I thought maybe she would not be so bad. "Money first, honey," I gave her the ten dollars. She got off the bed walked across to the chair where her purse was, and put the ten inside. By this time, I was undressed. "You ain't half bad," she said. My thought was *half bad, my ass,* I am down-right *physical.* And I was, after the many mornings of physical training and marches to the rifle range the past eight weeks. I was 6'1" tall, 192 pounds, with a 28" waist and a 46" chest. I was *bad*.

The action on the bed was all business. After I was in her, it was as if she was counting the strokes and she knew the exact stroke at which I would reach orgasm. "That's it, honey. You only paid for one time.' I protested, but she made it very clear by slapping my backside that the action was over.

Almost as soon as she left the room, there was another knock on the door, "Montgomery." A short, dark-complexioned girl said my girl was in LeCorne's room and we still had time for another quickie at half price. I passed and went to look for Jackson and Bearden, only to find that they had left for Fayetteville, North Carolina, and said they would see me in January 1960, in communications school.

I waited at the front desk for LeCorne, and in the short time it took for him to come down, I counted ten couples who signed in and out of the hottest hotel in Columbia, South Carolina, two days before Christmas 1959.

The fare to the Greyhound bus station was $1.50 each. It was my first visit to a bus station of any type. There was a waiting room for coloreds and one for whites. The station was full of GIs just out of basic, some of whom I knew. There were more blacks than whites; however, the black waiting room was much smaller, with no eating area. There was a sliding window, where you could order food from the white's side of the station. For the most part, the black civilians carried brown paper bags with food from home (mostly fried chicken, or lunch meat between white bread).

The waiting area seemed to be one big picnic. For a newcomer to these environments, like me, one would think that everyone knew each other. I was glad I had my ticket. I was already thinking this would be my last time buying a ticket to ride a Greyhound bus.

The activity in the area was almost the same as Taylor Street: Prostitution, greasy pig, and the money in the envelope trick. For the most part, the white boys were the ones being taken because the blacks had already been had at least once. It was almost unsafe to go outside of the station once you had made it in because, by one means or another, someone was going to get your money.

I checked with the person at the ticket counter for the departing time for my bus. I learned that the departing time for the bus to Charleston was 6:30 p.m. or 1830 hours military time. It was then 4:10, two hours and twenty minutes to wait in a place that was becoming more and more unpleasant by the minute. LeCorne was much more at ease. He had already made a trip to the little sliding window for food and drink. I wasn't hungry.

I began to assess who was who and tried to figure out where they were all going. For the most part, they were Carolinians going short distances within South Carolina. And others were going to northern states like New York, Chicago, and Washington, DC for the Christmas holidays. Some were complete families, with only a few days off from work who would soon repeat this process, after visiting families and friends, so they could be back on their jobs.

All the college kids had departed several days earlier, so almost none of the travelers were from Benedict College or Allen University. I was preoccupied trying to figure out why I felt so totally out of place with these people, when LeCorne was right at home. Was it because it seemed they accepted everything as normal and I felt it was abnormal to be barred from clean, decent facilities?

Finally, the Charleston bus departure was announced! I jumped to my feet to learn that that announcement was for whites only, and we would have to wait until they were loaded before we were allowed out of the waiting room. The second announcement was, "All coloreds for Charleston, your bus is now loading." I told myself again I would return by bus, but never again would I buy a ticket.

While boarding the bus, I saw trainees who graduated with me who now felt superior to me. I thought of King, who had climbed the rail of the theater in Columbia because we were not permitted to sit together. King had been kicked out of the army because he had been ruled not trainable. I wondered if he was still standing up for blacks and how much trouble he was having in his hometown back in Virginia.

As the bus pulled out of the station, LeCorne and I were one seat from the last seat in the bus, which was not a bad seat. I had the window seat and easily saw the hustle and bustle of the streets of Columbia. The bus departed the city that would always be a part of my memory.

Charleston was the city where my Grandfather Wallace was born. The bus made many stops between Columbia and Charleston. I saw all the personalities at each stop, both black and white. However, my mind mostly compared what I saw to what my grandfather must have looked like as a young man in these environments. I saw almost no one of the Negro race who stood tall, as I had on the parade field during passing review. For the most part, the older Negroes walked slowly with their heads to the ground, and the younger moved about with no particular sense of direction.

Charleston was a city of great beauty, the capital city of the South, the city with rich history, where the first shot of the civil war was fired. Charleston was founded in 1667. How long would it be before coloreds would display a sense of pride in these parts, and how could it be that with in this same region, with only a fence as a divider, black men stood tall, walked with their heads high? Why couldn't black men have the same authority outside the army as they had within it?

We arrived at the North Charleston bus station just short of four hours after departing Columbia; the only other rest stop had been Orangeburg. At Orangeburg, I saw only a few white folk and, seemingly, hundreds of coloreds, with none being in positions of authority.

In Charleston, the condition repeated itself. But there, I felt closer to the people because out there someplace, I had several great uncles, aunts, and cousins who I would never see, unless someone did a search of the

Montgomery family tree. A gene study. But who would ever have time to do anything like that? Maybe me? But when? I had no answers, so I shook LeCorne to wake him, for he had been asleep almost since departing Columbia.

As LeCorne and I departed the bus for the colored side of the bus station, I was in goose bumps. There were so many coloreds, of which many looked to be well-educated men and women. There was even a dining room for coloreds to eat in. LeCorne and I ordered hamburger platters from the grill, helped ourselves to a Coke from the Coke machine, and took a table to wait for the next bus to Jacksonville.

I could not help looking at all those coloreds, thinking that I could possibly see a resemblance of my father, uncle, or one of my aunts. I was sure blood kin was with in throwing distant from my table.

I can't remember my grandfather; however, I was told he often came to our house when I was just a baby and would take me for long walks, until my mother would not allow him to visit any more. She often had to hunt him down just to retrieve me. Afterwards, I was told he would wait until no one was looking and would steal me away from the family. Before I was old enough to remember, the family had him put away somewhere in Chattahoochee, Florida, just south of the Georgia line and only about 100 miles from my father's birthplace in Moultrie, Georgia.

As we waited for our next bus, my mind was completely engulfed with thoughts of my grandfather. I would trace his migration south to the birthplace of my father. Some two hundred and twenty miles south of Charleston. I would also pass within a few miles from where my grandfather died while still confined to the asylum in Chattahoochee. As I recall, this was in the fall of 1947. I don't recall a funeral being held. Possibly, there was some type of family observance, but it must have been a very hush-hush affair.

I was feeling a great deal of pain when the call came for the white folk to load the bus for Jacksonville. The city of Charleston, South Carolina, within itself represented a great deal of pain. It could be called the birthplace of slavery, or the point of debarkation for the North American slave trade, and also the place that started the war to defend slave practices. This was also a town my grandfather saw a need to flee, and I was waiting to load the bus after to those whose ancestors had inflected this pain upon me and upon my predecessors.

When it was our time to board the bus, I was thinking how I could again generate those feelings I had had just that morning during graduation. I looked on the bright side, and could only assume that someplace, somehow, I would again feel proud to be an American. However, for the next ten hours or so I would be covering territory that could only generate more pain.

LeCorne and I again took the seat, one ahead of the last, in the back of the bus. He was generous and let me have the window I had enjoyed since we left Columbia. Again, he was asleep before I could say ten words to him about the plight of my grandfather.

The bus headed south on Highway 17 to Savannah, and I remained awake with a million thoughts. For whatever reason, I thought of Al Joseph (the white man who painted his face to imitate blacks) and the Swanee River. *Why should I dislike him so? Was he not painting a true picture during his minstrel shows when he imitated coloreds?* We had our music, our love for the land, and our hope that one day God would end our suffering. Possibly, Joseph told our story better through his minstrel shows than what we ever could, simply because he had a better résumé—he was a white man. Then I thought there was little or no future in this country for coloreds, simply because we had so little to build on.

I was a young black man, subordinate first to older black men of my community, who were subordinate to white men. It is unlikely our voices would ever be heard, and my father's voice would only be heard through that of a white man, who would demand his total loyalty.

So it was as I looked from the window of the bus headed south on Highway 17 to Savannah. I knew I would be a soldier for many years to come because it would be as close as I could come to being my own man and having my voice heard in this country.

It was past 3 a.m. when the bus pulled into the Savannah station. The driver of the bus and several other people got off, and others got on. LeCorne had only a short distance to go before he would be home. I thought how much I would miss him. LeCorne was a man of very few words, but when he spoke, it was wise to listen. In basic, he had saved me many times, and I knew he would be a success in life because he was made out of the right stuff. I wished, however, that he would speak up for himself more often than he did.

The driver returned to the bus and walked to where we were to check tickets, punching those of new passengers and simply nodding toward LeCorne and me to acknowledge that he recognized us as through passengers from Charleston. When he had reached the front of the bus and checked his last ticket, we were on our way again.

LeCorne was wide-awake now and talked a little about this part of the country. He told me he had worked as far north as Savannah, picking and loading cotton for almost nothing. He preferred loading to picking because, while picking cotton, the bulbs would cut your hands and cause them to bleed if your hands were not toughened for the task. He also expressed a desire to not return to these parts because they held little or no future for a young black man. But he had not yet committed to being a career soldier; he thought he might seek employment in the city after the army.

I told him city or no city, colored was colored, which spelled little or no hope for a long and productive life. I told him I knew schoolteachers married to men who worked in the orange groves and other teachers married to teachers, and they too were tied down to the same old Saturday night routines as everyone else.

Teaching school is about the highest position you could have in the colored community, except being a doctor, and it wasn't worth it just to work for the colored community. Most coloreds had so little money, they couldn't pay. If you could be a funeral director or own a big nightclub, possibly you could have a future. But that takes a lot of money, so my option was to stay in the army as long as I could.

It was early morning when LeCorne pulled the line to signal the driver to stop. Somewhere between Waycross and Valdosta, Georgia, in the middle of nowhere is where I would describe it. But the driver pulled to the side of the road and stopped at a little country store. LeCorne found his handbag, and the driver got out and let him get his duffle bag from the bottom side of the bus. As we were pulling away, I could see LeCorne step up on the front porch to a telephone that hung from the front of the little building. I wondered who was on the other end of line. Probably someone who was very upset to be disturbed so early in the morning, especially with it being Christmas Eve, and one of the few days off from work in these parts.

LeCorne had been the only person in my platoon who had received fewer letters from home than me during basic, so from this perspective, I wondered how my family would respond when I made my phone call from the Greyhound bus stop just off Highway 50—less than a mile from Big Mama's house. *Who would come pick me up? How long would I have to wait in the poorer section of the white community of this very segregated southern town that I called home?*

It was Christmas Eve. No doubt, Mama would be busy cooking or out doing last minute shopping, for my younger sisters and brothers. Of the six, only Alexander was old enough to drive. I began to feel that coming home might even be a mistake—a disruption to a very busy family that was trying to make a living under the most adverse conditions. It was at this point that I decided not to volunteer anything about basic training or my experiences of the past two months while I had been away from home.

I had left home during very trying times. My father had just recovered from a serious accident, during which he had lost the three middle fingers of his right hand. My brother James was married with a new baby. Deloris was in her junior year of college at Florida A&M University. And she had also just had a baby that Mama would have to take care of until she graduated. A younger brother, Alexander, somewhat of a slow learner, had spent the past year recovering from correctional surgery to his feet and had also dropped out of school. My older sister Gloria and her family had just built and moved into a new house, almost as big and beautiful as Mom and Dad's new house.

It was pushing 6 in the morning, and the bus was coming into the city limits of Thomasville, Georgia, less than fifty miles north of Tallahassee. As it slowed down and I was able to see the shacks that coloreds lived in, I thought of my father and mother's house, boasting five bedrooms and three baths. I felt more secure about who I was and where I was going in life. However, not so secure that I thought life was good in my hometown.

For whatever reason, my older brothers and sisters would say that life was just great. They were equally as proud of who they were and thought they had good futures. I disagreed. I think life is not only about gaining wealth, though my family seemed to be on the right track to accomplish that. But rather, life was about establishing strong continuity between family members. In other words, building a family that could enjoy an uninterrupted success base. I did not see that in my family; instead, I saw almost from birth, stiff competition, and it seemed that from the very beginning I was at a disadvantage.

I thought it to be rare for my father to be a general building contractor in 1959 in the most southern part of these United States. But even more rare was for a black family to form an equal partnership between family members, such as incorporation so the success could be passed to each family sibling.

In the small southern town of Clermont, Florida, were several very successful black men, but I knew of no successful black family who had developed into a corporation as one unit. *Was it something carried over from slavery that coloreds were ordained to be in continuous competition with one another? Why was it that black heads of families were so insecure, that their members felt threatened by other members of the family?* In the short time I had been in the U.S. Army, I had learned to trust myself, and I also learned I was strongest when I enlisted both moral and physical help from others. Through the use of this support, there was nothing I could not accomplish.

The bus pulled to a stop in front of a weather-beaten structure that was marked with a metal sign, "Greyhound Bus Station." Several elderly colored women with cardboard boxes waited for its arrival. They were dressed as if they were going to Sunday meeting, including hats. As the bus stopped, each with two boxes struggled to the right side of the bus, where the driver was waiting to secure their luggage and take their tickets. There were several seats open just in front of me. I hoped until it was almost like a prayer that they would not take the open seats just in front of me. I watched them struggle up the three steps and down the aisle until they were just in front of me.

They had been talking all the time. I assessed that they were on their way to Jacksonville for Christmas, and their biggest worries were that there might not be anyone at the station to meet them upon their arrival. "Look at Soldier Boy," one remarked, and still not saying anything directly to me, commented, "I know your mother is proud. You can send her a little money each month."

My thoughts were, *Why is it that black adults looked upon their siblings as a commodity of some sort? or Why would she take for granted that I still lived with my mother?* It was a silly question; I could not have looked over eighteen, which I was not. Most mothers felt boys my age were not old enough to be on their own, and this old sister was no exception. However, when I thought of my old schoolmates, they were all married except one or two, and most were no older than I was. God, I thought! How will they ever make it? But surprisingly, most were doing very well—they even had cars and well-furnished apartments. In fact, most thought I was crazy for enlisting for a mere eighty-seven dollars a month.

For me, money wasn't what it was all about. First, I needed acceptance and respect. I wanted a career, and thus far, I had not seen any opportunity for any of the above in Clermont. The first direct question coming from the women who got on the bus in Thomasville was, "Son, how far are you going?" I answered simply, "Jacksonville."

"Do you live there?"

"No, ma'am. I live in Clermont."

"Ain't never heard of that," was her reply, and for the rest of the questions directed toward me, I did my best to answer with a "Yes, ma'am, or no, ma'am."

It was almost hard for me to admit that in my short eighteen years, I had almost lost all respect for the wisdom of the black community. I was living in hope that some black leader would come along to restore that respect, and the old women were not that somebody. At this stage of my life, I wanted absolutely nothing from the black community but maybe a roll in the hay with the woman of my choice, and I was willing to pay for that.

It was a quarter to eight when the driver called for a rest stop, pulling into the Tallahassee bus station. It looked almost deserted. It was Christmas Eve, and most people were already home with their families. I was thinking that maybe it would be best if I spent my Christmas some other place. But I quickly concluded I would go home and be as much help to Mom and Dad as I could during the two weeks I had off from training.

They had worked hard to make a reasonable life for me and my nine brothers and sisters— even if we never agreed on anything.

I was getting very tired and knew I had another six hours before I would be home. But, for whatever reason, it was impossible for me to sleep while traveling. For the rest of the trip, I promised myself I would try and get some rest. At a minimum, I could close my eyes and pretend to be sleep. Maybe the old women wouldn't direct any questions toward me.

I almost wished I had a girl at home or that I was more like everyone else, feeling good about all the little things of Clermont. Then I did a simple evaluation. First, a girlfriend. But what was there to do? Go to the movie. Go riding in a borrowed car. Park in the orange grove and become a father. That's what already happened to most. My old friend Eddie had fathered several kids. No, I wouldn't be looking for any girlfriend anytime soon.

The next thing in the community would be church participation. My brother James was big on church participation, and the only thing I think it had gotten him to date was a sanctified wife, a baby, and someone to tell him how to live his life. Not to mention how they seemed to take half of his money to support the pastor, who spent too much time around James' sanctified wife. The pastor might have been doing more than counseling. No, I thought I could do just fine for the short time I would be home without female companionship.

The other things that were special were fishing and hunting. People came from all over the United States for these sports. There were the Ocala National Forest for deer and boar, the wetlands along the Kissimmee River, Lake Okeechobee, Saint Jones River, and over one hundred other lakes in my hometown county alone. All this did for me in my early years was make more fighting because everywhere there were white men with guns who I didn't know.

There were almost always rumors that some black had been killed and buried in a cement vault designed especially for the purpose of covering up the rumor of missing blacks. The site of the vault was said to be someplace in the town of Montverde, just ten miles west of my hometown on Highway 50, in the same county.

I think at one time I was almost fond of fishing, until I had an experience with a truckload of crazy young white men with guns who fired several shoots in my direction while I was fishing on the side of the road at Lake Louise, in southwest Lake County. I ran off, even leaving my catch of warmouth and have not fished from the side of the road since. So, when I got home, I would probably stay close to the house or help Dad out in his construction business.

I had learned a great deal about myself in the past eight weeks: 1) I was very objective in nature. 2) I had a deep desire to succeed and find a way to circumvent most persons or things that got in my way. My mom and dad also had the need and energy to succeed. I am sure this is where my drive came from; but I was not willing to take or seemingly sell my most inner being to achieve success. In my hometown, many were, including Mom and Dad.

I always thought of a childhood rival, Lester Cole, as one willing to sell his own family if it would win him favor with the white man. My brother James was almost as bad. I felt both had sold me out in my first and only attempt to work for a white man in our home environment.

I think I inherited my personality from my grandfather, for I was almost always compared to him, which was not willing to do that which was necessary to make a living. As for me, this was not true at all. What was, and is true, is I have never been willing to sell others or myself short for a dollar or anything of a material value.

The driver made his usual calls to load the bus, and soon we were on Highway 27 heading south. We had passed the campuses of Florida State University, and Florida A&M University, my sister Deloris was still in school. We also passed the state capitol. Resting my head on my seat, I had pleasant thoughts again about who I was.

First, I had thought of the Hawkins Family, and Virgil Hawkins, attending the University of Florida School of Law, which was a first for a black man. Then I had thoughts of my very own sister with a college education, which would be a first for the Montgomery family. My own family and the Hawkins's. Those I felt very close to were indeed achievers. Mrs. Hawkins, Virgil's wife, had been my high school algebra teacher.

And I also felt good to be in my home state, even with all of its racial shortcomings. I closed my eyes and promised. myself not to open them again before Jacksonville. It was about 11:30 a.m. when the bus reached its final destination—Jacksonville, Florida.

I could only partly remember the three-hour trip. I remembered the chitchat exchange between the old ladies and looking up occasionally to see the beautiful Florida landscape along the highway, but nothing more, so my guess was I must have gotten some sleep. Here, I would depart company with the old ladies and would have to catch the through bus for Tampa. That would drop me off in Clermont, between Tampa and Orlando, on Highway 50.

I again thought, Who would pick me up? The departing time for the Tampa bus was 12:20. The larger cities before my stop in the road, were Saint Augustine, Daytona Beach, and Orlando, and the time elapse, about five hours. I would again try and get some sleep. It had been eighteen hours since leaving Columbia; I was just a little tired.

The Jacksonville bus station had a Christmas-like atmosphere. There was a skinny Santa Claus going from the coloreds' waiting area to the whites', asking young kids what they wanted for Christmas. Times were good. Everyone I knew had a job, so there was no reason to think that Christmas of 59 wouldn't be a good one for everybody. The kids were really excited— to the point that I thought, just for a minute, it would not be so bad to be married with kids of my own. But it was only a very quick and foolish thought.

When the announcement for coloreds to board the bus came, I took my now most favorite spot in back of the bus and positioned my tired body to rest without trying to see who else was getting on. I hoped my bags had been properly exchanged for my final destination.

As the bus wove through the city of Jacksonville toward Highway 1, I looked up several times to see the abhorred position of the black community. The moment of Christmas joy that the bus station's atmosphere had sparked was extinguished. My pessimistic view of the environment I would visit for the next few days was reestablished. Again, I was able to get a little sleep between stops and tried not to be distracted by others who were getting on and off the bus as it made its stops.

It was a quarter to six when the bus driver announced Clermont. I stood up to let him know I was getting off. I looked out to see the old army barracks that my father still maintained, where I had painted and done repairs. But I did not want to be caught in this part of town after dark.

Mr. and Mrs. Mims lived just across the streets from the small bus station, and they were almost like family, however white. Just down the street was the Pools' property—winery and all. Also, possibly Pee Willie Pool, who was known to be mean, real mean! My brothers, friends, and myself had been harassed, shot at, run off the road, and other things short of being tarred and feathered by the meanest white boy in Lake County.

My objective was to get my bags, call home, and get out of there as soon as possible. The driver opened the luggage compartment, and I reached in and retrieved the only duffle bag in it, checking to make sure it was the right one. Afterward, I dialed my parents' number and was lucky. Fred Pinkney, my sister Deloris's husband, was there. He and my sister were on Christmas break from Florida A&M University, and my mother told me she would have him come pick me up. In about five minutes, Fred was getting out of the '55 Chevrolet to open the trunk for my one bag.

I liked Fred a lot. We had so much in common. He liked to have a beer once in a while; so did I. Plus, he also had a car and would let me drive whenever he was around. However, I would not make that request of him now that he was married because I didn't want to get in trouble with Deloris any quicker than I would under normal circumstances. If she and I were in the same place over ten minutes, we would be in a fight. That was just a fact of life.

When we arrived at the house, there was no welcoming party—just my mother, who I kissed on the side of the mouth. I set my duffle bag down. Dad was out doing some last minute shopping, along with my three younger brothers, Mom said. My two-year-old baby sister was asleep. Deloris and my twelve-year-old sister, Marsha, were down at Gloria's house just two blocks down the hill from my parents' house.

Things at our house looked very productive. Our very large house—by our community standards—was indeed the envy of both whites and blacks. So was Gloria and her family home, and even I felt good about being apart of it all.

The greatest thing about being home was the food. Boy, could my mother and sisters cook! Food was everywhere: cakes of all types, sweet potato pies, pecan pies, hams, collard greens, cornbread, turkey, and dressing. I knew I would put on ten pounds, and that was not good.

When my brothers got home, I would have to arm wrestle with them or something to recognize their development, even though it been less than six months since they saw me. This held true for James as well. I would be asked to go fishing and hunting. I would have to prove how well I could shoot, now that I was a soldier. I knew I would not outshoot James. He was almost born with a gun in his hand. I would not attempt to out-fish him because this was an everyday part of his life since he was six years old. In these areas, I was considered a misfit. Because in their eyes doing these types of things was what made boys men.

My dad did not have very much to say, after asking how I got along with the sergeants once I told him I would be going to work with him after his one day off for Christmas. If it was not for my ability to box and wrestle in these part, I would have possibly been looked upon as a sissy. But because I was good with my hands and could probably outwrestle almost everyone in the community, I was just thought to be a misfit—to which I very much agreed.

Chapter 9

Expectations & Pain

It was the day after New Years 1960. The things being talked about were: Could John F. Kennedy be elected president over Vice President Richard M. Nixon? What would the United States do about the U2 spy plane incident? Integration of schools, after the landmark, the unanimous decision of Brown vs. Topeka Board of Education. Freedom Riders and sit-ins led by the Reverend Martin Luther King, who had been brought to national prominence, following the Rosa Parks, incident—when she had refused to give up her bus seat to a white man on December 1, 1955. And the slaughtering of Emmett Till, the fifteen-year-old black boy who was accused of flirting with a Mississippi white girl.

I was somewhat concerned with integration and the right to ride on the front of the bus, but I was more concerned about my family and me. *How would Daddy make it with so little help? What would my brother Alexander do, now that he had dropped out of school? Would his feet heal so he could be gainfully employed? What about my twelve-year-old sister, who had problems in school? How would my two-year-old sister develop, with my mother working as a maid for white folk and still having the responsibility of taking care of my older sister's baby when she still had another year to go at Florida A&M University?*

It was Fred who had brought me to the bus station and had agreed to wait with me until the bus came. We were in Lake County and could almost smell the fears of the blacks of this area, from the slaughters of times past slaughtered even by the very hands of those committed to protect us. Not to mention the likes of Pee Willie, who lived just down the road a little piece from the bus station.

The bus was on schedule, and as it pulled off Highway 50, we could hear the distinct roaring of its engine and its shifting down to break speed to make its very brief stop at the little Clermont station.

Fred opened his door and soon had my single bag. We walked toward the approaching bus and stood parallel to it as the driver applied the brakes and the bus came to a halt, with a sound of air escaping its valves. Without recognizing our presence, the driver descended the steps and opened the lower baggage compartment, where Fred stored my duffle bag.

The driver took several items off the bus and placed them in a bin outside of the small station designed for securing packages when there was no station attendant. He turned to me, passing me a tag and pen, "Here, boy. Fill this out and put it on your bag." Fred removed the bag without speaking as I filled out the tag with my name and destination. I thought the driver could have just as well greeted us when he first pulled into the station, as I had seen white folk being greeted by the drivers, and I commented to Fred: "You see how he let you put the bag on the bus without saying anything?"

Fred whispered, "He is just a common southern cracker, and you have to be careful with them." I shook my brother-in-law's hand, and his last advice as I climbed the steps of the bus was to take care of myself.

Seated in my favorite spot in back of the bus, I waved to Fred as the bus pulled out from the station, with him standing next to his 1956 Ford. I thought he would have a hard time making it in Lake County, even if he had already finished four years of college at Florida A&M University.

Fred was the only person in my family I could hold a conversation with without getting into a fight of some sort. We both believed that black men could stand on their own two feet and could make a living without the assistance of a white man. We both would rather run our own barbecue stand and earn fifty dollars a week than lay concrete blocks under the supervision of a white man for one hundred dollars a week. However, Fred was now an elementary school-teacher, and I knew he would not last long because as early as the sixth grade, I could tell that black teachers did not have a free hand to teach black children things they needed to know to stand on their own two feet. Thad refused my mother's offer to be sent to college to become a school-teacher simply because I would not have been able to follow the white folk who supervised our school's agenda, nor would my brother-in-law be able to. And when he refused to, he would suffer the consequences: The black community would label him a failure.

As the bus headed east on Highway 50 toward Orlando, I began to reminisce. There were two other college graduates in our community—my second cousin, Abraham Logan, who was now a second lieutenant and was already on active duty with the U.S. Army, and T. C. Adams, who had gone out west to work for some big company. I thought both had a much better chance of making it than my brother-in-law Fred.

Lester Cole, who [had fought with from the very first day I sat in class with him, would make it after his family had moved from north Florida, even if he had to sell out every other black in Clermont. In fact, he might even become mayor because he had that type of quality about him—the same as my basic training squad leader Private Whiteside. Most blacks called it "Uncle Tomish."

The Fogle brothers: Albert, George, Gene, and Mack were so close that if one made it, so would the others. They had been raised that way, and by a single parent, Mrs. Rose, after Mr. Fogle had left when we were all just kids in grade school. I had always envied those guys and wished my brothers were more like them.

Jimmy and Donny Freeman did not live in the black community per se, but rather with a white family for whom their father chauffeured and took care of the grounds of the its estate. And their mother was the white folks' maid and owned a beauty shop in the black community, where she styled black women's hair. They also owned a cafe and kept a house in the black community where others lived from time to time.

For whatever reason, I almost thought of the Freemen boys as not being colored; however, we went to school together. Both Donny and Jimmy would, for sure, someday become businessmen in one form or another and would have very little to do with the black community.

Buster and Charles Chandler also lost their father at an early age. I have always had a great deal of respect for these guys as well because of the strong leadership of their mother Mrs. Thelma. The Chandler's were a close knit family, and as with the Fogles, if one made it, so would the other.

Johnny King, a good running back for the Carver Heights Trojans, could have earned a scholarship to college. However, he did the right thing after getting Eddie Bass' sister pregnant. Even without a high school education, Jonnie would find a way. I wish I could say the same for Eddie.

And there was Lester's older brother, Ollie, who was just 180 degrees away from Lester's personality. Where Lester would sell you out, Ollie would throw you his very own life preserver to keep you afloat. There could have been maybe only two in our community who worked harder than Ollie. One was my brother James, and the other was Gloria's husband Abraham (alias "Speedy"). He had been so named because almost no one could keep up with him in the orange groves except maybe James, but between the two, it would be a race worth watching. Because of this, the two had bonded well.

Junior Floyd, at whatever cost, would be a success and would probably reach out to help many of his family members who lived throughout Lake County, Florida.

The successes of these, the best men of my community, would probably never be heard of outside of Clermont and Lake County, and the reason was simple: one lacked trust for the other.

My older brother and brother-in-law were already pulling away from my father and would probably never become general contractors or incorporate with Dad, who was already one. This was probably only because he was not allowed to practice his skills as a carpenter within communities at large, but rather was restricted to doing handyman work for white folk. After the civil rights legislation of 1957, under President Eisenhower, he was almost forced to take a general contractor's license. But even armed with this most powerful tool, it would not be used to the greater good of bringing the weaker of a family, race, or community to a level of self-sufficiency.

I was still thinking of the ills and pluses of the men of my community when we pulled into the Orlando bus station, and the announcement was made that the bus had reached its destination, and connections would be made there for points north and south. My thought as I exited the bus was that coloreds were haunted by some slavery syndrome and/or dilemma, and this impairment had prevented coloreds from looking out for number one. If they tried to help other coloreds, they would only worsen their own dilemma. Probably to some degree, those who were successful within the colored community were correct; however, if our community was to survive and become a major part of society, these practices would have to change.

How could a father demand a son be as strong as him? What about those who did not have a father to teach them to be strong? Could a man become a man just because he possessed physical ability? Or would his physical ability be used only to serve a higher intellect? I submit to you the latter; or especially in cases where the physical young man had no "father" to teach him the responsibility of manhood, physical ability could lead to an individual's own demise.

As I sat in the Orlando bus station, I thought of the young men in my community, some of whom I admired and respected—most just a few years older than me. Some with fathers, and some without. Mack Jones, the brother-in-law of one of the young men killed following the alleged rape of the white woman from the Bay Lake Community, was physically strong, good hearted, and worked from could to can't. His father, Mr. Rufus, was eighty years plus, but both had almost no sense of direction without maximum supervision and thus became slaves to the Lake County environment.

Mack had looked out for me as long as I could remember. If I didn't get anything for Christmas, Mack would make me something with his own hands that sometimes took days or even weeks. One of my fondest memories is of the tractor and trailer truck that Mack made me for Christmas of 1947. I was six years old. It was the year my grandfather Wallace died. The truck helped me through the hard times, and if I would have had the foresight to protect it, today it would be a treasure. It would have been just grand if Mack was the exception, but he was a sure reflection of other young men of this central Florida community.

Alex Newsom was raised by his grandmother and was just as protective of the younger boys of the community. He had on several occasions been accused of having sex with girls several years his junior, though, and I think there was some truth to these rumors. Almost everything I know about sex I learned from Alex. Boy! How all the girls liked him?

James Curton was one hell of a basketball player, but that is about all he would do. I think he had a father who did handyman work for the white folk. In addition to playing basketball, James served the ladies of the community, and from time to time would pick a few oranges. If there was any young man in my community said to have a sense of direction during these years, it would have been J. B. Forehand—the only person other than the black millionaire Mr. Dock Jones' sons, who had a high school education prior to my sister Deloris and her graduating class of 1952.

J.B. had been educated at the Orlando all-black high school, Jones High. I submit that blacks had little or nothing to do with this feat. It was simply the wish of the white community that he be educated, and so it was in this central Florida community. J.B.'s mother, Mrs. Babe, was a good hardworking, God-fearing woman who took in washing and could make a white shirt stand alone. Almost every businessman in Clermont required her services. And so it was the businessmen who made sure Mrs. Babe's son had an education and subsequently ensured that he had a job.

Almost as long as I could remember, J. B. Forehand was the only black foreman who supervised a complete operation of grove work, including payroll and vehicle maintenance. He always maintained good rapport with both the colored and white communities.

Abraham Logan, alias "June Bug" and T. C. Adams, were also able to attend college because of maid loyalty to rich white families. And I would also include the future of Donny and Jimmy Freeman, to the loyalty their mother and father displayed to the family they had kept all these years.

The irony of black men being supported and educated by their own families was simple: They probably would have a harder time succeeding. In the case of the black millionaire and his sons, the old slave syndrome would come into play: "I will have to watch you, or you will sell me out." Black men are always subject to being sold out by other black men, including fathers and sons.

So, in effect, Tom Wootson, who graduated with the class of 52, who my mother thought could become a foreman in the groves, would probably not be successful, even after given the opportunity, simply because he would be sold out by one or more of his subordinates. J.B., Jimmy, Donny, T. C., and June Bug had the security of the years of bonding between the servant and master family, and thus the chance of being sold out was much slimmer, and they probably would be successful. The chances of a prominent black man's son becoming successful in the fifties was lower than the chance of a son of a well-thought-of black maid who served powerful white families.

The more I thought about who I was and where I was from, the more I became sure of making the army a career. At the age of eighteen, I felt I had solved the plight of black men, even if no one would ever listen to my logic. It was simply to stay in a position of servitude or subordinate to the white community. For the most part, no one even cared how much money a black man made—as long as he did not encroach upon white men's territory or their women. Black men who understood this within our community would be successful men within their own right, and those of us who broke the rules would pay by one means or another. The rules were different in army: Just by the definition, "armed services," were subordinate to all civilian communities. I was able to live with is.

The call was being made for white folk to load the Charleston-bound bus. My thoughts were still back in Clermont, more specifically on my elementary school principal, Mr. William N. McKinney. Here was a man who had gone to college under the loyalty scenario: His mother had been a Godfearing woman and a maid for white folk. However, McKinney was an excellent athlete and received a scholarship after being accepted into Edward Waters College at Saint Augustine, Florida.

Under the servitude scenario, McKinney was highly successful. In fact, from many perspectives, the most successful within my hometown by black folk's standard. He had been a football standout at an all-black college. He had completed graduate work to become a school principal, and now he had two sons.

Then the call was for "All going north to Charleston, last call." I boarded the bus and took the very last seat on the left. I did not wish to become as concerned with the demographics of the Southeast as I had on my first bus ride south from Columbia to Clermont. I really just wanted to rest and be left alone. However, my mind would not rest; it seemed to have become a computer of some type, bound to give the formula for the most direct path to success for a disadvantage male youth. And that youth was me.

I thought of Butch McKinney, the oldest son of Mr. McKinney. Butch was thirteen at the most, but he was already one specimen of a man.

I had often protected my younger brother, who was about the same age as Butch, from Butch simply because he could not defend himself against Butch's superior strength. Butch was also a good student and a damn good-looking black youth. But from my observations, his chance of succeeding was minimal. First, simply being the son of the black community's top educator placed him on some pedestal. And there would always be challengers trying to knock him off. With him being the competitor he was, he would vigorously take on all comers, and chances were, occasionally he would loose. But even a greater threat was the changing times.

The victory in Topeka on the Brown vs. Board of Education case caused the United States Supreme Court to strike down the separate-but-equal doctrine under which blacks had for so long been legally segregated in schools. That had been six years past, but with 1960 being an election year, it would become a political ploy. Chances were, it would be enforced, and now Mr. McKinney would have to compete with white men for the job of school principal. I doubted his chances of winning, but if he did, the hand-some young McKinney would have to endure even greater pressures.

The Lester Coles of Clermont would always be looking to improve their stations in life. I even thought of my own family, as to the effect the enforced Topeka victory would have on Clermont and Lake County, Florida as a whole. The one conclusion I came to was, it would be bad for educated leaders of the black community and good for the "Uncle Toms."

Now "suck butts" could improve their station in life and get elected to different committees and boards, simply by sucking butt and selling out good black people. The businesses of the black community would also be affected in a negative way, and black colleges, as we know them, would almost become something of the past.

My father had been the president of the community PTA as long as I could remember. Now black people's participation in the educational process of their kids would become very limited, if at all. The victory of the Brown vs. the Board of Education of Topeka, Kansas, was possibly only a victory for Mr. Thurgood Marshall and his station in life and for suck butts who wanted to become assistants to white school superintendents.

As the bus headed north on U.S 1 toward Jacksonville—me in my brand-new army green uniform with basic training already behind me, I should have been rejoicing. There must be hundreds of young black boys who would change places with me. *Why was I worrying about the future of the black community of Lake County when even the members of my immediate family refused to write me?*

It had started to rain, and I could smell the scents of the earth and of the bus coming through the vents on this unseasonably warm January evening. Florida was the only place in the world that could produce this intoxicating smell. To understand what I am talking about one would have had to walk through the wetlands of the Kissimmee, or Saint John River or fish from the banks of more than a hundred lakes in Lake County, or ride along U.S. 1 on a warm rainy evening.

I could very easily understand how one could become attached to these environments; however, for me the price was too high. It would be hard for the prisoners to enjoy all the beauty of this wonderland from the inside of the state prison that sat just a few miles off U.S. 1, over by U.S. 301, in Starke, Florida.

It had been less than six years ago that I would have given anything to go to school with white folk. I could still remember the days I sat on the back steps of our house and watched white folk enjoy the athletic facilities that I wished we had at our school. That was before the run-in with Willie on my first attempt to hold down a day job. That was before seeing how black men sometimes kiss up to white men for even the smallest of favors and prevent them from being in charge of other black men, for even short periods of times.

It was also hard for me to understand how my father, brother, and brother-in-law could not form a productive company together that someday could benefit other family members later on in life. They were the best at what they did in the county; it should have been easy.

I remembered the first contract my father got, in an exclusive white community in Orlando. It was the summer of 1958. I had been restricted to mixing mortar and finishing up behind James and Speedy, who were both exceptional at laying block and bricks. If I had had my druthers, I would have been in management and sales; however, the argument was that I did not know enough about the business, and white folk did not buy from black men. I disagreed. I even made-up flyers and tried to get my dad to let me go door-to-door to advertise his business. My guess was, if I could show black men building a house valued over fifty thousand dollars and could be sold at a reduced rate, people would be glad to do business with us.

My father and brother only saw it as another one of my shams to get out of hard work. They were right, but had not the white man did the same? And had not his schemes worked to keep black men doing all the hard work? I never had and never would like work where it was all back and no brains. God had given me, a black boy, a brain! And I wanted to use it. Now what was wrong with that?

It had been five hours since I had said bye to Fred at the small bus station in Clermont. We were now coming into the big city of Jacksonville, and I could guess what the environment would be like there, where I was sure I would have to wait for a half hour or so for the next bus.

For whatever reason, I had come to want as little to do with the black community as I possibly could. Did this mean *I was some kind of freak of nature and had become a black bigot? Did it mean I was afraid of a relationship with a black woman? Or did it mean I simply had been rejected and was looking for a higher level of intellect?* I don't know the meaning of these feelings, but I knew I would keep searching and giving myself the benefit of whatever doubt until I could find the truth as to who I was.

The city lights of Jacksonville were impressive, and the only way I could evaluate what form of intelligence existed within was to compare it with other cities or towns. If I compared it to Clermont, I would have to multiply by some one hundred times, and if by the size of Orlando, only about three times, and if by Columbia, only by two times. These were the only places I had ever visited, and for the most part, I had only visited them with the hope of finding a quick piece of ass that wouldn't cost me over ten dollars.

So, in effect, Jacksonville would have one hundred times the whores of Clermont, three times the whores of Orlando, and twice the whores of Columbia, if that was possible. I doubted if any place could have more whores than Columbia, though. The cliché there was, "You have to close the whorehouse to have church," and it was close to being true.

The bus wound through the city streets at a speed of about twenty miles per hour. We were passing houses that looked as if they should be condemned. They had little or no paint on them, and almost all the houses' porches were overcrowded with children who were poorly dressed and had looks of despair on their faces.

It was just dusk, and the temperature was 62 degrees, according to the sign that advertised the First National Bank. Cafes seemed to be the leading business, with an occasional barbershop, with red-and-white peppermint signs every several blocks, and old buildings several stories high with dim neon signs that said Hotel. There were girls colorfully dressed, who seemingly made themselves available to whomever would stop to examine the inviting merchandise.

We were in the colored quarters of Jacksonville, and as we passed through the residential area approaching what seemed to be buildings of a more permanent structure, the bus driver announced, "Jacksonville. There will be a thirty-minute delay here. All persons continuing north may leave your belongings in your seat and may reclaim your seat when called to do so. This is Jacksonville."

There were only a few people on the colored side of the bus station, mostly servicemen returning to camp. I had once passed through here, but it had been early morning; now the area gave a totally different impression. There was action on the streets. I walked to the door of the waiting room to check out the action but was too scared to go any farther.

There were several sailors—all white, walking fast toward the bus station with a shiny new Caddie following. About one hundred yards or so from the station, the Caddie pulled upside the sailors and stopped. The door opened, and a big colored man got out with a razor pointing at the sailors. "Two of you guys owe me twenty dollars," he said.

The sailors, quickly remarked: "We don't want no trouble" but were going into their pockets at the same time. They gave the big colored guy forty dollars, and he thanked them and everybody seemed happy. Yet, as the sailors passed the colored waiting room, I heard one say, "I can't stand nigger pimps."

I saw a civilian-colored man demand something from some white men, and they met the demand. I was impressed. It was a first for me, and I looked around the colored waiting room for a person I could identify with, so I might make small talk. I saw no such person or persons. And again, I thought, who am I? My answer was, "a country nigger kid trying to find himself."

I thought of the black pimp confronting the four white sailors, and my question was, where did he get the authority to confront white men in a civilian environment? But I kind of liked the idea. I had no concept of a pimp and prostitute relationship, and felt it was wrong to take money from any man by threat or by force. Yet, somewhat twisted in the back of my mind, I thought maybe sometimes wrong could be right.

The call came for passengers north bound to Charleston to reclaim their seats. It was the only time I was permitted to board the bus in front of whites. I felt really good about getting on the bus alongside white folk, but the feeling changed once I was at the threshold of the seating arrangement, and by law, I had to make the long march to the back of the bus.

After [had reclaimed my seat all the way to the rear of the bus and was comfortable, I watched the other passengers, both black and white, fill up the seats closer to the front. The four white sailors were just four seats in front of me. I was able to assess from a part of their conversation that I overheard, that they were in route to Charleston Navy Training Center, for advanced navy training.

It had been the idea of the sailor who was familiar with the Jacksonville black quarters to go to a black whorehouse and not pay, and the others had no reason to doubt his authority to pull it off. I, too, felt almost any white man could have pulled this plan off with the smallest amount of resistance from the working girls of the black community. I know Pee Willie Pool and his gang, if they wanted to, could have pulled it off in my hometown. I never saw a pimp in Columbia, and working girls were everywhere, including on college campuses.

From listening to the four sailors, they were little or no different than me, looking for the same fulfillment in life. In fact, I probably could even have come to like them. But for a brief time in my life, and I am sure it won't be the last, I saw a black take advantage of a white man. I was sure this would be an indelible mark in my brain.

I thought of Private King again—how he had tagged along with me on our first trip to Columbia, and how he had always talked about how beautiful many black women were to him. I always got the impression that he wanted. me to turn him on to some black woman. But I had not yet experienced one myself and found ways of not revealing the truth to King. Possibly, King and I would have burst our cherries together, with black working girls, if he had not gotten himself arrested for the impersonation of an army captain. Even though I was glad to be rid of him, I still thought of the guy more favorably than negatively.

I had seen white soldiers on several occasions going in and out of clubs and quickie rooms with black girls, and had heard of black men with white women, but I had not experienced such a phenomenon. Not that I would not have liked to have. But every time I thought about a white woman, I first thought about my mother and how she told me I could lose my very life by just looking at one. Of course, Emmett Till had lost his.

It was shortly after nine when the bus pulled into Tallahassee. For the past three hours, I had been getting bits and pieces of the four sailors' conversation, and their biggest complaint was how far Greyhound went out of the way to get to Charleston. Their argument was, if the bus had taken Highway 17 straight north, we could almost be there by now, but the bus had taken Highway 90 instead, and it would be ten hours before we would arrive.

I thought Charleston to Columbia would be even another four hours for me. I was hoping that my friend, Robert LeCorne, would catch this bus at his little spot in the road, close to Valdosta. If I knew LeCorne, however, he would wait until the very last hour to leave because he had a girl.

It was very hard for me to consider having a girl. First, by my family's standards, she would have to be light complexioned. I had met only one girl who I liked a lot who fit the description. Her name was Vivialora Thompson, and I was sure she liked me. But she lived in Leesburg, and I lived in Clermont, twenty-three miles south in the same county.

We had several classes together at Carver Heights High School, one of two black high schools within Lake County. I had ridden the county bus from Clermont to Leesburg for the three years that I was in high school, until dropping out to help my father. I was sixteen when I left school; I felt the greatest loss was not having the opportunity to develop into a starter on the varsity football team. Secondly, not having the opportunity to develop a lasting and meaningfully relationship with

Vivialora. She would have fit into the family hierarchy of women just fine, which in our family was the higher authority.

She had fair skin and long brown hair that fell almost to her buttocks when she let it down, which she often did. Her lips were full, and she walked with quick short steps, causing her rear end to wiggle sensually under her skirt.

At the point of my dropping out, our relationship was only at stage one: I would get to carry her books and play with her long beautiful hair and pinch her butt. I think simply because I liked the way it moved under her clothes. She would furnish me with pencil and paper, and let me copy off her in Mrs. Hawkins's algebra class. Without her help, I never would have passed algebra. Vivialora was a very smart girl, and I am sure she would have a productive future.

The call came for northbound passengers to reclaim their seats. I was just finishing off a greasy hamburger I had gotten through the rear window of the white folks' snack bar from a colored boy who looked like he would rather not be there and was ill prepared to be anyplace else. Disparity was a hard thing for me to take. Yet, I had seen it in the eyes of a multitude of coloreds up and down the railroads and highways since Eddie and I first departed for army enlistment almost three months before. I was sure I would do anything not to come back to this Dead Sea environment where all hope had left its inhabitants' eyes.

I left the small waiting room almost at a trot, in part to relieve myself of the hopelessness I felt because there was nothing I could do personally to change these conditions. I noticed I was the only person left standing there; the others had already loaded the bus while I was caught up in the disparity of black folk.

We departed Tallahassee on Highway 319 and reached Thomasville, Georgia, just a few miles from the birthplace of my father. I had never been to Moultrie, Georgia, and could not help wondering what the birthplace of my father looked like. I also wondered why almost everyone I knew came from northern Florida or Georgia. I think I saw the answer in the eyes of the people—total despair. I thought of families in my hometown who were not from northern Florida or Georgia and wondered if they were better off than immigrants.

Mr. Dock Jones was born and reared in Lake County, and he was the only black millionaire I knew. Mr. Joe Odum was a Floridian, and he had owned three home-steads and drove a Lincoln. The Deans were Floridians, and I thought them to be well off. Maybe they were from Georgia or the Carolinas, or northern Florida, just like most black folk, except Mr. Dock, who I often heard bragging about how he had run the swamps of Lake County all his life.

The Coopers, too, must have been Floridians. They had money and property, and new cars. Almost every colored in Clermont lived in a Jones or Cooper boarding house and drank whiskey on credit from the Cooper liquor store. I always thought both of the Coopers and Mr. Jones were above the law and took advantage of all the poor colored folk. Any loan from Mr. Cooper or Mr. Jones would demand fifty percent interest, and not paying meant a trip to jail. Again, the bail bondsmen were the Coopers and Jones. The rule was, pay me one way, or pay me the other. The head deacons of the local churches were also Coopers and Jones. One could say the Coopers and Jones were the keepers of the immigrant niggers, from the North. However, there were some exceptions,

My father was an exception to the rules, and he had made good. In less than twenty years, he had owned two homesteads and several other properties. Mr. Cole and his family, from northern Florida, had beat the odds and owned their own home. However, both families had paid a great price for success—hard work on the part of the whole family and great personal sacrifice.

The bus was just outside of Valdosta, Georgia, on Highway 84. I thought it was where LeCorne had gotten off, but I did not see him, and knew he would spend up to the last minute with his girlfriend before reporting back to camp. So that meant he would be catching the next day's bus. As the bus continued on toward Savannah, I made up my mind to never live in Clermont, Florida again. Never to live in a town where I knew by name every family and family member of the black community and every surname in the white community. Never to live in a town with all the local rules, as they applied to colored folk. Where the avenue was paved for me to become a reasonably successful nigger.

My mother and father had seen to this by knowing and keeping their places. But my reasoning was simple: I could not live the subservient life that my mother and father had lived, and the army was my only way out.

I laid back in my seat and must have fallen asleep somewhere between Savannah and Charleston. I briefly awakened to hear the sailors talking about going to sea and did not awaken again until the driver announced, "Charleston. Final destination."

I was glad to be in Charleston. This was the only stop where there was a complete rest and eating area for coloreds. I wished I could meet a friend, but almost every story I had heard about meeting stringers in bus stations ended with someone getting ripped off. I had about twenty dollars, and that had to last until payday, which I hoped would be in a few days. Even then, I would get only forty dollars; all the rest went home to help Mama and Daddy with the family.

The bus pulled to a halt, and I sat and watched as everyone departed. White folk looked so happy, talking and hugging, as blacks hurried to the black waiting area to line up and order food. It was easy to understand: Whites could get food anyplace. For blacks, Charleston was their only hope other than the back door of the white folks' café. And even at that, chances where you would have to eat standing up.

As I departed the bus and looked at the clock in the bus station, it was 6:20, the morning of January 3, 1960. Times were good; everybody was making good money, and the craziest thing in the world was for me to be in the army. This is how my family felt about the whole matter.

I was not in a hurry; I got in at the back of the line, and when it was my time to order, I ordered eggs, grits, bacon, and toast. I took a table that was vacant and listened for the call for the bus to Columbia. That was less than four hours by bus, and I hoped I would make lunch at the mess hall.

About 7:15, the call for white folk to load was made, and five minutes later, I was seated at the very back of the bus that would take me to Columbia. Some twenty minutes of winding through Charleston put us on Highway 176 North. The countryside displayed farmland and unpainted shacks, and in many cases, conditions that were unsuitable for human habitation. I now understood why so many had come south to live in the citrus belt of Florida; at least they had a better chance of not freezing. I became almost obsessed with what I saw in the light of day, riding through the heart of South Carolina and made a promise that one day I would return here to do whatever I could to change these despicable conditions.

I thought again of my grandfather, and what life must have been like for him. I also thought I would one day do a genealogy study of the Montgomery family to find out more about my humble beginnings.

It was 11:30, or thereabouts, when the bus pulled into the Columbia bus station. I departed the bus, and stood to wait for my bag, as several taxis waited to take a carload of GIs to Fort Jackson. The irony here was that white boys and black boys were loading into the same car in the presence of God and the whole world that did not allow the mixing of blacks and whites. The difference was that the cabs could not operate on base unless they operated on a first-come, first-served basis. My thought was, people could change, but the price had to be right. In almost any other city of the South, this scene would have been impossible, unless it was a military town.

We loaded the cab: five white boys and I, and I asked to be dropped off at the 5th Training Regiment Consolidated Mess. I made lunch, and afterward, found a bunk at the reception station and waited for LeCorne.

Chapter 10

Limitations

As I lay on my bunk at the reception station, I attempted to put the last few days behind me, or to try and find something positive in my experiences over the Christmas holidays. The only positive thing was, my family was healthy and had jobs. The prospect of the future, for the great majority of my hometown community, was bleak indeed. The saddest report, however, was very few knew they lived in a dead sea, with few if any rivers flowing into it to replenish it so it could spring to life again.

    The school system I had been so critical of would soon be replaced with a system over which coloreds would have even less control than the community had under the present dictatorial white-regime system. Black male youths like myself would be doomed to work for minimum wages for eternity, and our young women who were having babies as fast as one could count would gain little or no sense of direction to sustain themselves or their new families. In other words, my once very proud community would soon be a welfare state that would come under the direct supervision of some subservient "Uncle Tom" nigger, like Lester Cole or some other kiss-ass, who drew his breath through the butt holes of the dictatorial white regime.

    It was Sunday, 1400 hours, January 3, 1960. LeCorne was probably catching the bus, so he would be in camp for the evening meal and Monday morning reveille. I was worried about him because he fell in love so easily and would probably be caught up in the no-win situation of an uneducated black man trying to support a wife and family. I almost knew he would not reenlist. All he knew to talk about was his woman back home. Why couldn't he be satisfied with a quick lay in town, at ten dollars a shot— a lot cheaper than trying to support a family?

He got less mail than I did, and his woman was probably doing his best friend when he was not around. After all, she had to eat, and the eighty-seven dollars a month the army paid us was not going to support a woman. I thought this would be a good opportunity to walk around Fort Jackson. The next military formation wasn't until 0600 on Monday morning, and it was now three hours before supper.

I was already dressed in my army greens, less my jacket. I grabbed my jacket, put on my cunt cap, and just outside the door stopped to survey the organizational layout of this World War II era training facility. The temperature was about 40 degrees, which was just about right for a good walk when dressed in the very heavy woolen army green uniform.

Looking northward, I saw the big water tank sitting on a hill that trainees referred to as tank hill. To the South were a pine grove and the area we had come to know as the confidence course, or obstacle course. It had been on the obstacle course that I learned I had a long way to go to measure up to the best. It had taken all I could do to make it through the course, and for whatever reason, I thought I was in pretty good shape. I thought of my older brother and his friends, and knew this course would have been right down their alley. However, it probably would not have been safe to try and negotiate any of the obstacles with them, simply because they would have had little or no concern for personal safety. I would have been the one to get hurt. It always seemed to work that way when I was around those guys.

To the west was the gym for the fifth training regimen. I had been on the boxing team and used the gym daily. In preparation for my first fight, however, I was sick on fight night and lost by forfeiture. Early on, I had learned I really did not want to become a fighter, even though this was about the only thing I could beat all of the guys at back home. I think I did not like boxing because I knew, sooner or later, somebody would kick my ass.

At the base of tank hill was Fort Jackson Boulevard, which ran west toward gate one and east toward the east gate. My decision was to go north to Fort Jackson Boulevard and discover what I could find of interest on Fort Jackson's main drag. It seemed almost unreal to be walking freely along a major roadway, with little or no fear of anyone. To this point, I had found few places that I as a young six-foot, 180 pound black teenager could walk freely, with little or no fear of physical harm.

I enjoyed this feeling of freedom and walked toward the east gate. I stopped along the way at a snack bar I discovered on the boulevard and ordered a hot chocolate and sat down to drank it and to listen to the chitchat of the crowd that was already there and was more familiar with Fort Jackson than I was.

I had spent eight weeks of training here, but I had seen little other than the training range and the inside of the fourth platoon training area. One thing I learned from listening was, in the advanced individual training mode, one would have almost total freedom after class was out for the day, including passes on a limited basis.

I had never had total freedom under any circumstance. In fact, the most freedom I had had to date was the recent bus trips, and even then, I was afraid to leave the bus terminal or waiting room. By my observation, even the adult men of my community did not have freedom of movement and were very much afraid to travel alone. I would have to learn how to handle this new freedom that I would now be afforded, like the freedom to sit in a public eating area with other ethnic groups and whites and have a hot chocolate.

I had never done this before. After finishing my hot chocolate, I continued my discovery walk along the boulevard. As I walked, I began to reflect back on things I was sure I had learned, but I did not know where or how important they were to me.

My first feelings could have surfaced as early as preschool, in the infamous house on Highway 50, where Big Mama lived. The premise established there was, fair skinned people were superior to people with dark skin. I had made several attempts to dispel this premise; however, it was clear that I had not. I felt guilty, sitting with whites in the snack bar, as if I had not earned the right to be in their presence.

I had stood up for myself, as early as fourteen, when I had refused to give Mr. Willie my hard-earned money after a foolish bet, and lost my very first job and the respect of my family. And I had kicked the Mississippi bigot's butt and seemingly had been rewarded. I also had been taught in basic training that men were limited only by two real phenomena: physical and mental ability, or the lack of them.

On the right side of the boulevard, I discovered a golf driving range and knew it to be that because I could read the sign. I had never seen a golf driving range, but I was amazed with the accuracy and distance with which the players hit the little white ball.

I stood and watched for several minutes and promised myself I would play the game as soon as I got the opportunity. While I was standing there, I thought, if I was so confused as to who I was and what authority I had as a man, what about other black boys who had looked up to me for being in the army, standing up to Mr. Willie, and kicking the bigot's butt? In the sight of the only three other blacks who I knew would be in my advanced individual training class, I was a hero. But they did not know the real frightened black country boy that I really was.

The thing I was most frightened of was making it through airborne training after advanced training. I had made the twelve-minute run, which was a faster pace than double time, and had done all of the required sit-ups, pull-ups, squat thrusts, and the forty push-ups in five minutes—the whole works. Yet, I had not told anyone how my knee had swollen after doing all the required exercises. There was a reason I had not told anyone: I was afraid I would be kicked out of the army if the knee was x-rayed and required major surgery.

I liked being looked upon as a hero and did not want to appear weak to those who had elevated me to that status. I just could not go back to the Dead Sea community of Lake County, Florida. Especially, not as a failure. I would just have to put up with the pain and occasional giving away. It could possibly be stopped with an ace bandage.

After reaching the east gate, I walked through the picnic area that was at the very end of the post, sat on a bench, and looked through the fence at the passing civilians and across the highway at the exclusive all-white community. I was not jealous of the houses of the community across the highway because my family also lived in a big ranch style house back home.

There was, however, something I did not like. I think it was because all this money and opportunity was concentrated in one area, and seemingly, the rest of the world was their servants. They could complain and everybody would come running. In my community, we could complain for a lifetime and conditions would not change.

That was what caused me to become angry when I looked at or passed through these exclusive, privileged areas. I thought of the shacks of the heartlands of South Carolina, where so many of my ancestors lived. I saw several blacks cleaning yards and wondered if they lived in houses like I had seen when I was on the bus earlier that day.

It was now 4 p.m., and I wanted to see what was at the other end of Jackson Boulevard before supper. I headed west, stopped briefly to watch the people on the golf driving range, and gave special attention to the several blacks who were hitting the little white ball. For whatever reason, I felt better, just by being close to blacks who took part in more than a fifth Sunday meeting, festivities, and the twentieth of May celebration of freedom day in Florida.

I had been to several football and basketball games that had been played in the black school district of central Florida. Those were good times in the black communities. The athletes of the area were exceptional; many had received college scholarships to various black colleges in the South. However, I doubted if their education would advance their station in life.

For whatever reason, I have always watched the progression in my community—almost took it as some inherent responsibility. I think because I have never had any confidence in the system that we had to depend upon for our livelihood, and if one left the subservient umbrella, to become independent, chances are one would drown.

My dad's independence was a tightrope act— working cheaper and doing better work than his white peers, and building homes in the black community with an independent financier, a Jewish gentleman who owned most of downtown Clermont. Everyone knew the setup, but no one could afford to cross the rich Jew. Speculation was that, when the Jew died, the Montgomery's would stop being productive. The Jew lived and was active until about the age of ninety, and afterward, his son-in-law kept the same arrangement with my father.

On the right side of the boulevard, I discovered a theater. The movie of the day was "A Summer Place." The early movie started at five, and I opted to take it in, as opposed to hearing about it back at the barracks. The movie was about first love and a young girl losing her virginity. It starred Connie Stevenson, and some faggot, supposedly superstar by the name of Troy Donahue.

It was suppertime, and the mess hall was a mile away. I took off at a double time, praying my knee would not give way. I reached the mess hall just in time to find LeCorne, Jackson, Bearden, and a black private who was introduced to me as Private Wheeton, from North Carolina. They were coming out of the mess hall. I shook hands with the new comer to our ranks and made a beeline to the serving line. The menu was meat loaf, potatoes, broccoli with cheese sauce, bread, and milk. I was able to get a double serving because the line was closing down for the evening, and I was glad I was able to eat along without all the tales about the girls back home. However, I knew as soon as I got to the reception station sleeping billets, everyone would be talking about the girl they left behind.

I made it back to the barracks about seven thirty, and Bearden, Jackson, Wheeton, and LeCorne were hard at a game of Bid Whiz. Wheeton was the loud one, and from his carrying on, one would have thought it was hogkilling season back home.

"Montgomery, find yourself a partner because this one is all over but the shout. I am running a Boston on these mothers." I had no idea what he was talking about. Back home, it was a sin against the church to play cards, and I had never considered it as a game just for fun. Wheeton had an engagement ring displayed beside him on the foot-locker that he used as a bench. He took time out from the game to pass the ring to me.

"Montgomery, feast your eyes on that; it is for my woman, and you are invited to the wedding. I am getting married in my airborne uniform as soon as this course is over." *Damn, I thought all these guys were crazy. Or was it me? How could any of them support a wife? How could they be married and be so far from their new bride?*

I looked at the ring and passed it back, and told him I never played cards. I looked through my duffle bag, took out my boots and shine kit, brushed the boots to an acceptable shine, and found a uniform for the following morning. I heard Jackson tell Wheeton to put up his girl's engagement ring before someone took it.

Wheeton pulled out a straight razor, "I want everybody to see this. I will cut a nigger's balls off, a cracker's too, if anything is taken from me." He let the ring remain displayed on the footlocker.

It was about 9:30 when I returned from the shower. The card game was over, and I noticed the jump boots Wheeton had displayed in front of his bunk. One could shave in them.

"Montgomery, how you like them boots?" I went closer to get a better look. "I'll show you how it's done. It takes about three hours. I learned this from real airborne troops back home, at Fort Bragg." I felt pretty bad about my boots, but I was not going to attempt to match this guy.

It was drawing close to ten o'clock, and I knew it would soon be lights out. As I lay on my bunk with the lights out, my first thought was how Wheeton got away with carrying a straight razor, and if he really would cut someone. Second, I thought if I had not established a reputation as one who stood up for himself, this group of guys would not even talk to me.

From my own perspective, these guys were far more advanced in life than me. With this group, sex was a full-time involvement. From their conversations, sex was almost like food, a three-times-a-day requirement, and the rest of the day would be confirming their individual prowess. My only experience with sex was the visit to the whorehouses in Columbia. As far as I was concerned, there was no real urgency to become totally involved with one woman. But still, in the pit of my gut, I wish I had had some personal sexual conquests to boast about.

From my position, the three other coloreds in my platoon had almost no limitations and had experienced a full life, almost like my friend Eddie Bass. My life had been very controlled and sheltered, and I had many limitations. As our second training phase ended, I know one could win without taking on the challenge. I felt like a winner in life.

I had taken on three very serious challenges. These conquests could very well be my impetus to manhood. I would never forget standing up to Mr. Willie back in 1964, nor would those who were there as witnesses in the orange grove that hot summer day. Beating the Mississippi bigot during basic training was a test that won favor on my behalf and gave me some degree of confidence that I was ready for the next test that life would send my way.

Chapter 11

My Knee And Ankle

Advanced training was altogether different from basic training. It was more like training at a regular school. Books (field manuals) were assigned, and there were problems to be solved. The field communications crewman course was not a hightech course. Circuit boards and installation of switchboards were the only areas that required one to think. Other circuit installations required simply following the illustrations in the field manual.

School was eight hour a day for eight weeks. After the eight hours, the rest of the day, except for the evening meal, was free time. Bunks were not stacked, and I did not have to put up with the big guy from Mississippi. There were still acting platoon and squad leaders, though. Their jobs were to make sure assignments were posted on the bulletin board and weapons and gas masks were maintained.

Robert LeCorne was my single friend during advanced training. He even convinced me to go to church with his one Sunday morning. After church, he introduced me to a young high school girl named Virginia, who I saw several times while in advanced training. It was all so awkward for me. My early visits to Columbia at age 18 had taught me girls meant automatic sex, and Virginia was not about that. It was different. I can't say I really had fun with Virginia. There was always something missing, and our kisses only magnified the problem.

After I stopped seeing Virginia, LeCorne still made visits to Columbia to see his girl. I asked him if he was still in love with his girl back in Georgia. He said she had stopped writing. Of course, she never did write. I continued to visit the USO in Columbia, where connections could be made with the university and college girls who were working their way through school.

For a guy like me, times were good. In advanced training, there was nothing physical except climbing telephone poles, which was a one-week block of instruction before graduation. One was required to climb a four-foot pole and from that height play a game of catch with a basketball. My knee and ankle barely stood the pole-climbing test, and I hoped that they would be one hundred percent when I graduated from advanced training.

Airborne training would be all physical. Twelve-mile daily runs were not easy. I did the twelve miles to qualify, but that was a one-time thing. I also needed to hold the physical image that I established among the colored boys in basic training. I was so afraid that if my knee and ankle did not hold out, my career with the army would be over.

What would my life become?

I thought of my feelings toward women, not needing them except for sex. I didn't need a girl like the rest of these guys. They would die and go to hell just to be seen with a girl in public. One day, I knew I would find a girl who I wanted to be with, and I was sure I would marry her and we would settle down and have kids, just as my mother and father did. But at eighteen, no way!

Graduation was nothing like graduating from basic training. It was held about ten o'clock on March 4, 1960. After lunch, I had my bags packed and was loaded on a two- engine prop aircraft with about thirty other airborne bound individuals.

This was my first flying experience. I thought the aircraft was overloaded. The turbulence was terrible. I thought the plane would fall at any moment. However, shortly we were landing at Fort Campbell, Kentucky, home of the "Screaming Eagles" Airborne Division. I had come to accept that my knee and ankle would not hold out; however, I had no idea what the army would do with me.

At Fort Campbell, I was assigned to an artillery unit, 319 Battery D, 105 Millimeter Houser 319 Battalion. I was on the second floor. Everything on the floor shined. Wheeton, the kid from North Carolina, would be at home on this floor. I wondered where Wheeton was. I was sure he was with some airborne unit, comparing his boots with the guys' in his unit or in the brig for cutting some GI with his razor.

I was assigned a bunk and two lockers—one foot and one wall locker. I looked around the one, very big room with no wall and saw perfect displays on top of each wall locker that separated one sleeping area from the other. Under each bunk were perfectly aligned boots, shined to perfection. It was enough to scare a normal fellow to death. I was afraid to unpack, and I was sure this was not the place for me.

A Mexican trooper had been assigned to help me get settled in, and I asked him how everyone was so uniform and strike. He told me I too would fit in; it took time. I would be given the help and time to bring my area up to par. With that, I unpacked my duffle bag and put my belongings into my lockers.

Alex, my assigned trooper, showed me around the battalion area and afterward gave me some pointers on how to put an airborne shine on my boots—a process that would take three to four hours the first time. After three hours of water and Kiwi shoe polish, my boots were beginning to look airborne-qualified, and I was not afraid to display them under my bunk, with the knowledge that they still needed some work.

My next stop would be the supply room—to be issued. my field gear, which would be displayed on top of my wall locker. I had already wrestled with field combat gear in basic training. I thought I would never get it right. And I am not so sure that I did because it never felt right on my back on those long marches to the firing range.

The next day would be my first day of pre-back training. One must pass this training before entering jump school. It was mostly running and calisthenics. If I passed this phase of my training, I would become an airborne trooper. If not, I would suffer the fate the U.S. Army handed me.

The next morning, I dressed, had breakfast, and reported to the physical training area. My trainer was a stocky Mexican Sergeant First Class about 5'8" and about 210 pounds. I stood 6'2" and about 180 pounds. If you did not know otherwise, you would have thought I was the trainer and the Mexican the trainee. Several others soon arrived —about six men, including me.

The Mexican was a man of few words. He called the roll and announced that we would be going on a six-mile road run to start the pre-back training period, and with a few facing movements, we were off. The six-mile run turned out to be a twelve-mile run—six miles one way and six miles the other. The fat little Mexican did not break a sweat and only had two quick times that lasted about two minutes each.

On our return to the training area, my ankle had swollen so badly, it was hard to remove my boot. I was taken to the aid station, and a medic took me to see an orthopedic doctor. The first question the doctor asked was, "Do you want to stay in the army?" Of course, my answer was yes. He said that he would recommend I be assigned to a holding company, where I could receive treatment for my ankle and knee, and then I would be reassigned from the holding company.

When pre-backs wash out, normally their equipment is thrown out of the window, and they are identified as quitters over the battalion intercom system. I was afraid I would get the quitters treatment, but I did not. Someone was assigned to help me with my bags, and a company jeep was assigned to take me and my equipment to the holding company. This was March 7, 1960.

The holding company was made up of several WWII-type buildings warmed by a coal furnace. Persons assigned to the holding company had no assigned duty but to keep appointments and KP, on occasion. There was an assigned vehicle to take personnel to and from appointments. One had to have special permission to go into town. I had resolved that my intension would be to get better, if that was possible, and to look forward to my next duty assignment, wherever it was.

I had lots of time to shine my shoes, and for the first time, I wished I had a girl to write to. You see, there was nothing to prove at the holding company. It was almost like being confined. The diagnosis of my ankle was a high-ankle sprang. With an ace bandage and staying off of it, in several weeks it would be fine. I had crutches to keep me mobile, and pain pills to relieve the pain.

In early April 1960, I finally got my assignment for Hawaii's 25th Infantry Division. All I had ever heard about Hawaii was that it was a paradise. The question was, *a paradise for whom? Did this paradise include eighteen-year-old black boys?*

In any case, I had a thirty-day leave; afterward, I would be sailing from Brooklyn Army Depot on May 19. The biggest question I had upon receipt of my orders was what I would do for thirty days at home. I did not have a girl, and the girls who hung out in Clermont were not attracted to me. I could work with my father. God knows, he always needed help. But what about the ankle and the knee? It would be difficult to do construction work in my shape. I guessed I would just play it by ear.

The question now was, how would I travel to Florida? I had said I would never take the bus again, so that left the train or air. My flying experience was from Fort Jackson to Fort Campbell, and it was not a good experience. I had taken the train from Jacksonville, Florida to Fort Jackson, South Carolina, and it was pleasant experience. I concluded that I would visit a travel agency to work out my options. After talking with the travel agency that I located on the army post, I decided to take the train.

I bought a one-way ticket from Hopkinsville, Kentucky, to Orlando. The problem I had now was, who would find time to pick me up from the Orlando train station? On April 14, at 7:30 p.m., I boarded the train with destinations Orlando and all stations south. The oddest thing happened to me: I was seated in an all-white coach.

I could hear the chatter, "There's a nigger soldier over there," but for whatever reason, the train attendees did not seem to care. I thought of Martin Luther King and the sit-in marches, and I was just a bit scared, to say the least. To add insult to injury, a white girl boarded the train and had the nerve to sit beside me. Right away, an older white gentleman said, "Young lady, we have room up here for you. You don't need to sit there with that nigger boy." The girl got up immediately and found herself another seat.

I was not hungry. I had eaten at the mess hall, but I wondered if I would be permitted to eat in the dining car. For sure, I would be hungry before reaching Orlando. I thought it would have been smart to ask the conductor for another seat. However, I felt it was the sixties and I too needed to do my part for equal rights. I had no idea what the conductor was thinking when he seated me there.

The first stop after leaving Hopkinsville was Clarksville, Tennessee. A few passengers entered my coach. Everybody noticed me, and for a moment, they thought they were in the wrong coach. I knew I would not get any sleep before reaching Orlando because I was not comfortable with everybody watching my every move, as if I was a caged animal or something not human.

Yet, I felt good about myself. I was going to stay in the army. I had an assignment. Hawaii did not sound like a good place for a black person, but I would make it. I might even like the beach.

The conductor announced that the next station would be Nashville, Tennessee. A lot of the passengers were getting their things together to depart the train. I wondered if any were country singers, Nashville being home of the grand old opera and the musical capital of the world. But it was not a town for a black boy looking for things equal.

My first train ride from Jacksonville to Fort Jackson had been altogether different. I had had freedom of movement. I also was able to use all the facilities on the train. The only thing sad was seeing the living conditions of black folk along the tracks. I still think the living conditions along the tracks from Hopkinsville were deplorable, but on this trip, I felt like a trapped slave. I was afraid to leave my seat. I felt like I have always felt when I was in the presence of white people. I felt they had the power to do whatever they wanted to do to me, from calling me a "nigger boy" to taking my life, if that was what they wanted to do.

It was a long way to Orlando. There were lots of towns that the train would stop at. I felt less secure when the train was at a stop. This is when the most comments were made about a "nigger boy" being on the same coach as white people. It would have been so easy for them to have thrown me off the train or form a lynch mob and do whatever they wanted to do with me. This is the way I was thinking as I set frozen to my seat. For the most part, I had no defense.

From Nashville, there were eight more major southern cities before Orlando. I needed to go to the bathroom, but I decided I would wait until the train was moving, and I would ask the conductor what bathroom to use. I would also ask him if I could use the dining car and get something to eat. After the train was moving, the colored conductor passed, and I stopped him and asked him about using a bathroom. He said he would show me. We walked several cars just past the dining car to find a place where I could relieve myself. He also sat me down in the rear of the dining car and gave me a great meal. Now I did not feel so terribly deserted. I had made contact with a caring and considerate human being. With his assistance, I made it back to my seat. I still felt very much out of place but a lot more comfortable after going to the bathroom and getting something to eat.

Our next stop was Chattanooga, Tennessee. I was not as scared as I had been before, but I did not feel like one of the boys either. I wished I had felt comfortable enough to get on and off the train, as some of the white passengers did, when the train made a major stop. I almost wished I was on a bus. At least you could see from the window. But on the train, it was hard to see from the window what was going on the outside in the train station. I only knew I was in Chattanooga.

When the train started south toward Atlanta, it was about midnight. Too dark for me to see the black families in their unpainted shacks, but I knew they were there in the dark. I was a part of them— scared living in the hope that all the white man wanted from us was a "yes, sir" or "no, sir," but too often in this part of the country, he took much more, including life itself.

Looking back over my young life, one would think I was not afraid of white men. Maybe I wasn't, that is one on one. At fourteen, with a pruning knife, I stood down a white man in his element and lived to talk about it. But when a white man's total environment was included, I was afraid. There was so much he tried to protect. First his pride, secondly his woman, thirdly his position as it related to his woman and himself. If a black man was caught up in the white man's triangle, perceived of doing wrong or otherwise down here in the South, he could quickly loose his life.

Groveland is just six miles west of Clermont. On the day in the orange grove with Mr. Willie, I had been lucky to survive my challenge with the white foreman. I now had challenged two white men from the Deep South and survived. However, neither occasion was like being in the Deep South. Everybody in the barracks thought the big Mississippi bigot had picked on me one time too many, and it was about time I challenge him. So I guess I was pretty much in my element. I think Mr. Willie decided I was just fourteen years old, and nothing positive could come of him challenging me.

On the train, my uniform was a factor in my not having been seriously challenged. I'm sure soldiers were common on this train route— but maybe not black ones in great numbers in a car with white folk. The objective of the Deep South was to put the fear of God All Mighty in blacks. In the case in Groveland, the whites did not only shoot one black to death and whip another to death; they burned down four hundred houses and forced the entire black township into the woods and swamps.

For all the beating, killing, and burning, the sheriff got three confessions —from Samuel Shepherd, Walter Lee Irvin, and a sixteen-year-old boy named Charles Greenlee. All three men were convicted. In the trial in Lake County, Florida, Frank Williams—Thurgood Marshall's assistant, had defended the three colored men: Shepherd, Irvin, and Greenlee. Samuel Shepard and Lee Irvin were sentenced to death in the electric chair. Charles Greenlee was given life because of his age. The NAACP lawyers, headed by Thurgood Marshall, appealed the conviction, and another trial was granted, with a new venue in Ocala, Florida.

During the wait for a new trial, Sheriff Willis B. McCall was transferring Shepherd and Irvin to another jail. They were handcuffed together when McCall shot the men. Shepherd was shot to death, and Irvin was shot three times—in the shoulder, chest, and neck. Irvin survived by lying face down in the mud and playing dead.

Sheriff McCall's brutal actions caused an uproar. Newspapers from around the world sent reporters to cover the incident and the upcoming new trial. Judge Truman Futch was assigned to the trial. In December 1951, Judge Futch ruled that Marshall and Jack Greenberg were not allowed to represent their clients because the NAACP, according to the judge, was a group of agitators who had "stirred up trouble in the community."

Marshall did not back down, and called on the black church community of Florida to give him the support he needed. Because of the threats, Marshall had two bodyguards with him at all times, and he did not stay in the same place two day in a row. In fact, the black community took turns housing and feeding Marshall and his staff. Harry T. Moore, head of the NAACP in Florida, was not so fortunate: His home was bombed and he was killed.

Under threats of further appeals, Marshall finally forced Judge Futch to allow him back into the case. Even though the trial was back on, Marshall still received death threats from Sheriff McCall's deputy. The jury was all white men. While Marshall was talking to the jury, he noticed they all had on Shriners' pins.

Once the case was given to the jury, it took them ninety minutes. One court observer later told Marshall they took that long because the men wanted to smoke their cigars. The verdict was guilty. Irvin was sentenced to death. Marshall appealed the case at every level until the Supreme Court refused to review it. But the lengthy appeals delayed the execution and gave Marshall time to work on other options to keep Irvin alive.

Using political and NAACP contacts, he put public pressure on the governor and generated bold headlines week after week about various details in the case. With the pressure building from all sides, Governor Leroy Collins, three years after Irvin had been assigned to death row, changed the sentence to life in prison.

Several years later, Irvin was finally released. In 1951, when Irvin was convicted and given the death penalty, all of black America felt violated, but there was no public outcry. Colored folk were born into racism. It was the job of our parents, schoolteachers, and church pastors to teach us our place and how to appease the white community.

One example is when you talked to a white person over the age of fifteen, you would look toward the ground and remember to say "no, sir" or "no, ma'am." You were not permitted to look them in the eye, for that would constitute disrespect. For this, you could lose your job, or even worse. There was no place for smart niggers in these communities. So, when Irvin won release from prison, there was no public celebration.

The train was reaching Atlanta, Georgia, "The Capital of the South." This was a major stop, and people would be getting on and off the train, but I did not have the nerve to move. I knew the rules and would not try and change them single-handedly. The other cities we would probably stop at before Orlando were Macon and Tifton, Georgia.

I'd listen to my father talk about colored working conditions and how colored men were whipped if they caused the white man any trouble. Savannah and Valdosta, Georgia were cities where coloreds would run away like slaves to get away from their white bosses. Many of these runaways ended up in central Florida just to start the process all over again.

The next stop would be Gainesville. The big thing there was the first colored to be accepted in the University of Florida Law School. There had been some demonstrations but nothing to equal the burning and killing we had in Groveland in 1951.

In a few minutes, I would be getting off the train in Orlando. I would have to call for someone to pick me up. If I had not been afraid, I could have called from Atlanta, then someone would be waiting at the station for me.

It was April 15 at 10:15 a.m. when I used the public phone to call for someone to pick me up. The Orlando station was clean with nice seats. It was not a bad place to wait. I was surprised when my sister pulled up to the station about 11:30 in my mother's new Buick Wildcat. I asked her if she had any problem finding the train station. She said she knew where it was and asked how my trip was. I told her good, with the exception of my fear of southern white people.

We were now on Highway 50, the main highway from Orlando to Clermont. The distance was about twenty-four miles. On the outskirts of Orlando in the town of Ocoee, it is rumored colored were lynched and buried in a common concrete vault. It is said that no one ever questioned the men who were part of the lynch party, even though everyone knew them by name.

I would be home for thirty days, plus I had another five days for travel time. That is a lot of time when there is nothing to do, especially with a bad knee and ankle. If this were my brother James, he would fish for thirty days. James, he fished anywhere and everywhere, but not me. I had tried fishing, but almost every time I went, I ran into white men and, sometimes, they had guns.

My older brother was a master of the lakes and swamps of central Florida. He was thirteen when lynch parties burned out and killed our neighbors in Groveland. I was ten; those times had a greater effect on me than they did on James.

My ankle was almost one hundred per cent, so I would find some work clothes suitable for construction work, and I would work with my dad for the next thirty days and would visit with my aunts and uncles. There were ten of them. With them, I would confirm my heritage from South Georgia to central Florida.

My mother's linage was some colored but mostly Seminole Indian. All of my mother's sisters and brothers lived within two miles of each other in Clermont. They would enjoy the opportunity of telling stories of South Georgia and the three hundred and fifty acres where my two older sisters and James were born.

I am the first of the family that was born in central Florida. My six other sisters and brothers younger than myself were also born in Clermont. The difference between me and my sisters and brothers where I never could learn that coloreds had to be respectful to white men. For some reason, I felt I was as good as they were.

I was afraid of white men. I guess you can sum it up by using a dog-andman connotation: Man can control the dog, however, if the dog is cornered, it will fight back, sometimes overcoming the man. I told my family that the army was good for me because in the army, even a black man could be in control and be held responsible, and that was good.

I was able to help my dad for a month, and that was good. My knee and ankle were almost 100 percent. I did go fishing with my brother James once, and it was a good fishing trip. Now [had to get to the Brooklyn Army Terminal to meet the USS Mann for a seven-day cruise to Hawaii.

After having the experience of traveling on a civilian train and a bus, I selected the bus to travel to New York. The bus departed at 11 on May 14. My brother-in-law Fred had brought me to the Clermont bus station and waited with me until the bus came because I was not comfortable waiting alone.

Pee Willie Pool, a known racist, lived just down the road, past the Mims' apartments, a section that my father and I were responsible for maintaining for all my high school years and even after I was out of school. Mr. and Mrs. Mims were my friends, and I had visited with them whenever I was home. This bus trip would be different: It would be the first trip north of the Mason-Dixon line. This meant I could ride in any seat on the bus, eat in a public restaurant, use a public toilet, or board public transportation carriers at the same time as whites.

Martin Luther King, Jr. and his followers were fighting for these rights in the South, but whites thought he was only stirring things up. Whites in the South were meaner than ever before. This bus trip would be the same as my first bus top.

In the cities, I would see the poor and downtrodden. Once in a while, I would see a soldier with his bags trying to make it to his next duty station, the same as myself. If we come in contact, we would exchange information about our travels and about our new duty stations and other pleasantries.

My bus had reached Ocala, a town seared into my brain. It is one almost every colored in central Florida remembers. The intensity of the Marshall Marion County fight for the right to defend Walter Lee Irvin against the charge of rape, I get cold chills thinking about it.

First, the fight for a black lawyer to defend a black man in the Marion County Courthouse was unprecedented. The fight for Thurgood Marshall to practice in the county courthouse was a victory. However, after loosing the case, it was a fight for him to get a retrial. Irvin was fighting to stay out of the electric chair.

During this second trial, Irvin was again convicted and sentenced to death in the electric chair. It had been eight years since the last trial, but just passing through the area gave me a feeling of helplessness.

Sitting in the rear of the bus as we pulled into the station, I couldn't help but wonder how whites remembered the Irvin trial. To them, they lost, even though they won the verdict to send Irvin to the electric chair. The idea of a colored man practicing law in the South was enough but, in their courthouse, was about as much as they could take.

Thurgood Marshall was the first colored man to practice law in the Marion County Courthouse. This had a profound effect within our community and within our families. The widespread brutality sure affected the way mothers and fathers raised their children in the colored community subsequent to the death of three black men being shot to death or whipped to death.

I felt unprotected. My question was, *Why would a colored person live in this area?* The answer was, it was home.

At one time, we felt it safe to walk in the woods, go fishing, hunt, or take a swim in one of the one hundred lakes in Lake County. I had nine siblings and a very protective mother and father who were suspicious of every white person they did not know. Our first thought when we saw a strange white person was, maybe that person was a member of the KKK, and we remembered how four hundred houses were burned and how we were run into the swamps, how several young men were lynched, and the national guard had to be called out for our protection.

Life changed for most of us. My brother James and several of his friends were the exception. They still fished the lakes of Lake County and went hunting in the county. They caught a ton of fish. But they were the exception.

I will tell you about my family at their best. My mother was a strong physical person, about six feet in stature. She was equipped with only a sixth grade education; however, most would have assumed that she graduated from one of the nation's finest universities. She was also an enterprising person. She and her husband were building a home construction business that would support this family fifty years into the future.

Mama was born to Mr. and Mrs. George Walker on December 2, 1918, in the South Georgia town of Fitzgerald. There were also eleven other siblings in the Walker family and some three hundred fifty acres of farm and timberland to manage. Thus, they all received their diplomas from the "Walker Family School" of timber management, as well as cotton management.

Mama accepted Christ at an early age and became a member of Mt. Calvary Baptist Church in Ben Hill County, Georgia. She married my daddy, James W. Montgomery, on November 23, 1933. Thirteen months later, my oldest sister Gloria was born. Then Deloris followed. So, around 1939, the Montgomery family relocated with three children to central Florida and established a homestead in the small town of Clermont in Lake County Florida.

I was the first Floridian of the Montgomery clan, with six others to follow, every two years or so. However, childbirth did little to slow Mama down. Within the central Florida heartland, the citrus capital of the world, those who knew Mama would tell you she held her own in the groves, among the best man or woman, even during the eighth month of pregnancy.

In the early forties, The Church of God in Christ came to Clermont. Mama was one of the organizers and was assigned as missionary of the Young Women's Christian Council. For many years, she worked as a teacher and mentor for young Christian women while continuing to work in the fields and to raise a most productive family. Mama's skills rivaled those of an experienced ship captain navigating his ship through rough and dangerous waters but always sure of the state of its cargo.

The bus pulled off Highway 301 North into the city of Jacksonville, a bus station I had been in several times in the past six months. It was the same old station—a side for the colored and a side for the white. This was a break station, meaning you could get off the bus if you wanted to. I elected to keep my seat and watch the activity in the station from there while I continued to think of my highly productive family.

My sister Gloria, the oldest of the Montgomery siblings, had always been like a second mother to me. She fed me when I was hungry, fought my battles when the odds were too great, and was often an intermediary when things got rough between siblings. Gloria is a born leader of the highest order. She and her extraordinary husband Speedy and my brother James broke away from my father to start their own business.

I think Mama always expected Gloria to be successful because I have always known Mama to lay heavy assignments on her, and I am sure Gloria at times thought them insurmountable, especially when there was so little to work with. I wondered if she always thought she would do as well as she had. She was now an employer, were in the past only whites were employers in Clermont and Lake County.

As I thought of my next oldest sister, Deloris, a young schoolteacher in Lake County who had graduated from Florida A&M University in 1959, the bus was pulling off USS. 301 into Brunswick, Georgia. As long as I can remember, Mama wanted Deloris to be a schoolteacher. And, as long as I can remember, Deloris has practiced that role. Even when she was just in elementary school, she had that very special reserve about her that was expected of school-teachers within the black community.

Wherever any scholarly task needed to be performed, the family called upon Deloris. She would do letter writing whenever Mama needed to communicate with relatives back home in Georgia. Deloris wrote the rent receipts when Mama's tenants paid their weekly rent. She helped Daddy keep books in his construction business.

To go to college, Deloris picked oranges. She took other odd jobs, including babysitting at night for not-so-respectful white men, whom Deloris had to depend on for transportation home. On occasion, I noticed

Deloris had tears in her eyes when she came home, and Mama would talk to her in private.

The first year out of high school was not enough time to raise the necessary money for Deloris's education, so she had to sit out a year and work fulltime. Many would have given up, but giving up was never in Mama's vocabulary. Deloris, too, was willing to hang in there. She started college in 1956, and in 1959, she was in her last year of school, graduating in just three years with a B.S. degree in education.

As the bus pulled out from Durham, North Carolina, I thought of my brother James. For most of my young life, I had wanted to be like him. He had Mama's work ethics, the physical ability of Hercules, and endless friends. Almost everyone loved him. He used these assets to make Mama proud.

He had great earning ability at a very early age. Almost no one compared to him within the orange groves of central Florida except Speedy, my sister Gloria's husband. James was always employed by someone, doing something. During the school months, he waited tables within local hotels that catered to the snowbirds from up north, who were hibernating in sunny Florida. I had tried my hand several times at waiting tables, but I was too dark-skinned, or I was not able to keep up with the fast pace that James usually set.

James took his pleasures from the environment. I can safely say James and his friend Pop Hodges knew where almost all of the 100 plus lakes in the county were located. But I was scared of the woods after the lynching and burning in Groveland.

There was also a third party, Abraham Jones, who made up the fearless threesome. This was the team I most coveted during childhood. Possibly, the saddest I have ever seen James was when one of the three sons was taken away. Abraham's life ended when he wrecked his new 1956 Crown Victory Ford north of Tallahassee, Florida.

James and Pop's fishing continued and came in handy during the lean months of summer, when their catches so often were served for our evening meal. During the winter months, coon hunting started at dusk and ended at day-break. You could almost always find James and Pop in camp with their blue-tick and red-bone hounds. Coon meat was a delicacy within our community.

As the bus pulled out from Lynchburg, Virginia, heading for Washington, DC, I thought of my brother Alexander. He felt he had nothing to look forward to. Alexander had deformed feet and could only stand but for a short time without crying out in pain. Often, he would sit on the front porch and cry because he could not play with the rest of the children. He could not play basketball, baseball, or football like we could, and he was not very studious. However, Mama had plans for all of her children. She would always say, "Alexander is going to be all right."

Several months before I enlisted in the army, he was admitted to the crippled children's hospital in Orlando. He was still in the hospital when I finished basic training and when I received my assignment to Hawaii. I saw him only once. At that time, both feet were in casts with traction. I was sure he would be all right because Mama said so.

My brother Willie aka "Fats" was about twelve years old, and everything Alexander was not, Fats was. He was a twelve-year-old who believed he could win at anything. He could not remember the burning of Groveland and the killing and lynching that I could. He was not afraid to go into the woods to play.

My other sisters and brothers were too young for me to remember much about. Marshanell was a sweet little nine-year-old who was still playing with dolls. Wilbert was seven years old, and I can't remember anything about him except that he was dark-skinned like me, and I wondered if he would have a hard time in this extended family, as I had. Lawrence was five years old and was the baby boy in the family, with lighter skin than Wilbert and probably would have an easier time. Maryon was two years old and got the attention of all the family. She was pretty little, with short, nappy hair. She loved being held and sung to.

We were not a poor family. Since Daddy had his own business and we lived in a large, beautiful house, we were probably the envy of both white and black families.

It was about 11 p.m. when the bus pulled into the Washington, DC, bus station. I was pleasantly surprised to see black folk dressed in good clothes and high fashion, and yes, there were a number of soldiers, sailors, navy, and marine troopers in the station. I felt safe again, and left the bus for some refreshment. Everyone in the station was colored. I thought, this is a world I could live in.

The stop was for about twenty minutes. I reclaimed my seat, and after everyone was loaded, the bus was on its way to Baltimore, Maryland. The bus was approaching the North, where coloreds did not have to sit in the back of the bus or eat standing up outside of restaurants in a designated area. North Baltimore was the end of the South. When the bus left the Baltimore bus station on Highway 15, colored folk were sitting all over the bus.

For some, this was a new day. However, I just became more suspicious of white folk. How could a leopard change his spots overnight? I was still in my back seat when the bus pulled into Port Authority in New York City.

Port Authority was one big station where connections could be made to all parts of New York City and the rest of the country. This was the end of my bus ride. I would connect here for the Brooklyn Army Terminal. There were lots of soldiers and lots of cabs lined up. The cab drivers announced their destinations. I got my bags from the bus and listened for the cab to announce Brooklyn Army Terminal. I selected a cab with three white boys. We were all army and all assigned to the USS Mann, the troop ship bound for Hawaii.

They were all excited about their assignment to Hawaii. I was wondering how a colored boy from the South would survive Hawaii. It was May 15, 1960. The ship would sail on May 19. The cab ride was about one hour. It was 3 p.m. when we unloaded our bags and squared up with the taxi driver.

Inside the building were signs directing soldiers where to sign in for the USS Mann, bound for Hawaii on May 19, at 0700. We signed in and were assigned a bunk and reminded to keep our bags locked at all times.

For the next three days, we had nothing to do. There were Ping-Pong, several pool tables, and card games—some illegal poker and illegal crap games. I was lucky at craps and won several hundred dollars during the next three days. I was told that the crap games would be bigger on the ship, and I looked forward to playing.

First call at Brooklyn Army Terminal was at 0530, headcount at 0600, and breakfast at 0630. Headcount for physical training was at 0700. The next headcount would be at 1700. On shipping day, first call was at

0500, headcount at 0530, and breakfast at 0600. Headcount for loading was at 0630. The USS Mann departed port at 0700.

The USS Mann was named for Private Joe E. Mann, a Congressional Medal of Honor winner during WWII. I was not comfortable on this hunk of iron called a ship. It was about the size of a football field, which I thought to be small when it was taking on the Pacific.

The captain announced that the trip from New York to Hawaii would take seven days. He also announced that first call each morning would be at 0530 and muster would be a 0600. The afternoon formation would be at 1700. All formations would be on deck.

There were about three hundred, including soldiers and crew. Our sleeping arrangement was hammocks stacked three high. Our bags were secured to the center post that secured the hammocks. Below deck were activities such as poker and dice games, and nobody seemed to care as long as there was no fighting, which would land you in the brig.

For seven days, I spent my time playing one dice game or another and watching sperm whales and dolphins on top side alongside the ship. In six days, I won three hundred dollars. Along with the money I won at the Brooklyn Army Terminal, I would have a good start in Hawaii. I took five hundred dollars and locked it in my bag, and kept two hundred to gamble the last day of the trip. The dice were good to me. I won another four hundred dollars. Now I had over a thousand dollars. Considering that my monthly pay was only $89.01, I was rich. I locked all my money up except ten dollars and would not gamble anymore before reaching Pearl Harbor.

Chapter 12

Oahu, Hawaii

The ship docked at Pearl Harbor on the May 2, 1960, at about 1500 hours. I was glad to leave the ship, but it would be hard to find dice games to match the games onboard ship. Once off the ship, the sergeants in charge on the ground had us form a mass formation. The instructions were to listen for your name. When my name was called, I was assigned to Headquarters Battery 2nd Battalion 9th Field Artillery.

I was told to load on truck number one with bag and baggage. Once all five trucks were loaded, we departed for Schofield Barracks, about twenty-five miles up the mountain. The temperature was about 80 degrees, and going up the mountain were beautiful flowers, green trees, grass, and pineapple fields as far as you could see. This was paradise. But I thought it was too good for a black kid who had known nothing but discrimination in his life.

At our next stop, the division commander, Major General Richardson, welcomed us to the 25th Infantry Division. He told us how lucky we were to be assigned to the 25th. "Here, we work hard and we also play hard." He talked about the brigade football teams that played every Friday night and about other brigade-level games: basketball and baseball. He said if you were good enough to make the brigade team, you could be exempt from normal duties and play sports full time.

Then he called to the sergeant, "Get these men to their units." Again, we were ordered into formation, names were called with the units we were assigned to, and we were told to get on a truck. It was about 1500 hours when the truck stopped in front of my new unit, Headquarters 2nd Howitzer Battalion 9th Artillery in section K of the 25th Infantry Division.

The charge of quarters signed the new recruits into our new unit. We were assigned a bunk with sheets and blankets and told we would be assigned a foot and wall locker the next day. This was home for the next three years. I made a friend in a new recruit named Willie J. Harris. We both had the same assignment, Headquarters Communications Platoon.

An artillery organization is broken down by batteries. In a headquarters battery, there are the following sections: Battery Headquarters Platoon, consisting of the commander, normally having the rank of captain. The first sergeant, normally having the rank of E-8, the second highest enlisted grade in the army. A battery clerk, normally having the rank of E-4. The commander's driver, also an E-4.

The mess section, consisting of a mess sergeant (E-7) and two first cooks (E-6s). There were two shift leaders (E-5s) and four cooks (E-4s).

The medical section consisted of the medical sergeant (E-7), one senior aide (E-6), and four aides (E4s). When the battalion is in a tactical mode, medics are signed out to line units.

The survey platoon consisted of the platoon sergeant (E-8), three team chiefs (E-7s), three assistant team chiefs (E-6s), three recorders (E-5s), and six tape men (E-4s). The survey platoon was responsible for surveying in gun positions.

The communications platoon consisted of the platoon sergeant (E-8), wire section sergeant (E-7), radio section sergeant (E-7), three wire team chiefs (E-5s), nine wiremen (E-4s), three radio team chiefs (E-5s), one senior radio repairman (E-5), one radio repairman (E-4), and three radio operators (E-4s).

The headquarters Ammunition Platoon had a platoon sergeant (E-7), an assistant platoon sergeant (E-6), six truck drivers (E-5s), and six assistant truck drivers (E-4s).

Battalion headquarters had the commander LTC (colonel), executive officer major, (sergeant major, E-9). S-1 Section had the rank of captain, S-1 sergeant (E-7) and four S-1 clerks (E-4). S-2 Section had the rank of captain, S-2 sergeant (E-8, Sergeant Pryor) and S-2 clerk (E-4). S-3 Section had the rank of major, S-3 sergeant (E-8, Sergeant Jones). Battalion Fire Direction Center, fire direction officer, major, S3 sergeant (E-8), chief computer (E-7), three fire direction operators who were E-5s, and two fire direction operators who were E-4s. The S-3 Section is the heart of an Artillery Battalion.

The key thing about this organization and all military organizations is that each function had a slot. In most cases, the platoon sergeant assigned the slots. In some cases, the commission officer in charge assigned slots. Each slot had a rank and/or grade. One could not move up in rank unless he was in the proper slot. For example, an E-5 could not be promoted to E-6 unless he was in an E-6 slot and met all other qualifications: education time-in-grade and a written proficiency evaluation for the slot he was being promoted into.

The 2nd Howitzer Battalion 9th Artillery, stationed at Schofield Barracks, Hawaii was a reasonably just organization. Master Sergeant Pryor (E-8) was in charge of the S2 section. The S2 section was responsible for the security of the battalion, including security clearances for need-to-know personnel.

Master Sergeant Pryor made his rank in the old Negro army that started integrating into the regular army in 1948, by order of President Truman. MSG Pryor was a highly intelligent individual. He had no coloreds in his section; however, his presence made it easier for coloreds in other sections.

Master Sergeant Jones was the other colored E-8 in the battalion. He was the S3 operations sergeant. Operations was responsible for running the battalion. As operations, Master Sergeant Jones was responsible for day-today training: firing guns, and special training such as jungle warfare.

Both Master Sergeant Jones and Master Sergeant Pryor sat in on enlisted promotion boards. This gave colored soldiers the feeling that the boards were fair.

There was no senior-colored sergeant in the communications platoon. There was one stepping, fetching Uncle Tom sergeant E-5 by the name of McAllister. As a private, I had established good report with both the senior sergeants and the other enlisted men of the platoon. I was selected for almost every wire-related communications work assignment.

On this day, Sergeant McAllister had been assigned to install an overhead wire line from the garrison to a field terminal. He selected me to help him install the line. We loaded the equipment on the truck and made it to our work site. Sergeant McAllister explained what we were going to do and gave me the pole-climbing equipment.

I have always been a good climber, but to climb four miles of poles on my bad knee and ankle was asking too much. However, I took the equipment and put it on. On my first pole, my knee buckled and hit the side of the pole, and I fell to the ground.

Instead of helping me, McAllister continued to work on the wire line until he concluded that he could not do the job by himself. He asked me if I could get up off the ground and walk. I told him to come and inspect my knee. When he did, he was scared what the doctor would say by not getting me to a doctor sooner.

Somehow, he got me on the back of the truck. He took me to the division artillery aid station, and with some help, dragged me inside and laid me on the floor. It was another hour before the doctor saw me.

Once he did, he called the ambulance driver and two medics and told them to take me to Tripler Medical Center, located twenty miles from Schofield, near Pearl Harbor. I had nothing for the pain, and it was unbearable. It took almost an hour to cover the twenty miles and to go through the red tape and get into a doctor's care.

I was given something for the pain, and my trouser leg was cut away from the knee. There was not very much hope in the doctor's eyes. That caused me to wonder if I would walk again. They moved me onto a gurney and rolled me along the long corridor into an elevator. The elevator stopped at the fourth floor, and I was rolled down the corridor and deposited in an empty bed.

About twenty other soldiers, sailors, marines, and others had one type of injury or another. I was given more pain medication, and I tried to get some sleep. But the staff had other ideas. Together, with one doctor, staff personnel took me to the x-ray room and x-rayed my leg. Afterward, they took me to an operating room, drilled four holes through my bone, and put big long pins through my leg.

Once we were back at my bed, they put my leg in traction with about forty pounds. I could lie only one way, and that was flat on my back, with my left leg extended to the ceiling. I would stay in this position for another month, with the doctor coming by every two or three days to drain my knee of fluid. I had been in Hawaii for less than a month, and what I had always been afraid of had happened —a serious injury to my knee. I wondered how long my ankle would hold up.

My birthday was less than a month away. I would be nineteen. The colored soldiers said to forget about finding a girl in Honolulu. To Hawaiian girls, blacks were invisible. They said the only possible sex for a colored soldier was with Big Red and her girls at $20 a shot. Big Red was a six-foot, very good-looking colored woman. She ran shop out of clubs on Hotel Street in downtown Honolulu. I think Big Red was a very wealthy woman. There were also some very good-looking nurses in the hospital, who I know got an eyeful of all the GIs who had abs of steel and were not bad looking themselves.

I think I thought of sex 24 hours a day, and a pretty nurse passing every once in a while, added more to the imagination. No matter how pretty the nurses were, it was not fun when one had to bring you a bedpan. Being confined to the bed was no fun. For one reason, there was constant pain. Pain medication was only given about twice a day unless you made a lot of fuss. Then you might get an extra shot.

One morning, I was surprised by the battery commander, 1st sergeant. My platoon sergeant visited the hospital, and had a bedside ceremony to promote me to Private First Class while I was flat on my back. The promotion was only to pay grade E-3, but to me this was a big thing.

Sergeant McAllister had told me a colored soldier of equal intelligence could not compete with a white soldier in the same career field. He said, after the grade of E-5, colored soldiers could seldom or never get an evaluation equal to a white soldier, unless the evaluator was colored. Without a superior evaluation, you could not get promoted unless you were competing with all colored soldiers.

I thought of Master Sergeant Pryor and Master Sergeant Jones, who were in charge of the fire direction section and intelligence section. They had gotten their promotions mostly in the all-colored army and were now in charge of two sections that had no coloreds.

It was very easy to see that these two sections got faster promotions than any section, except maybe the gun section in A and B batteries, with almost all colored soldiers and with colored evaluators. The difference between these sections—other than one being all colored and one being all white—was that Master Sergeant Jones and Master Sergeant Pryor, both black, were the evaluators for the all-white sections.

Most of the whites had college degrees or at least some college. And most of the colored sections had little or no college, and a high number of them were high school drop-outs. As long as they competed among themselves, they got promoted to E-6 and to E-7. When coloreds competed with whites, being equal in all areas, whites usually won, sometimes making the grade two to three years ahead of the colored soldiers.

In most cases, the colored soldier's job would be line duty, working with his hands with heavy lifting and exposed to the elements—snow, rain, mud, and so forth. Within the communications section, where I was assigned, the duty was heavy lifting of snow, rain, and mud, with about fifty percent white and fifty percent colored.

Sergeant First Class Portwood was our platoon sergeant and evaluator. I think he was a fair white man. In most cases, I think he evaluated E-5s, E-4s, and E-3s fairly. If he had to evaluate an E-6 or E-7, and one was white and one was colored, I think he would give the edge to the white soldier. Basically, that was the way Sergeant McAllister explained it. He had been in the army for almost twenty years and was just an E-5.

I was excited about my first promotion, and I would work very hard to compete with all soldiers, white or colored. For my next promotion, I'd need to overcome my injuries. That could take two or three years. My next promotion would be E-4. Even though I was in the hospital, I would work hard to be the next E-4 in the communications platoon, even if the platoon was fifty percent white.

I was told that I would be going back to surgery for a knee reconstruction. This meant I would be in the hospital for a minimum of three more months. The first thing good about going to surgery was that my leg would come out of traction. After surgery, the leg would be put in a cast, and I would be given crutches. I could not wait for my cast, so I could get around the hospital area.

There was a club on the Pearl Harbor side of the hospital. I was looking forward to sitting in my wheelchair at the club and sucking on a gin and tonic. I was only nineteen, and drinking age in Hawaii was twenty-one. However, I was told they did not check ID cards at the club.

The club was about one hundred yards downhill from the hospital on the Pearl Harbor side. I was sure the hill could be negotiated on crutches. I was not told how soon it would be before my knee reconstruction; however, I was told the recovery period would be about three months. And I would remain in the hospital for this period, due to the severity and special treatment this type of injury required. Doctor Tensely would be the head surgeon in this case and would brief me before the surgery.

Several days later, Doctor Tensely talked to me about the upcoming surgery. He said the kneecap would be removed and a rasp would be used to file and reshape it because it had been cracked. Some cartilage would also be removed from the bone that interacted with the kneecap.

He said this procedure constituted a total reconstruction of the knee. He said it was a time-consuming procedure and would require a great deal of effort on my part if the knee were to ever be normal again. I told the doctor I would do my part because I wanted to make the army my career.

Surgery was scheduled for June 21, 1960. All I can remember was lying on the operating table and being told to count backward, starting at 100. I remember getting to about 95. The next thing I remember was waking up in recovery with fifty or more stitches in my left knee. There was a nurse in the room to make sure I did not hurt myself and to be there until I was fully aware where I was. I was asked to tell the nurse where I was and to state my name.

For the next two weeks, I was in bed with an ice pack on my knee. The doctor came to draw fluid off my knee every few days or so. This was an excruciating experience. After about a month, my leg was put into a cast. During this time, I also had a birthday. There were no gifts. I was able to walk with the aid of a crutch and was able to explore the hospital grounds for the first time since my hospitalization.

On the hospital grounds was a hobby shop for leather crafts, basket weaving, woodworking, and so forth. There was also a concert hall where entertainers came to entertain the patients. I looked forward to these concerts. I also made my way to the small club and had my first gin and tonic. I did not visit the club again because it was not legal for a nineteen-year-old to drink, and I wanted to be an example of what a soldier should be.

For the next two months, my leg was in a cast, and I was a fixture in the hospital area, visiting from one place to another. It was boring, and my leg itched like crazy.

When the cast was removed in early August, I had been in the hospital for almost four months, and physical therapy had not yet begun. I was introduced to the physical therapist, who explained the exercises I would be going through: 1) warm-up exercises, 2) flexing of the muscles, and 3) weight lifting. After each session, there would be the whirlpool, at 112 degrees for thirty minutes. This routine would be each day at 0900 hours in the morning and at 1500 hours in the afternoon until the knee was again one hundred percent or near that. After a month or so, I was lifting about eight pounds with my left leg and was directed to use the loom in the craft shop between 0900 hours and 1500 hours to make a rug.

The loom was powered by paddling with the feet and using the hands to put material in place to construct the rug pattern. It took me about a month, working about an hour a day to construct my first rug, which I sent home. I hoped that this would establish better communications between home and me. I did get a letter telling me how much they liked my handmade rug and that they hoped I would be out of the hospital soon.

I was discharged from the hospital in October. I was reassigned to the communications platoon and was given temporary duty as division petroleum and gas clerk at the division artillery. This duty required me to supply the division with gas and oil and to keep record of the gas and oil used by division artillery.

In September 1961, 1 was assigned back to the communications platoon as the senior switchboard operator, and in October 1961, 1 was promoted from private first class to specialist 4th class. This caused a lot of fuss in the platoon because I was in the hospital from May of 1960 to October of 1960 —six months. And from the time of discharge from the hospital until September 1961, I was assigned as division petroleum specialist another eleven months—for a total of seventeen months and was the first to be promoted.

The platoon sergeant, Sergeant First Class Port, would explain that I carried myself in a professional manner and demonstrated extraordinary leadership traits. To this point, even with all of my setbacks, I was on track to have a successful army career. Now I was back to regular duty. I thought I would check with personnel to put in an application for flight school, only to learn that I was not qualified because of the knee operation. Now I would have to decide if I wanted to stay in the army.

Chapter 13

The Big Island, Hawaii

Preparing to go to the Big Island for training required all of the unit's vehicles to be brought up to a high degree of readiness—all fluid levels and maintenance up to par. The load-out point was Pearl Harbor Naval Base. A battalion- sized unit would be loaded on a navy ship (LST) and barge. This included about one hundred or more vehicles, counting the headquarters battery and two-gun batteries— A and B.

The headquarters battery was responsible for ammunition for the guns, fire direction (S3), security (S2), and maps, as well as S1 personnel and S4 supply, and all of their vehicles and equipment. A and B batteries were responsible for their guns, vehicles, and equipment. All vehicles and equipment had to be secured within the ship and on the barge. That took several days to accomplish.

The voyage would be from the island of Oahu to the Big Island, passing Molokai, Lanai, and Maui. Along with the vehicles and equipment, the voyage included about five hundred officers and men. It was about a two day and night voyage, culminating at the landing site some two thousand feet below our training camp.

The road from the landing site to our campsite was almost straight up. My three quarter-ton truck and trailer had to use every gear to make the climb. It really was a tricky undertaking to make the climb up the mountain. The site was between Mount Kilauea, an active volcano, and Mauna Kea, the highest mountain in the Hawaii chain.

On one side of the camp was a snowcapped mountain, and on the other was a spewing volcano. The meant the temperature was about 40 degrees.

Our training took place in the lava beds of the mountain terrain. The lava beds were treacherous. A pair of combat boots lasted only about a week when training in the lava. They were cut to bits by powder-like residue left by the flowing lava of a hundred years past.

Nearby was the Kings Ranch, which had become a tourist attraction for hunters. I understand there were bighorn sheep and pheasant on the ranch. On two occasions, we took a break for some fun on the beach and at a Kona resort hotel. In Kona was a cook out of barbecued lobsters and shrimp, and dancing girls who were untouchable. There was lots of beer and mixed drinks. Drinking age was not an issue.

Our second break was at the beach, with just sleeping bags. We had the locals wrap a pig in banana leaves and cook it underground. This is called a luau or a Hawaiian barbecue. There were also dancing girls doing the Hawaiian hula, but they were also untouchable.

Training at the Big Island was demanding. It lasted for four weeks. Then the process reversed itself. If going up the mountain was rough, coming down the mountain was even rougher. Some inexperienced drivers burned out their brakes and required the assistance of a tow truck. Loading the ship and barge was accomplished in a day because we had a greater workforce. Every section was responsible for loading their own vehicles and/or guns, with the supervision of the noncommissioned officers of the section.

Since my ankle swelling at Ft. Campbell and the pole accident that required six months of hospitalization, I just made it through a major training exercise. Along the way, I had done pretty well. I still had $900 in the 1st National Bank of Hawaii.

There had been poker games and dice games at the training site on the Big Island almost every night that we were in camp. I had made the games whenever I could, but being the senior switchboard operator took up most of my time, both at camp and during field training. I lost a few and won a few. I think I was about $50 dollars ahead. Gambling was not legal, but everybody gambled. It was the only way we stood a chance of having enough money from one month to the next. I was lucky. I often won when I gambled. There was no gambling on the voyage of the LST between islands. I think because there was so little room, everyone was topside most of the time.

Topside, you could see dolphins running alongside the ship. I was sure I had impressed my platoon sergeant, First Class Portwood, Sergeant McAllister, and the section sergeant of the battery because I had made sure each section within the headquarters battery had communications with the battery switchboard and could communicate with other sections, as well with the civilian switchboard, so they could call home whenever possible. Only one terminal in camp could reach an outside line and that terminal was open to Headquarters A and B, so it was busy most of the time.

Back at Schofield, I had it pretty good. I had money, even if there was little chance of finding a girl or a reasonable working girl. I went to the best spots once or twice a month. Waikiki Shell for concerts with my friend Willie J. Harris. (I always called him Willie J.). Willie J. was in the communications platoon and made Specialist 4th Class in November 1961, a month after me. We did everything together. He always had money to spend and did all right with dice.

Training on the island of Oahu was just as demanding as training on the Big Island. The difference was red mud instead of lava. Mountains were almost as hard to negotiate, and there was jungle training, negotiating mountains with artillery pieces using block and tackle. We trained against an aggressor force that had capabilities equal to our own with like-real prison-of-war camps and with umpires to decide who was winning the war games, using guidelines determining the number of kills captured, or loss of equipment. This type training was almost constant within division artillery units.

In the jungle terrain of Oahu, we rotated from the training site to garrison, and back to the training site every two weeks or so. It was usually raining. The mud was ankle deep and hard to wash off once back in garrison. Wash pads or "racks" as we called them were always busy using high-pressure hoses to try and wash the everlasting mud from our combat vehicles.

On return from the field training sites, after vehicles and equipment were washed and cleaned, they were displayed on Saturday morning for inspection by the battery commander, the battalion commander, or the division commander. There was always an inspection of some type on Saturday mornings.

Section equipment in a headquarters battery for the communications section would include all of the equipment used for combat training — radios, telephones, vehicles, reels of wire, equipment for laying wire lines, and so on. Along with the display would be a loading plan on how the equipment would be loaded for field or combat deployment.

S3 fire direction would lay out equipment such as charts used to compute artillery fire, slide rules, computers, map, and so forth. Individual soldiers would lay out their individual field equipment between the section equipment, including mess gear, tent halves called shelter halves, tent poles, entrenching tools (small shovels), and other equipment necessary to survive comfortably in a combat environment. All sections, including the gun batteries, would lay out their equipment for inspection every Saturday morning when in garrison. The 25th Infantry Division was a combat-ready jungle division, fully trained in jungle warfare.

Chapter 14

Thailand

On February 1962, the 2nd Brigade of the 25th Infantry Division including the 2nd Battalion 9th Artillery was designated to airlift to Thailand fully combat-ready. This included live ammunition for each combat ready trooper and basic loads for each artillery gun section. The threat was the North Vietnam Communists.

The load out was from Hickam Air Force Base, close to Schofield. Equipment loads out was on C 130s Hercules Aircraft. One aircraft could carry two-gun sections, with ammunition or about four two-and-one-half-ton trucks fully loaded. The troops loaded out on C 147s.

The destination was Korat Thailand Royal Air Force Base. From there, we would travel south on Thailand Friendship Highway about ten miles south of Korat and set up base camp. The camp would be called Camp Friendship. It was on the edge of the jungle, and under every bush was a snake of some type, mostly cobras, and lots of spiders.

Cobras were so common that I was soon picking them up by hand before they could come to a striking position and cutting them in half with a machete. Machetes were a must for the jungle. For the spiders, you wore a long-sleeved shirt and kept your pants legs tucked into your boots. You made sure anytime you went to bed that your mosquito net was tucked in.

If Hawaii was almost void of female companionship, Thailand—known as the sin capital of the world, made girls available 24/7. Upon arrival to our base camp, strips or sin cities were already set up in makeshift huts across Friendship Highway from our base camp. The girls wore western attire and made every attempt to get the attention of the GI, which was not hard to do.

By world standards, they were very attractive women. There was almost no restriction on visiting "Sin City." However, the medical section that issued protection upon request preached safe sex. The strip across the highway offered other services, such as haircuts, cold drinks, and laundry.

One objective of the 9th Field Artillery was to test the mobility of a field artillery unit, using both track and wheel vehicles in the jungle of Southeast Asia. The 9th would cross Thailand from bottom to top, starting from the most southern tip to the most northern tip of the country. This included following along the Macon River and along the Laos border. There was also a mountainous area to be negotiated.

Every time we moved, the "Sin City" would follow by one means or another. I am sure they were not always the same girls but girls from the closest village to make up what it took to service hundreds of American GIs. Upon arriving in Thailand, a GI could get a girl for about one American dollar. After about a month in the country, it was five dollars. I guess you had to pay for the price of doing business travel and all.

The duty in Thailand was considered combat duty; however, there was almost no contact with the enemy. Special Forces had gone across the Macon River and had reported contact, but they were with us only a few days, and I don't know what their mission was or if they had any killed or wounded in action. Once we reached the Macon, I was tired and ready to return to Schofield in Hawaii. I had one encounter with a very young girl who I would always remember, even though she was a working girl. I am sure, if given the opportunity, she would have done well in America. Of course, this is possibly true with many of the girls who were forced into prostitution. I spent a lot of time with her.

I thought of the working girls back at Fort Jackson and how different they were—or was there any difference? Some of the GIs fell in love with these girls and even wanted to marry them. I don't think I would ever go that far—maybe under the right circumstances. Some of them were downright knockouts.

Even the high-ranking officers had hang-ups over some of these girls. On one occasion, a girl put on a show in a makeshift club. A stripper show. Two officers had a fight "over who would spend the night with her. So it was not just the enlisted men, it was also officers as well. And West Point said they were gentlemen.

It was now June of 1962. We had been in Thailand for four months, and November of 1962 would be my time to make a decision.

Would I reenlist in the army? I could not be an airplane pilot, so chances were, I would not stay. But I had almost nothing to look forward to back home. I would probably work for my brother James, and I have never done well when working with him. But maybe? I understood there was lots of work, and the pay was good. I could buy a car. I still had money in the bank in Hawaii—more than enough for a down payment on a late-model car. And maybe I would find a girl.

The communications officer was an adventurous guy, so I got to see a great deal of the country. We visited restaurants and sampled all types of Thai foods. We met girls who were willing but did not work in forced prostitution. Other cities that we visited were Phitsanuloke, Chiang Rai, Mae Hong Son, and towns along the Macon River.

It was now June of 1962. We had been in Thailand for four months: two months at Camp Friendship, fighting cobras, and two months crossing the country, fighting fewer snakes. We saw lots of elephants doing logging work in the jungles. They were amazing workers.

Once we struck camp at Camp Friendship, there was no need of a switchboard, and for the past two months, I had been given the duty as the communications officers' driver.

The battalion returned to Hawaii in late November 1962. A Mexican specialist 4th class by the name of Presidio was promoted to sergeant E5—a promotion Sergeant First Class Portwood and I thought I should receive. I made up my mind that I would not reenlist.

On February 4, 1963, in Oakland California, I was honorably discharged from the U.S. Army. Willie J. Harris and I had a pocket full of money—more than a thousand dollars, with the money that I had drawn from the 1st National Bank in Hawaii, and my last payment from the army, including travel pay.

Both Willie J. and I were invited to a coming-home party by one of the soldiers being discharged with us. He lived in Oakland. We accepted. We all pooled our money for a taxi for about a thirty-minute ride over to the colored side of town, to our new friend's house, where there was music, barbecue, and mostly family members of our new friend. We were introduced to his family and enjoyed barbecue and beer until dark.

This was not really what Willie J. and I were looking for. We wanted to hear some jazz music, interact with some women, and do the town. We wanted to hear Coltrane, Monk, Miles Davis, or some of the better-known jazz artists of the day.

We thanked our friend and his family and called a taxi. We asked the taxi driver where the jazz artists were playing. Not in Oakland, he said, maybe across the bridge in San Francisco. It would be a fifty-dollar fare to checkout San Francisco for that kind of action. He would have to call and find out what nightclub had live music.

We gave up on the idea and asked him to take us to a decent local hotel and maybe round up a couple of decent girls for the night. He said he could do that for twenty dollars. We agreed, and in less than twenty minutes, we had two women in the car. Both were good-looking and well dressed, with no resemblance to a hooker.

We made small talk, told where we were stationed, and asked how much money we would be spending for their services. We gave them twenty dollars, which was acceptable for an hour. However, when my girl and I got to our room, she said she was not a hooker but made dates when she knew what she was getting into, and that she trusted the cab driver. Besides, soldiers had too much to lose to get into trouble.

She said if I ordered something to eat and gave her another ten dollars, she would stay the night because I looked like a nice guy and she thought I would one day make a nice girl a fine man or husband. I thanked her and gave her twenty dollars to order some food, even though I was not hungry. I thought I might be before the night was over. She went out and returned with greens, rice, beef tips, candied yams, and cornbread. She said there was a Seoul kitchen around the block from the hotel. We both disrobed with the light on and touched and admired one another's bodies.

She asked where my home was, and I told her Clermont, Florida, and that it would take several days to get there. We talked some more, and then we made love with the light on. Before the night was over, we made love several times, and when the morning came, she kissed me on the cheek and asked me to take care of the girl I would find when I got home. She said not to forget her, and she would not forget me. I gave her another twenty dollars, and she left me alone.

Chapter 15

Home

During my first week at home, I bought a 1960 maroon Thunderbird. My mother and father had to co-sign for me. I also started seeing a girl named Odessa Marie Brown, whom I had known all my life and thought was a knock-out. She was in college fifty-seven miles north of Clermont, in Ocala.

I also started to work for my brother. The workday started at 6 a.m. and ended about 6 p.m. Then I would make the drive to Ocala to see Odessa. I am sure I was in love with her. However, we only had about three weeks together before I told Odessa I was going back into the army.

She wanted a "token," as she called it: an engagement ring. I was not ready for that because I had no idea where I would be assigned. On the February 25, 1963, in Jacksonville, Florida, I reenlisted in the United States Army and was assigned to the 6th Battalion 9th Artillery at Ft. Sill, Oklahoma.

It was a newly formed organization with 175-mm guns—the biggest in the army inventory and 8" Howitzers—the second biggest gun in the army inventory. When I arrived at the 9th Artillery at Ft. Sill, there were just a few men assigned to the unit. Once the organization was complete and tested, we would be assigned to a station in Germany. 1 had completed three years of active duty and was sure my sergeant E5 promotion would be within the next few months.

The army regulations stated that unless you were in pay grade E5 or E4, with four years of service, you could not ship a privately owned vehicle to an overseas command. I wanted to take my 1960 Thunderbird to Germany with me. It would be the perfect car to run with the German Mercedes on the autobahn. The Thunderbird had 160 on the speedometer, and the autobahn had no speed limits.

I requested an extended leave past October 14 that would give me four years of service. After working very hard to prove myself with the battalion commander, my leave was granted, so I would have over four years of active duty. I would be able to ship my car, plus I would have more time to see Odessa, who still wanted a token.

I wrote her several times a week up until my leave started on October 2. On leave, I had money enough not to work. We did a lot together, but there was no sex. She said she was saving herself for marriage. We did everything except have intercourse. We kissed every time our eyes met, and we touched every part of each other's body. One time, she let me get my hand inside of her pants, I touched her most sensitive inner part, and she had an orgasm right in my hand. Of course, she slapped me and never said anything about it.

While I was home, she transferred from the junior college in Ocala to a four-year college near Jacksonville. This meant I had to drive a greater distance to see her. I drove it and visited her at her dorm. At night, we visited the local nightclubs and took long walks along the beach.

I was in love for the first time in my life, but I could not commit to marriage. Before coming home on leave from Ft. Sill, I had worked at two jobs and never went into town. I was due for the next sergeant E5 promotion, and I wanted to make sure I got it.

The battalion was filling up fast, and training had begun. I volunteered to work with Personnel (S1) and Operations (S3) when I was not leading a wire team in the field. In garrison, S3 had the duty of establishing the manning chart or the required workforce for each section, called TO&E for the battalion. S1 had the duty of cutting the order to assign each man to a position within the TO&E. S1 would cut the stencil, and I would run the hand-operated printing machine to produce the orders.

There were 542 members assigned to the battalion: 511 enlisted men, 28 officers, and 3 warrant officers. Each member got three sets of orders, so I hand-printed 1,626 copies of orders and made the proper distribution through the message center that I worked from when I was not in the field.

There were four wire teams: Jones', Weekly's, Goldstein's, and mine. Each team had four men assigned, with ten miles of wire. Within this battalion, a common wire line would run for about 20 miles. This meant each team would do about five miles on a common line. I think my team always did more than our share.

One day, while rushing to complete a line and testing the line between two points about a two-mile distance apart, I was at one point and my driver was at the other. I encouraged him to hurry and pick me up, and in the process, he turned over the truck, with three men aboard. This was in early September 1963. I was sure this would cancel the promotion I had worked so hard for.

The accident was discussed, the men had minor injuries, the truck was a lost and was replaced, and no one said anymore to me about it. I continued to work at the message center when I was not in the field with my new truck and new crew.

On October 12, 1963, several men and I left Clermont, going to upstate New York to a work camp around Peekskill to pick apples. Passing through Georgia, a man we called O.C. was driving my 1960 Thunderbird. We were speeding —doing about eighty in a sixty-mile-an-hour speed zone. The music was loud when the local police pulled us over.

The officer addressed us as "boys" and asked for O.C.'s driver's license and the insurance for the car. O.C. showed his license, and I got the insurance from the glove box. The officer reviewed and kept the license and insurance and asked us to follow him. When we got to the county courthouse, he asked who Julius P. Montgomery, whose name
was on the insurance, was. I told him I was.

He said the driver of the car had to go before the county judge and pay a fine or go to jail. The judge came in took the insurance and license and asked the officer what the charges were. The officer said, "These boys were doing eighty miles an hour in a sixty-mile-an-hour speed zone." The judge said the fine would be $120 dollars or one week in jail.

We pulled together and paid the fine. The judge admonished us and said, "You boys try and obey the law, you hear!" From Georgia on, we looked out for speed traps. We traveled nonstop, except for gas through South Carolina, North Carolina, Virginia, Washington DC, Maryland, and Pennsylvania. We made the trip from Clermont to the work camp close to Peekskill in about two days.

From there, I would have to travel down past the Hudson into New York City to Brooklyn Navy Yard, where I would load my car for shipment to Germany. At the work camp, I met a young man who said he was going into Harlem, and if I gave him a ride into Harlem, he would help me get over to Brooklyn Navy Yard. I agreed. It was October 14, 1963, and I did not have to be at the navy yard until October 19. My flight for Germany would be on the 21st.

I thought I would spend some time in Harlem, which I did. Ieven met an old neighbor named Juanita Curry from Clermont on 125th Street. I also met the young man who I picked up from camp's family, and had a few beers. Then we all loaded into the Thunderbird and drove over to the navy yard. [had let the young man drive. He pulled me right up to the building where I had to check in.

I went into the building with a copy of my orders and was logged in on the manifest. I was told where to park my car inside a containment area with the keys in the switch. The car had to be in place no later than 1500 hours on October 19. My orders were stamped and given back to me. I was told that the orders would get me breakfast and a place to sleep until my flight left for Frankfurt, Germany, on the morning of the 21st.

When I returned to where my car was, there was no car. I went back inside and reported that my car had been stolen. The military police were called and got me in contact with the detective of the New York 25th Precinct because that was where the suspect was from. We looked for the car for two days, and the case was turned over to the FBI.

They asked where had I been in Harlem. I told them in the area of 125th Street. We went to that area, and within two hours, we found the car parked in the backyard off 125th Street. The car was very clean and had a new shine. The officers knocked on the door and announced they were the FBI. Four young men came out into the yard with their hands on top of their heads.

The FBI asked if the man who took my car was among the four. I pointed him out. It was now about eleven o'clock in the morning. I was told had to go downtown to the judge's office, where this man would be charged with grand theft auto. I would have to press charges against him, and he would be put away for several years if convicted.

I was told I did not have to be present for the trial and was given my keys. The car was full of gas, and I followed the FBI downtown, feeling very relieved but a little shaken. It was now October 16. I still had three days to get the car to the containment area and catch my flight.

Since leaving Clermont, I had learned a lot. I thought I was smart, but I learned I was lucky. In fact, very lucky to have found my car in the biggest city in the United States, after trusting someone whose name I did not know with the keys.

I parked my car on the afternoon of the 16th. My flight departed New York at 0900 hours on October 21. The pilot said it would be about a nine-hour flight to Frankfurt, Germany, and that we would be landing at Frankfurt Military Air Base at about 1800 hours. Waiting for my arrival at the air force base was an army van. After the driver identified me, we went to baggage claim and picked up my duffle bag, I had one other carry-on. I was the only passenger in the van.

We drove through the streets of Frankfurt to McNair Kaserne, Hoechst, Germany. It was a small base—just big enough to hold the battalion. It was freezing. Ice was on the ground, and I was ready to get inside. I was assigned quarters with one other sergeant, Sergeant Jones. This was good. I knew I would be making sergeant soon; if not, I would have been assigned to the squad bay.

My knee was close to 100 percent. With all the training at Ft. Sill, it had not given me any problems. Jones told me my wire team was waiting on me, and we would be going to Graffinville, a training site, in about a week. I did not have much time to get my team ready for the move.

Graffinville was about a hundred km away, close to the east sector. I had never been there, but I had heard a lot of war stories about the place. It was talked about all over the army by careers who had experienced the cold, mud, and poor living conditions associated with the training area.

Our section sergeant was Sergeant First Class White, an E6. Some SFCs were E7 and some were E6s. It had something to do with the changing rank structure in the army. SFC White was an old timer who had been to Graff, as Graffinville was called, and had horrible stories to tell about the place. His instructions drilled into the wire section of the communications platoon were, make sure you have all of your equipment and all of your personal field gear—overshoes, field trousers, gloves, hats, and scarf, and so on, and make sure that the section equipment is survivable.

Field training test was for thirty days. We were required to stay awake 36 hours at a time, and I was told the mud and snow was knee deep. Four-wheel-drive vehicles often were not able to move in the mud and snow, and required chains on the wheels. Guns and heavy equipment had to travel by rail to get to Graff because they were not allowed on the autobahn.

The wheel section of the battalion departed for Graff on October 27, 1963 and arrived at base camp late on the same day. Each section was assigned one hut to store our equipment and one for sleeping quarters. Our sleeping quarters had a single coal-burning stove in the center of the floor. Each man had an individual cot to sleep on. A fire had to be started and maintained in the stove. There was no toilet or shower. There was a community toilet and shower facility at the end of the row of huts, with hot water heated by a coal furnace. This fire too had to be maintained.

There was also a common mess facility with gas-burning cooking units. The mess facility was very sufficient; this was our base camp. On October 29, we started field artillery training. We would train for 36 hours without sleep, moving from one designated firing position to another, firing the big guns and laying miles of field wire from the fire direction center (FDC) to the observatory post (OP). Radio communications also had to be maintained.

Our mission was to move, shoot, and communicate effectively, as if we were in a combat environment. Wire lines had to be laid between each gun battery and the headquarters switchboard. A, B, and C batteries were responsible for their individual wire lines, and headquarters was responsible for the twenty-mile wire line to the OP. This responsibility was divided between four wire teams: Jones', Weekly's, Goldstein's, and mine.

Back at base camp on the October 31, 1963, I was promoted to Sergeant E5. I had four years, seventeen days in the army. Sixteen years to go. [had decided to make the army a career. I wrote Odessa and told her about my promotion. I also told her I did not have a picture of her. She sent me a picture and congratulated me. She also asked if this meant I would be sending her an engagement ring. I knew that I would not.

I thought I should tell Odessa I did not want to marry until I was back in the states. In the next letter I got from her, she told me she was going to get married to a guy who she had been seeing before she began to see me. His name was Sam McGee. For some reason, I did not think she would be happy; however, she wanted to get married. I wrote her and told her I would always love her and hoped she would be happy. Someone told me she moved to Detroit with Sam.

To drive in Germany, you needed an international driver's license. You also needed a U.S. Forces license plate for your car. I took the test for the international license and passed. I also got license plates for my car. On return from Graff in early December 1963, I picked up my car from port. Driving back from port was a new experience. The Thunderbird was able to hold its own on the autobahn. I toped it out at one hundred and fifty-four miles an hour, passing everything on the autobahn. But I was sure there would be other days when I would be left in the dust of a Mercedes or Porsche, or some of the autobahn hogs.

In the Thunderbird, on my first visit to Frankfurt, Specialist 4th Class Brown from the wire section and I met two crazy Germany girls who wanted to have a foursome. So! The first time I was in bed with a white woman, there were two of them. I did not know what to think when the girls said we would share a single room for the night.

At first, l asked what we would do in just one room. The answer was, "Don't you want to make love to us?" I said, "I think so!" My next question was, "Will I make love to both of you?" They asked, "Do you want to?" So, Brown and I agreed to make love to these two not-bad-looking girls. Both had dark hair and were about the same size—5'9" and about 130 pounds. They said they were nineteen and twenty.

We all got into the Thunderbird, and they gave me directions to the hotel where we would spend the night. It was Saturday, and there was no formation at camp on Sunday. The hotel was several blocks away from the bar. I drove the distance and found a safe parking space. They asked for money for the room and went to pay the clerk and to get the key.

The room was sixty German marks, or about twenty American dollars, and was on the second floor of the hotel. We took the elevator. When we got to the room, I had another surprise: There was only one queen-sized bed. It was no surprise to the girls. They both undressed and sat on the bed and asked, "What are you waiting on. Do you want us to undress you?"

They were both having fun and laughing to beat all get-out. So, I thought I would join in the fun and requested that I be undressed. The nineteen-year-old took me up on my request. And the twenty-year-old began to undress Brown. Once we were all undressed, we all were in the small space of the queen-sized bed together, touching one another and going through various stages of having sex and enjoying one another's bodies.

I was surprised again when both girls refused to change partners. My girl and I, with her in the middle and me on the outside, stayed on our side of the bed, and Brown and his girl stayed on their side, with him on the outside and her in the middle, until morning. We all went and found the Thunderbird safe, and found a McDonald's for breakfast.

The girls wanted to hang out with us for the rest of the day; however, Brown and I were not so sure. We wondered why the two girls were inseparable. *Did they feel safe when they were together or what?* I was not so sure that I enjoyed the night as much with two girls and a guy or if I ever wanted to have a foursome or threesome. I think one girl at a time is the best way to go.

Chapter 16

Germany

From my first night on the town, three years in Germany was going to be a new experience for "Mama's black child." A solider who had spent several years in Germany told me that my 6'2", 195-pound frame would not escape Germany without being married to a German fraulein. I disagreed with him, of course. I was sure I would marry some day; however, when I did, it would be to a black woman, and I would have black children. I learned early on in Germany that frauleins were attracted to me, so I would play my own game. I had a beautiful American car, I dressed well, and I was a 22-year-old sergeant in the U.S. Army. I had almost everything going my way.

In December 1963, in-between one-night stands, I meet a nineteen-year-old fraulein by the name of Virginia. I liked her a lot. On weekends, I would pick her up at the Frankfurt Train Station, and we would get a hotel room for the weekend. We would go out to the local clubs near and around Frankfurt. Virginia was a freak for good sex; she never got enough.

One night we were at this nightclub when three African gentlemen approached me. One had a knife. He pulled it and asked, "What have you been doing with my woman, man?" Virginia jumped in front of me and said, "No!" Out of nowhere, a friend of mine I did not know was in the club put a pistol to the African gentleman's head and told him to get out of the club or he would drop him where he stood. Afterwards, I asked Virginia who the African was. She told me he was her old boyfriend, who wouldn't leave her alone.

I thanked my friend for coming to my rescue. I took Virginia to the train station and did not see her again for several months. In January 1964, I was assigned to the 7th Army Noncommissioned Officers' Academy

Bad Tolz, Germany. The academy was the most prestigious NCO leadership school in the U.S. Army.

The school taught drill and ceremonial, ground navigation, public speaking, lesson plans, principles of leadership, leadership traits, physical training, and combat operations orders. Many students failed to pass the course. There were 132 students who did pass. I graduated 47th from the bottom of the class: Student number 45, Montgomery, Julius P. Headquarters Battery 6th Battalion 9th Artillery Graduation Standing #85. This was not outstanding, but as many as 50 students failed to pass. I was happy to graduate.

Graduation day was on February 28, 1964. Three days after the battalion moved from Frankfurt Hoechst, Germany McNair Kaserne to Rivers Barracks, Giessen, Germany. Making the move were 511 enlisted men, 28 officers and 3 warrant officers. From January 24 until February 28, the Thunderbird was in a compound at Frankfurt Hoechst Germany. I had to go to Frankfurt to pick up my car, so I thought I would look up Virginia for one last night with her.

I found her at her favorite nightclub, The Sloes Bar. She wanted to know where I had moved to, so I told her. We agreed to ride to Giessen in the Thunderbird and for her to take a train from Giessen back home. We selected a nightclub in Giessen, and then had a few drinks and got a hotel for the night, Virginia was her old self. I thought I was going to miss the great sex we enjoyed together, or that I would look her up again in her favorite hangouts in Frankfurt.

I knew she was not a one-man woman, but neither was I a one-woman man. We were two of a kind, made for each other in the early morning hours, lost in a sea of lust and pleasure. On the morning of March 1, Virginia caught the train from Giessen back to her home near Frankfurt. I reported to my new duty station in Giessen. I was sure there would be many new frauleins willing to be seen with the tall black soldier in the maroon Thunderbird in and about Giessen, Germany.

Rivers Barracks, Giessen, Germany was a small compound when compared to an army post. It had a motor pool for the large guns (each gun section had a small building to house equipment necessary to maintain a gun section) and another for wheeled vehicles. Large hanger-like buildings to service the large guns and another building to service wheeled vehicles. There were smaller buildings for communications equipment, such as radio and wire sections.

In the center of the compound was a parade field for military ceremonial events. At the head of the parade field was the flagpole and a two-story large building that housed battalion headquarters. Large two-story barracks that housed personnel faced the parade field on two sides. And at the end of the parade field, facing battalion headquarters, was another large building that housed the NCO Club, a snack bar, the reenlistment office, the chaplain's office, and a general meeting room.

Other buildings included an enlisted men's club (the Rendezvous), a chapel, a barbershop, and the USO. There was a parking lot for privately owned vehicles. The compound was enclosed, with a front and rear gate. Guards were posted at the front gate, and the rear gate was opened only during training exercises.

The barracks capacity was approximately six hundred men. NCO rooms were separate from squad bays that were the quarters for personnel in pay grade E4 and below. A young sergeant just out of the Seventh Army Noncommissioned Officers' Academy, SFC White, the chief of the battalion wire section, wanted me to bunk with him.

This was the last place I wanted to be. I knew it would not last long because I would have a busy schedule, plus: 1) I needed a lot of room for my civilian clothes and shoes. 2) I would be coming and going most of the time. 3) I did not have the time to devote to talking about army and troops all of the time, and I knew that was all he was about.

I put in for an after-duty job as a bouncer at the Rendezvous Club. The manager hired me, and I would work there for the next three years. I enjoyed the work of keeping the peace. Everyone soon learned I was a no-nonsense, fair guy, so I had very few problems with the enlisted men, who were about my age. There were always a few who wanted to test me, but after I threw several out head first, they got the message.

The Rendezvous closed at 2200 hours each night. Bed check for soldiers in pay grade E4 and below was 2400 hours. For me, this was a good time to go to downtown Giessen to check out the bars. Most of the soldiers had already returned to post, leaving their girlfriends free to do as they pleased.

Early on, I had met a young fraulein who was a bar girl (girls who got men to buy them drinks that were only colored water but very expensive). She had asked me to buy her a drink. I told her I did not buy drinks for girls I did not know. She said she would buy me a beer, and she did.

I asked her what time she got off. She said she got off when the bar closed and after she got paid for her night's work. I asked if I could drive her home. She asked what kind of car I had—" a Mercedes because you dress so nice? Like someone who would drive a nice car." I told her I did drive a nice car, maybe nicer than a Mercedes. She said she would think about me driving her home.

I sat at my table alone, and she sent over another beer. When the club was closing, she asked me to wait for her. I waited for her with the third beer she had bought me, and once she, the other girls, and the manger got through talking in German over the night's profits, she came to my table and said, "Let's go!"

Her name was Renada, and if I could think of someone, she looked like, it would be Elizabeth Taylor. Renada lived in a one-bedroom apartment on the second floor of an apartment house about a half a mile from Star Bar, where she worked. The apartment had very few furnishings and was heated by a steam-heat radiator.

After we were in bed and had made love, she asked if I would let her drive my car. I asked if she had a driver's license. She said no. I told her when she got a driver's license, she could drive my car. She said, then I would be her gigolo.

I asked her what a gigolo was. She said someone kept by a woman. I ask her if she was saying she was willing to keep me. She said yes, as long as I was good to her and did not hit her or abuse her. I told her I would try to be her gigolo.

She asked if I would pick her up from work every night from Star Bar. I told her I would when I could. This was in March 1964. What Renada wanted from me was to be there to pick her up and to sleep with her.

She did not keep me. I had a paycheck from the army and a paycheck from the Rendezvous each month. I had a car payment and a tailor who kept up my wardrobe up. I had to buy shoes and gas for my car.

No, she did not keep me! We had a good agreement that I would be there for her, the sex between us was good, and I did not have to give her any money.

On weekends, we did things that I paid for. We went to other nightclubs and did other things together. We had an agreement that I would not sleep with any of the other girls from Star Bar. But that did not work. On two occasions, I broke this agreement. One was with a very young blond girl who always flirted with me, even when Renada was present.

One night, she played sick and asked if I would take her home. As soon as we were in the Thunderbird, she kissed me on the lips and asked if I would make love to her. I asked her where, and she said she would show me. She stopped me on a dark street, and we made love in the back seat of the Thunderbird. Afterward, I dropped her off in front of her house and watched her go in.

On another occasion, I was visiting the bartender's house from Star Bar, and a young girl who worked the bar on weekends was there. Somehow, she got me to make love to her on the couch in the living room, with others in the dining room.

Renada learned of both occasions and told both girls to keep their hands off her man or she would kick some ass! She said I was her man and that she knew what she had to do, whatever that meant. The relationship between Renada and me lasted for the full time that I was in Germany, with me breaking the agreement with a one-night stand occasionally. The opportunity always presented itself at the Rendezvous. There were always willing frauleins, even in the back seat of the Thunderbird. The soldiers at the Rendezvous called me "Superman."

Duty at Rivers Barracks in Giessen, Germany, was not all bad. We kept the equipment ready for combat. We had about two load-out alerts a month. The big guns would go to designated firing positions, and all other sections would go to their assigned positions. These were mostly practice alerts. If it was the real thing, we would also go into combat from these positions. These guns had nuclear capabilities and were prepared to take on any Soviet threat.

Our other training was at Graff, once in the summer and once in the winter to fire the big guns. Our old wire chief, SFC White was not allowed to reenlist after many years in the army. We had a new wire chief—SFC Duncan, who was more civilized and able to manage the section with everyone pulling his weight.

Under SCF Duncan—a black man, Graff was much easier. The impossible was not attempted. For an example, SFC White had attempted to lay wire lines across country without first surveying it. He would look on the map that may or may not be up to date and instruct the wire teams to take the closest distance between two points, often times running into impassable terrain such as swamps or ditches. We would waste hours winching our way out or call for assistance.

Our platoon sergeant master, Sergeant Rominger, would reprimand SFC White for taking shortcuts, and he would still try taking shortcuts again and again. He was almost never successful, making the entire wire section look inefficient.

Under our new wire chief, SFC Duncan, the wire teams followed known routes, sometimes laying two to five miles or more wire but getting the job done. In garrison, under SFC Duncan, we had a more constructed training program such as SOI and SSI. This gave communications personnel the ability to receive and send coded messages. Training that is a must, should a unit go to combat.

With the new leadership in the wire section, this gave the communications platoon a new direction, and duty at Rivers Barracks Giessen, Germany was good. With alerts only about two times a month and training at Graff only two months out of the year, the small concern had a lot of time for parades and ceremonies. The small parade field got lots of use. This made the concern more patriotic. With two units, there was a parade every Saturday morning.

With my 6'2", 195-pound frame, I was one of the honor guards (color guards), who led the parade for the almost three years that I was at Rivers Barracks Giessen Germany. Another honor guard was Sergeant Gross, also about 6'2", 200 pounds. He was also a black soldier.

Being an honor guard called for standing for sometimes thirty minutes at a time then marching. This caused my knee injury some problems, but I liked the spotlight, so I did not complain. Working at the Rendezvous Club, being an honor guard, having a steady girl to pick up every night, and being a wire team chief made time pass fast. I did find time with Renada when she took off from Star Bar to go to other nightclubs and restaurants.

Renada never stopped bugging me about driving the Thunderbird. One night when we were out on a deserted road, I gave in to her request. She took the wheel, hit the gas, and ran directly into the guardrail on the side of the road, causing several hundred dollars in damage to my car. All she could say when I said, "See you have destroyed my car. I knew I should have never let you drive!" She said, "Yes, but we will make great love tonight!"

At that point, I was not so sure I wanted to make love to her, or to even put up with her anymore. But I took the wheel, and we went on to the next town, to a small bar in the country and ordered a bottle of wine.

She tried to talk about all of the other girls she knew I was sleeping with. I told her that was just talk, and I was going to make her pay for the repairs on the car. She said that she would, but she insisted I was sleeping with other frauleins. I asked her if that was why she ran my car into the rail. She smiled. I told her if I thought she could drive and run my car into the rail on purpose, I would beat her ass.

She wanted to dance, but I did not feel like dancing. I knew I would get the car fixed as soon as I could. I looked in the German telephone directory and found a body and paint shop that would repair the car and paint it for seven hundred dollars. The following week, I put the car in the repair shop and changed the color to a metallic blue. I did not like the blue as much as the maroon, but it was okay, and people did not recognize the car so easily.

I did smack Renada once. She was bugging me again about sleeping around and said she could do the same if she wanted to and that there were several sergeants that knew me and had asked her to be their woman because I was not good for her. I smacked her and told her not to be discussing me with other men, but I think she did sleep with a couple of guys in the Giessen area. We never had a real fight about it because I think we had a good sleeping arrangement. She worked the club for drinks and I picked her up once I got off from the Rendezvous Club. The sex was good, and we enjoyed being together around and about Giessen in the Thunderbird.

Without notice, on April 26, 1966, I was called to battalion headquarters and was told that my tour of duty in Germany had been curtailed. I had served in Germany from October 1963 through April 1966. Two- and one-half years. SFC Turner was detailed to drive my car to port for shipment to New Jersey. I was told I would depart Germany for Fort Dix, New Jersey, from Rhein-Main Air Force Base on April 30. I was authorized thirty days leave, and would report to the U.S. Army Artillery Missile Center no later than May 6, 1966, upon arrival at Ft. Dix.

With the paperwork for my Thunderbird and my orders, I traded the 1960 Thunderbird for a 1966 Chevy Super Sport. I drove nonstop (except for gas) to my hometown of Clermont, Florida.

I felt bad that I did not tell Renada good-bye. I wondered how often a GI had left Germany without telling his fraulein good-bye. Renada had asked me to marry her on several occasions. I had told her my mother would not approve of me marrying a white woman. She had asked if I would give her my mother's address so she could write to her. I never did. I never thought I was too good to marry a "bar girl." I just thought maybe I loved her or maybe not. I also thought that a mixed marriage in Florida would not work in 1966. However, some black GIs from the South did marry their frauleins. Odessa was now married, so there was no one girl in Clermont for me.

Chapter 17

Home Again

At home, I made myself available to playing the field. Within the three weeks that I was in Clermont, I slept with four or more women who were there for the taking, and the black community of Clermont is a very small community. I remember when Eddie and I were first leaving Clermont in 1959. I had been reluctant to approach a woman for sex. Now, after Fort Jackson, Thailand, and Germany, it was not a second thought and was at the forefront of my every thought. I guess it has always been, but I had been taught to respect women. I still do. But I have also learned that women are little different than men about the subject.

In Fort Jackson, it was sex for pay. This was quite simple and uncomplicated. In Thailand, it was also sex for pay—at a very cheap price. In Germany, I never met a prostitute; however, some towns were as famous for prostitutes as the strip in Las Vegas. I am also sure some "bar girls" in Germany did sex for pay, but I was never approached that way, nor was I ever approached in Clermont to pay for sex. The times that I paid for sex were because it was convenient for me to do so. Like in Oakland, on my return from
Hawaii. I thought the woman was going out of her way to render a service. We had no other connection, nor did we wish to have any other connection. It was just convenient!

I had feelings for maybe only one girl in high school Vivialora Thompson. I was only sixteen, and there was Odessa. Renada, too, was an arrangement, but maybe I did love her. But now I was on my way to Fort Sill for the second time in my short career of four years.

During my last tour at Fort Sill, I was trying to get promoted and too busy for girls. This time, I was sure it would be different. I was now a sergeant with a new sports car, and I was sure I would have more time than I had had when I was last at Fort Sill.

In 1966, the Equal Accommodation Law of 1965 had just been passed, and motels in the South were still not accepting coloreds. From Clermont to Fort Sill was about sixteen hundred miles, so I would drive straight through, stopping only for gas and rest stops during daylight for an hour or so at a time. For safety reasons, I was afraid to stop at night.

The drive took twenty-four hours. Upon arrival at Fort Sill, I was assigned quarters at the staff and faculty battery, with others who taught at the officer candidate school. My 1966 Chevy still had temporary license plates, so I visited the Department of Public Safety, got a driver's handbook, and got Oklahoma plates for my car. A week later, I took the driver's test and failed the driving part. The instructor said I drove with only one hand on the steering wheel and the other on the gearshift. It would be two weeks before I could take the driving part of the test again.

As an instructor, I taught officer candidate students radio procedure, standard signal instruction (SSI) and standard operational instruction (SOI). There were no formations for instructors who had quarters at the staff and faculty battery. There was a bulletin board where information was posted twice daily. I had a friend who was also my driver during my last tour at Fort Sill. He had wrecked my truck with two others aboard, and I had sweated getting my promotion.

Major Boardingham lived in a small town, Anadarko, north of Fort Sill. He also had a sister who I had seen only once. I thought she was really cute. I wanted to get to know her then, and now maybe I would.

On my first weekend at Fort Sill, I drove to Anadarko and looked up Major. He introduced me to his sister (Alfreder). This was the beginning of a six-month relationship. The following week, I re-took the driving part of the driver's license test, and this time, I kept both hands on the steering wheel. I passed the test and got my Oklahoma driver's license.

During the next six months, other than Alfreder, I talked to only two other women (who were just friends). The drive from Anadarko to Fort Sill was less than an hour's drive, and I would make it every day. The town was small, and there was no motel available to coloreds so most of Alfreder and my sex encounters were on a country road in the back seat of the Chevy, except when we were in Lawton or Oklahoma City, where there were coloreds' motels.

I made friends with several other Fort Sill soldiers —Sergeant Jackson and Sergeant Watson, who had girlfriends in Anadarko or Chickasha, a town just west of Anadarko. We would meet at a small restaurant (Sarge's Place) in Anadarko with our girls for hot links and beer.

Across the street was a barbecue restaurant with the best barbecue in Oklahoma. It catered mostly to white people. Barbara, Major's wife, worked there. We would often have take-outs of pork ribs and beef brisket. Anadarko was al-most like home: The comradeship between us was good, and we knew almost every family within the small colored community.

Major had a good job according to colored standards, working at the local carpet factory as a carpet-dyeing expert. With his wife, Barbara, he had a nice home for themselves and two children. He was someone who was looked up to within the community.

There was also a great deal of respect for young army sergeants such as Watson, Jackson, and me. So, times were good. The only thing to worry about was being shipped out to Vietnam, which we all knew would happen sooner or later. In the meantime, being an instructor at the Artillery and Missile School for Officer Candidate Students at Fort Sill was a real important and prestigious job. Each block of instruction was subject to inspection by a superior officer, who would often be critiqued, and if found not to be up to par, the instructor's annual evaluation report could reflect that.

Getting ready for a block of instruction required research and practice. Annual evaluation reports were the means by which a soldier's career was dictated. Among the lot of us, Staff Sergeant Jackson was the most respected. 1) He was one grade higher than the rest of us, and 2) because of his job as an artillery fire direction expert, which was rare for a colored soldier in the sixties. The job required one to be well versed in math, slide rules, and logarithms. He worked in an artillery fire direction center, the heart of any artillery unit.

Often, during the summer, colleges and universities' reserve officers training candidates who would become artillery officers would train with the school. I was assigned to teach SSI and SOI class for college and university students. In one of my classes was a university student from Clermont by the name of Mack Fogle.

Mack was from a single-parent family. His mother was Ms. Rose. All of his brothers were outstanding. Albert, who was my age, was a community organizer. George was an outstanding football player who, unfortunately, was killed in a car accident before he could play at the next level. Gene was an apartment and property manager. After completing his military obligation, Mack owned property in several cities, including Clermont, which his brother Gene managed.

On October 7, 1966, I received orders for Vietnam with a departure date of November 15. The orders read that the individual would arrive Vietnam wearing khaki trousers and a short-sleeved shirt, and would have in his possession basic required summer uniforms, work uniforms, and combat boots.

On October 15, I visited Anadarko for the last time and told everyone I was in route to Vietnam, after a thirty-day leave that I would spend with my family in Florida. I asked for addresses so I could write. I headed the Chevy toward Chickasha on Highway 62. From there, I would take Highway 81 to 35 to 10 to 75 onto the central Florida turnpike into Clermont. The trip would take about 24 hours, and I would have traveled across Oklahoma, Texas, Louisiana, Mississippi, and Alabama,

I would leave my car with my sister Gloria and her husband Speedy and fly out to Fort Lewis, Washington. My thirty days at home would be more of the same in the small town of Clermont. With the old Jim Crow southern laws, there was little for a colored person to do for entertainment in 1966. For the most part, girls were willing, and again the entertainment was in the back seat of the Chevy on a country road. There was no golf at the country club or drinks at the local bar with the guys. Nor were there motels available for a guy and his girl. But there was war. And soon, I would be in the heart of it. On the November 12, Speedy took me to the Orlando airport, where I bought a ticket for Tacoma, Washington, to be processed for air departure from Fort Lewis to Vietnam.

Chapter 18

Vietnam

On the morning of the 15th, other troops and I were bused to McChord Air Force Base for departure to Camp Alfa, South Vietnam, with a layover in Japan for refueling. During the layover, we were not permitted to leave the aircraft. For 23 hours, we were on one aircraft.

Upon landing in South Vietnam, we departed the aircraft in single file for a single gate. The compound was encircled with razor wire, with guards in elevated sandbagged bunkers and machine-guns every fifty feet or so. It looked like a war zone! We were housed in large tents with sandbags about knee high around each tent. I did not feel safe.

We were briefed and were told if the loudspeaker announced incoming, we were to get on the floor until an all clear was given. There would be three formations a day, and at each formation, we would be given an assignment to a unit somewhere in South Vietnam. I was in a war zone without a gun!

After two days on the morning of the November 17, 1966, I was given an assignment: 1st Battalion 69th Armor in Pleiku, the central highlands of South Vietnam. At about 1000 hours, I was on a Caribou Army Cargo aircraft headed for the central highlands of South Vietnam. It was about an hour and a half flight.

Upon landing in Pleiku, a 6'3" tall white soldier with starched jungle fatigues, an M-16 rifle, and a 45-pistol strapped to his side put his hand in the air and said, "Anyone for the 69th Armor?" I held up my hand. He walked over to me with his hand extended and said, "I am Sergeant Summerville, better known as 81 Charley Fox Trot. I am the company supply clerk and your transportation to Company A. The company is presently on road security with forward base camp, about 15 miles south of Pleiku. I'll take you out tomorrow, after we get you your basic issue. Are you a tanker?"

I told him I was a communications sergeant. He said, "Oh! You will be replacing Sergeant Jackson. He has been looking for his replacement for some time. He is our commo/operations sergeant, mostly operations.

Sergeant Summerville was a very friendly, likeable, and talkative individual. He gave me a quick history of the unit. The unit was really the 3rd Brigade of the 25th Infantry, from down south around Hobo Woods that escorted the 4th Infantry Division to the central highlands. They were on loan to the 4th Infantry Division. The 4th Infantry Division 3rd Brigade was still down south with the 25th Infantry. We still wore the 25th patch. We called our base camp 3rd Brigade Hill.

The ride from Pleiku Airstrip to the Third Brigade hill was a short one, and upon arriving, Summerville told me I would sleep in the supply room for the night; "Let's get you your issue." I was given a cot, a sleeping bag, a shelter, half tent pegs, a rope, tent poles, three sets of jungle fatigues, three olive drab T-shirts, shorts, jungle boots, an M-14 rifle, a bandolier of ammunition, a steel helmet, and a bullet-proof vest. He told me to pack my khakis and other gear in a bag that he gave to me with a tag to put my name on, and gave me a place to store it in the supply room. "You will need them a year from now," he said.

The following morning, we headed for the forward base camp. Once outside of base camp, he told me to put a clip in my rifle and put on my bulletproof vest. We were doing about forty miles per hour on the dirt road, with jungle on each side. He said, "This is combat." He also said our tanks were positioned at each checkpoint along the jungle road, with infantry in between. It was time for him to check in with forward base camp by radio to tell them he had departed base camp, with the new "81Zero communications/operations sergeant." "81Zero. This is 81CharleyFoxTrot,Over." "81CharleyFoxTrotThisIs810,Over." "810. This is 81CharleyFoxTrotDepartingBaseCampWithTheNew810.Wil

Checkpoint Alfa was now a hardtop road, and we could see the M48A3 main battle tank with its crew on road-security duty. Sergeant Summerville pulled into the checkpoint and introduced me to Pappy, platoon sergeant of the third platoon, and three of his men, who put in an order for beer and sodas on his next trip out.

Summerville contacted forward base camp and reported that we were departing Checkpoint Alfa for Checkpoint Bravo. As we passed Checkpoint Bravo, we waved and radioed to forward base camp that we had passed Checkpoint Bravo and would report in at checkpoint Charley, the last checkpoint before reaching forward base camp.

Beer, soda, and cigarettes were issues for combat troops and could be picked up at the G4 lot at base camp. Ice was another story. That had to be bought off the local market. We reported passing Checkpoint Charley and would be at the forward base camp in fifteen minutes.

Upon reaching forward base camp, I was introduced to the company 1st sergeant, a man of Asian decent from Hawaii. He introduced me to the company commo/operations sergeant, Sergeant Jackson, a colored sergeant. Sergeant Jackson was a laid-back kind of guy who played the guitar. His assistant, Specialist 4th Class Cathguarth, also colored, was the company radio repairman. Road security was a laid-back kind of duty, for a tank company. It was the same old thing every day, so there was not much for a commo/operations sergeant to do but take sit-reps (situation reports) from the checkpoints. Most reports were negative reports. Infantry was also on duty with each tank. Both the tankers and infantry reported to the tank platoon leader, who was a lieutenant.

The lieutenant reported to the operations sergeant every hour. The operations sergeant made a record for the company commander. However, without this security, supplies and re-supplies could not reach division-sized units, there by cutting off operation within an area or theater. Road security in combat operation is a must—if not by tanks, then by escorts, heavily armed wheeled vehicles that led supplies through a suspected enemy area. My armored tank company during the Vietnam War was made up as follows:

Five tanks per tank platoon and two tanks were assigned. to the headquarters platoon. The company commander had his own tank. He also had a jeep with a driver.

The 1st sergeant supervised the dozer tank. He had his own jeep and driver.

The supply sergeant had a ¾-ton truck and a jeep driven by the supply clerk.

The mess section had a 2 ½-ton vehicle, a driver, and five cooks.

The motor sergeant had ¾ ton truck, vehicle/tank retriever, and five mechanics.

The ammunitions sergeant had a 2 ½-ton vehicle with two helpers.

The communications/operations sergeant had a M-113 armored personnel carrier modified to carry radios used as the combat mobile headquarters for the company.

Everything that happened within Company A, 1st Battalion 69th Armor came through the mobile headquarters. The mission was received by code and had to be decoded by hand. This sometimes took hours, using SSI. Road security was the exception because there were few, if any, changes.

Each tank's personnel number consists of the platoon number, followed by the vehicle number. There was no number one; instead, the number six was used as the universal command number. The following shows the tank platoon organization:

Company Commander 6
Platoon Leader 1st Platoon 1-6 (1st Lieutenant)
Line Tank 1-2 (Staff Sergeant)
Line Tank 1-3 (Staff Sergeant)
Platoon Sergeant and Second in Command 1-4 (Sergeant 1st Class)
Line Tank 1-5 (Staff Sergeant)
Platoon Leader 2nd Platoon 2-6 (1st Lieutenant)
Line Tank 2-2 (Staff Sergeant)
Line Tank 2-3 (Staff Sergeant)

Platoon Sergeant and Second in Command 2-4 (Sergeant 1st Class)

Line Tank 2-5 (Staff Sergeant)

Platoon Leader 3-6 3rd Platoon (1st Lieutenant)

Line Tank 3-2 (Staff Sergeant)

Line Tank 3-3 (Staff Sergeant)

Platoon Sergeant and Second In Command 3-4 (Sergeant 1st Class)

Line Tank 3-5 (Staff Sergeant)

These are the tankers' responsibilities:

Tank Commander: Responsible for the vehicle, its maintenance, and performance in battle; also, the most likely to be killed in battle

Gunner: Normally in control of the main gun; the second in command of the tank.

Loader: Responsible for feeding all weapons and keeping supplies stocked

Driver: Drives tank and maintains engine, tracks, and electrical system

As commo/operations sergeant for Company A, 1st Battalion 69th Armor from December 1966 to November 1967, working as the extension of the company commander, I received operations orders sometime in code with groups that exceeded one hundred. While on road security, the operations order was within a known area and would probably read no change from one day to the next. However, in every enemy contact or during normal operation, as operations sergeant I was available to assist if the tank commander needed ammunition, fuel, air support, medical extraction of the wounded (Medevac), food, vehicle extraction or repair, radio repair, infantry and engineering support, maps, and directions to known enemy contact where a tank could assist.

In Vietnam, my call sign was 81-0, which was available to Company A, 1st Battalion 69th Armor 24/7. On one occasion in February 1967, while on road security with the forward base camp stationed at the

Oasis, a platoon of Company A, tanks were moving on a road south of Pleiku, near the rock quarry when command-detonated mines exploded, disabling all five tanks.

The platoon leader called 81-0 for assistance. I called Captain DeMont, who was the company commander during that time. His instructions to the platoon leader were to buckle up and load canister rounds, and if the enemy mounted any tank, for each tank to fire a canister on each other.

In the meantime, I called into the air force to deliver napalm on each side of the road where the tanks were downed. I gave the air force the location on the map. Upon identifying the target, the pilot radioed, target identified, and two low-flying aircraft dropped their load of napalm on each side of the road of the downed tanks. I called for infantry to search the area for bodies or enemy activity. We received a negative report. The infantry-maintained security for the tanks until they were repaired. Engineers were called to sweep the road for mines, and both the infantry and engineers stayed with the tanks until they reached their new position.

This was the most activity I experienced during road security in my short time as operations sergeant for Company A. The following week, however, while still at the Oasis, I received a 106-word group for the tanks platoon with assigned infantry to search suspected areas for rice in 50–100-pound containers and retrieve it.

Upon receiving the day's mission (which took me most of the night to decode using a gas lantern), and the assigned SSI, Captain DeMont somewhat doubted the mission until he had confirmed it with the assigned infantry company commander given a rendezvous point to meet with the tank platoon. The day's mission was an active one, with tanks calling in each time they discovered a stash of rice. Several hundred pounds of rice were found. They were retrieved and given to the Montagnard chiefs of the central highlands, who had first discovered the rice and reported it to higher headquarters. This was a major accomplishment. It had reduced the Vietcong food supply for several weeks or even months.

In March of 1967, Company A, 1st Battalion 69th Armor was given a new mission. The company was assigned to support the Ist Cavalry Forward Division at LZ English (Bong Son). The orders were for Company A to road march to Qui Nhon and board a navy ship (LST) on the South China Sea north to make a beach landing on the Bong Son Beach—about a twelve-hour voyage. The plan did not work. The navy ship was not able to make a beach landing because the ship bottomed out, and the tanks would sink if they tried to go inland.

The plan was revised. The ship returned to Qui Nhon, and each vehicle of Company A was assigned to a single landing craft, and made the twelve-hour voyage back north on the South China Sea. Seventeen tanks, each weighing 52 tons, were assigned to single landing crafts. A vehicle tank retriever, also weighing 52 tons was assigned to a single landing craft. Two 2 ½ -ton trucks were each assigned to single landing crafts. Two jeeps were assigned to a landing craft. A ¼ truck was assigned to a single landing craft. The M-113 communications/ operations vehicle was assigned to a landing craft. Each unit had radio communications with the other.

I was assigned to a tugboat with a radio and maintained the status of each unit. The idea was, if any landing craft got into trouble, the tugboat would come to its rescue.

The combat voyage beaching at Bong Son Beach was reminiscent of the Normandy invasion. We took the beach without any causalities, and road marched into Bong Son City and on to Landing Zone (LZ) English without any major incident.

The outstanding memories of Bong Song are the day-to-day enemy contact at the forwarded location of the company and the impact awards of the Purple Heart, Bronze Star, Silver Star, Soldier's Medal, and Medal of Honor also:

"General Orders Number 87816 April 1970 AWARD OF THE VALOROUS UNIT AWARD TC 439 The following AWARD is announced.

By direction of the Secretary of the Army, under the provisions of paragraph 202 1g(2) AR 672-5-1, the Valorous Unit Award is awarded to the following named unit of the United States Army for extraordinary heroism while engaged in military operation during the period indicated."

The citation reads as follows:
"COMPANY A, 1ST BATTALION, 69TH ARMOR, 4TH INFANTRY DIVISION distinguished itself by extraordinary heroism while engaged in military operation during the period 30 May

1967 to 3 July 1967, in Binh Dinh Province, Republic of Vietnam. While in support of the Ist Cavalry Division (Airmobile), unit personnel participated in numerous tank-infantry assaults on well entrenched and heavily armed North Vietnamese Army and Viet Cong forces. Using the shock effect of armor to the fullest, they aggressively engaged the enemy with 90-mm guns, coaxial machine guns and, often times due to the close quarter fighting, utilized hand grenades to dislodge the enemy from his well fortified position. Demonstrating great determination and a remarkable grasp of the tactical situation, the men of COMPANY A, 1ST BATTALION, 69TH ARMOR, 4TH INFANTRY DIVISION skillfully located hostile emplacements and ably supported ground assault troops by delivering the heat of battle, tank crewmen employed their vehicles as shields, and despite intense enemy fire, they courageously dismounted their vehicles to assist wounded comrades and evacuate them from the battle zone. Their brave and selfless action saved many lives and won the respect and admiration of those with whom they served. The men of COMPANY A, 1ST BATTALION, 69TH ARMOR 4TH INFANTRY DIVISION displayed extraordinary heroism and devotion to duty which are in keeping with the highest traditions of the military service and reflect distinct credit upon themselves and the Armed Forces of the United States."

The impact award of the Medal of Honor was awarded to SFC Hazelip (and was late downgraded to a Distinguished Service Cross). The Silver Star was awarded to SFC Baggly. The Bronze Star Medal was awarded to Staff Sergeant Trump and to several other members of Company A. The Purple Heart Medal was awarded to Sgt Bell, SSG Watanabe, and many others of Company A.

The Medal of Honor was also awarded to Dwight H. Johnson, a friend, of Company B, 1st Battalion 69th Armor. Johnson's citation states that the medal was awarded the 15th of January 1968. This was a misprint. I was in country when the award was made and I departed Vietnam in November 1967.

In November 1967, upon arriving at Pleiku, from the Bong Son plains by way of Qui Nhon and Mang Yang Pass, Company A set up base camp south of Pleiku on road security. Captain Allen was Company A's new commander. All of the men of Company A were restless. Road security was boring, and now Company A was in a no-fire zone, after being in a free-fire zone for the past eight months.

Infantry and military intelligence had searched all the local villages. Dogs had been used to detect anything out of the norm. Intelligence had left with me a frequency to call in case of suspected enemy activity. However, SFC Baggly, the first platoon sergeant reported receiving fire from a nearby village and requested permission to take the village out! I told him we were in a no fire zone. He requested to speak with the company command, Captain Allen.

I called Captain Allen and First Sergeant Quinton to the operations bunker and told them the first platoon sergeant, SFC Baggly, had called and reported receiving fire from the local village. I gave Captain Allen the information from the intelligence report. Captain Allen requested that I get SFC Baggly on the radio, so I did. He asked First Sergeant Quinton what his evaluation of SFC Baggly was.

First Sergeant Quinton told Captain Allen that SFC Baggly was a noncommissioned officer of the highest caliber and recipient of the Silver Star Medal. After a few words between Captain Allen and SFC Baggly, Captain Allen gave Sergeant Baggly permission to fire on the village. On the command radio net, the command was given: "Cease Fire! Cease Fire!"

Those in the village that were still alive were immediately evacuated by helicopter (Medevac). However, I saw many who were not alive, and others that were dying. There were broken limbs and mangled bodies. All were women and children. It was a massacre.

The following day, SFC Baggly was relieved of his duties. I was picked up by the military police and charged for another infraction—fraud. My records were flagged, but no action could be processed against me.

Chapter 19

Fort Meade, Maryland

My file was assigned to 6th Armor Calvary. Regiment. Fort Meade, Maryland. After leave, I reported to Fort Meade in December 1967. For several months, while under flag, I had no assignment to a TO&E slot. After my record had been reviewed, and after several interviews with the local commander at Fort Meade, the flag was lifted in March 1968, and I was assigned to 2nd Squadron Battery A 6th Armor Calvary Regiment.

On April 4, 1968, an assassin's bullet killed Reverend Martin Luther King. The violent death of Dr. King brought an immediate reaction of rioting in black ghettos around the country. The 6th Armor Calvary was only twelve miles from the Washington, DC area.

The unit was quickly assigned to the area to assist local law enforcement. It was rumored that the rioting in the area was controlled by the likes of the Black Panther Party, Stokley Carmichael, and H. Rap Brown. I was attached as a radio operator with the Police Department, who assigned me to a patrol car that reacted to hot spots and/or sightings of Carmichael, Black Panther Party members, or H. Rap Brown.

Fires were everywhere, in fact, it seemed that the entire city was on fire. My job was to inform the commander where the army troops were needed for riot control, or where the heavy concentration of would-be rioters were.

During the rioting, everyone was a looter. Police car trunks were filled with everything thinkable, from stereo equipment and jewelry to cases of the best whiskey, which they off-loaded from time to time in key locations within the city.

During the rioting "The Godfather of Soul," James Brown, agreed to put on a special concert to calm the riot. He was pumped through all the television channels, and he requested that everyone go home and stop the burning. The 6th Armor Calvary Regiment boasted about six hundred members. How Battery made up about 120 members, the number that was under my control. The riot lasted about a week. We slept in gymnasiums at high schools, in our sleeping bags within the city communities. Each soldier was armed with an M-16 rifle, and ammunition could be issued upon the request of the commander.

These were serious times in this country. Once the cities throughout the country came to a calm, military units were reassigned to normal duty at their respective military installations. At Fort Meade, I was assigned as communications chief for How Battery and was promoted to SSG E6 on August 27, 1968.

During those months that I was under flag, I supported myself playing poker with a partner, 1st sergeant Joseph Barker, who was a card shark. He taught me the way around a poker game. In fact, during that time, I bought a new car—a 1969 442 Oldsmobile. After the flag was lifted, and after the DC riots, I stopped playing poker for a living because I had an army paycheck. Playing poker for a living is not easy as one may think. In fact, it was an odd way to try and make a living.

The Washington, DC, and Baltimore areas were full of action. There was everything you could think of from orgies to opium and pot-smoking parties. However, I continued to see several of the girls I met during those times. One was Gladys, from Lumberton, North Carolina, who was living with her sister Betty, in Baltimore. Betty was one of Sergeant Barker's girls. Both sisters loved to party, and Gladys, only eighteen, had no sexual hang-ups. She lived for sex.

Another girl I met during my flagged period was Eleanor, from Annapolis, Maryland, who was a divorcee and wanted to get married. She always talked about building a hope chest. She introduced me as her future husband to everyone she knew. When I told her I was not in love with her, I had to call one of her friends to stop her from crying. She said she would sue me for breach of promise. When I told her I never promised her I would marry her, she said she had witnesses that I did. There were many other women whose names I can't remember; however, I remember their personalities, sex drive, and how much they liked the nightlife of DC and Baltimore. I was so ready to leave Fort Meade.

Chapter 20

Korea

Upon reenlisting on February 24, 1969, I requested an assignment to Korea. My port call date from Fort Lewis, Washington was April 29, 1969, and I would arrive at my new duty station on May 1, 1969. I would do two additional months at Fort Meade—March and April, and I would have one month in Clermont.

During this time, I tried to stop seeing Eleanor; however, she called my bachelor enlistment quarters (BEQ) nonstop. I saw Gladys, who wanted to set up camp at my BEQ, and did a pretty good job of it. I saw her even when I did not want to see her. It was always about sex.

In early April, I told Gladys I was going home. She said she would meet me in Clermont after she went home to North Carolina, if I would send her airfare. At first, I told her I would. However, after being home, I called and told her I did not have the money because I had to travel to Fort Lewis at the end of the month. She was upset.

Clermont was always the same. The same old girls were always available and willing. However, this time it was a little different. I had to make a decision who I would leave my new Oldsmobile with. For whatever reason, I decided to leave the car with my young brother Wilbert, who did not have a car.

The reporting time to Fort Lewis was no later than 1200 hours April 29, 1969. Enlisted members would arrive wearing khaki trousers and short sleeved khaki shirts, and have in their possession the basic allowance of uniforms. The flight departed Fort Lewis at 1600 hours and arrived Seoul, Korea midday on May 1, 1969.

Korea was a cross between the training areas of Germany in Graff and Vietnam. The living arrangements were like Graff, and the working conditions were more like Vietnam. The troops were housed in Quonset huts, heated with radiators. There were common toilet and shower facilities at the end of each row of huts, except for senior noncommissioned officers or those who were in senior noncommissioned officer's positions, who had private facilities. Officers' quarters also had private toilet and shower facilities.

In a battalion-sized organization of M-110 and M-107 artillery guns capable of delivering a nuclear warhead into North Korea, the battalion was made up of three-gun batteries, Service Battery and a Headquarters Battery. There were small villages made up mostly of women and some men, who worked on the military concern as houseboys and shined shoes and cleaned quarters for officers and senior noncommissioned officers, for a price.

Women offered the America GI anything that a wife would offer, from home-cooked meals, Korean style, to sex. This was a contractual agreement between the GI and the Korean-kept women called "yobos." These small villages were set up outside of each battery area to better serve the GIs. Many GIs married their yobos and brought them home to the states.

I was a staff sergeant E6 who worked in senior positions from the time that I reported for duty in Korea until I left a year later, after being given a quarters assignment. My first order of business was to find a good houseboy. I found one in Mr. Kim. Then I visited the village to find a yobo.

I was introduced to a cute young thing with an American name of Debby. Debby had a young daughter about two years old. I agreed to try Debby as a yobo for one month, and if it worked out, we would think of longer terms. The cost for rent for the first month was forty dollars. It was understood that other costs, such as food, would be as needed during the month. I paid to Debby the forty dollars up front. I was set.

My first senior position was as communications chief, an E8 position assigned to Headquarters and Headquarters Battery. The communications chief was in charge of a platoon of about forty men. The sections that made up this platoon were as follows.

A field wire section that was normally headed by a sergeant first class E7, but under my command, was headed by a fellow staff sergeant E6, with about twenty men.

Men and equipment common to a field wire section were: Five ¾-ton trucks, each with a sergeant E5 team chief, an E4 assistant team chief, an E4 driver, and two E3s. Ten miles of field wire, an A frame for laying field wire, and two field telephones for testing wire lines. A switchboard section with one %4-ton truck with trailer, two switchboards with necessary terminals, and four men—one E4 and three E3s. A radio section chief headed by a fellow staff sergeant E6, two radio operators E5 per radio trucks, and four AM radios single-side band AM-106s with radio teletype capability to communicate with the United States. A radio repair section with an E5 and an E4.

The communications headquarters section was made up of one captain, the communications officer, an E4, and me, who were responsible for SSI and SOI, and in general, the operations of the communications platoon.

The mission of the battalion was to 1) move, 2) shoot, and 3) communicate. Communications was key in every facet of delivering a warhead on a designated target. Upon the arrival of an E8, Master Sergeant Berry, I was assigned to another senior position within the battalion. This time, it was the Intelligence (S2) section, also a section within the headquarters battery of the battalion.

Early on in my assignment to Korea, I had received two alarming letters from home, from two different sources. A letter from Gladys telling me that she had missed her period and could be pregnant. A few days later, I got a letter from her that she had started her period. I was relived.

The other news from home was that my brother Wilbert had wrecked my new 442 Olds, and State Farm Insurance had said it was beyond repair. They had paid off the finance company — $2,626.40. The insurance company also sent me a small check that made up the difference of the appraised value of the car. I visited the post exchange and applied the check toward the down payment on a 1970 Corvette.

The intelligence (S2) section of the battalion was almost like the communications headquarters of the communications platoon but with a wider scope. Manning the section was Captain Waltman, Specialist 4th Class Churchill, and me. The files of the battalion intelligence section covered every facet of the battalion's operations. The S2 files were classified from unclassified to Top Secret: storage of a nuclear warhead, moving of a nuclear warhead, security, inspection of nuclear facilities, types of alerts in preparation to fire a nuclear warhead. A nuclear site is under constant inspection, and there is no room allowed for errors. Errors in an inspection, depending on the error, could mean the removal of the command structure of the unit.

In this job, there was little time to spend with your yobo in the village. Files were always being taken from the S2 section, and it was my job to make sure the file was in the right place when it was returned. A file out of order could cause breakdown of continuity for the battalion. I was on "top of my game, and during the time that I was the intelligence sergeant, the battalion had no problems within the S2 section.

Another job of the S2 section was to process all security clearances within the battalion. This required direct communications with the FBI and NSA for background investigations to obtain security clearances. Everyone within a nuclear battalion required a security clearance. Processing clearances within itself was a full-time job.

After several months, I was relieved from the position and was assigned to another E8 position—operations sergeant (S3). This was also a demanding job, responsible for training within the battalion. My replacement was Master Sergeant E8 Stanley. Shortly after Stanley took over the S2 section, the battalion failed an inspection, due to filing errors within the section. This caused alarm throughout the battalion.

The battalion sergeant major had a nervous breakdown and was sent back to the states. For several weeks, the battalion received assistance from higher headquarters until it was on equal footing again. For whatever reason, no one was relieved of their command; however, several reprimands were given, which could cause serious problems in future assignments and promotions for persons of the command structure, including the battalion commander.

S3 sergeant, my third E8 position within the battalion since my assignment to it, was another high-profile and heavy workload position. I was responsible for all the training within the battalion on a daily basis. Special training included familiarization and zeroing of personal assigned weapons. I was also responsible for field training and firing of the M-110 eight-inch Howitzer and M-107 175-mm guns that could deliver a nuclear warhead into North Korea.

These training exercises sometimes took place in the dead of winter, in -20 degrees weather, along the demilitarized zone of South Korea. The most demanding exercise within the battalion, though, involved almost every member and could be called at any time: When a nuclear alert is called, this required members of the battalion to man their assigned posts.

Three authentication cards from three separate safes located in the S2 section required three key personnel to open an assigned safe and pull their assigned cards, called "cookie jars" from each safe. When the cards are opened, if they all match, this could mean all systems go for firing of nuclear warheads on their designated target, unless there was a follow-up call to stand down.

Nuclear alerts were called several times a month, both day and night, and key personnel had to be ready to act. Reaction time was within the hour, so persons in senior positions had to stay close to their posts. This meant that oftentimes senior personnel's yobos visited them within their quarters, which required an escort for security.

Between assignments from battalion intelligence sergeant to battalion operations sergeant, I was assigned as chief of firing battery. Within a battery of the battalion, this was another key position responsible for four eight-inch gun sections, which were the nuts and bolts of an artillery battalion. I was assigned as chief for only a brief period — long enough to learn and experience the real hardship of field artillerymen.

A projectile or warhead weighed several hundred pounds, with fuse fitted to the projectile. It was required to be loaded into the breach of the gun by two men and rammed into place by an automatic rammer. Black gunpowder called charges was measured and put into place behind the projectile, and the breach was closed. A detonator was placed into the breach.

The data from the fire direction center was relayed to the chief of section and fed into the gun instruments. Data including deflection, elevation, and so on were given to the chief of section before he gave the order to fire the gun. When the chief of section gave the order to fire, a rope attached to the trigger mechanism on the breach was pulled, firing the gun. This was basically what a member of a gun section experienced when firing an M-110 eight-inch gun or an M-107 175-mm gun. However, much more than that was required.

First, an orienting angle was established, and the battery was laid at the battery level. At the headquarters level, surveying teams spent many hours surveying in targets. Also, at the headquarters level, fire direction used instruments, maps, and computers gave accurate and effective data to the guns. And without good radio, AM and FM together with wire communications, none of the above was possible.

As the S3 sergeant, I was also the platoon sergeant for S2, S3, the forward observer, who directed artillery fire from an observation post many miles from the gun in placement, and the fire direction section. During my assignment of one year in Korea, I served in every key NCO position except survey — another E8 position within headquarters battery.

I was only an E6 with nine years of service. From my own observations over the years, if I was white, I would have been promoted to E7 during this period. On several occasions, the subject of promoting me was brought up, but it was turned down because of time in grade and time in service, so they said.

I also had one account on my records of disrespect of an officer at Fort Mead. I think if the black mark was not on my record, they would have had to promote me based on my track record during my year in Korea. But this was the sixties.

There was one other thing during my assignment. A black E6 from the medical section who was about seven feet tall said I was an uppity nigger, and he wanted to kick my ass. He gave me a hard time every time he got the chance, especially during meals around other blacks. He was three hundred pounds or over, and I was 6'2" and about 190 pounds. I agreed to fight him in a boxing match with an official referee. I explained that I had no reason to fight him, other than to get him off my back. I had nothing against the big guy.

The fight was set up as a battalion event and would be held at the concern gym. SSG E6 Gray of headquarters battery would be the referee. I was much faster than the big bully and got in some good punches during the first round. I think everyone in the gym was pulling for me. However, in the early minutes of the second round, the big guy caught me with a haymaker and knocked me out. I am sure I had a concussion because a month later I was still having headaches from the devastating blow to the head.

I served in Korea from April 1969 through March of 1970. I should have served through April of 1970, but 1stSG Colon of Headquarters Battery worked a deal with personnel to cut my tour short because it was rumored that a private from the communications platoon, together with a 2nd lieutenant, would bring charges against me for hitting the said private.

I don't remember hitting anyone, but I do remember giving orders to several enlisted men in a restricted area who had too much to drink and/or were high by other means. One had said he would tell his lieutenant that I had physically assaulted him and would bring charges against my black ass.

I suspect the lieutenant himself was buddies with the said private and may have also been a bigot. 1SG Colon said the private had several witnesses and the lieutenant had agreed to press charges against me. I agreed with the 1SG and agreed to leave Korea a month early.

A lot had to be done to get me out of country. 1) I had a lot to pack because I spent so much time in my quarters due to my duties and had a lot of stuff. I had stereo equipment: a reel-to-reel Sony tape recorder, a record changer, two large speakers, a Kenwood amplifier, and stacks of records and tapes. I also had my basic military issue. 2) I had to have an assignment. The 1SG said the assignment could be received by telephone, and I could be out of country within days, or as soon as I was packed.

He said this could not be done for just anybody, but I had served the battalion well and should not have to go through something like this. He also said this would probably mean I would not be receiving any medals I deserved, but I had a long career ahead of me—time for medals and accommodations.

I had saved the boxes that my stereo equipment came in, so I was packed within several hours after getting the word from the 1SG. My stuff and my military issue were taken to I Corps Headquarters and would be processed out upon getting an assignment.

Chapter 21

Fort Hood, Texas

The following day, I got my assignment to Fort Hood, Texas, Headquarters 7th of 6 Infantry of the 2nd Armor Division. I was assigned as headquarters company communications chief. I was again in an E6 position, after serving in several E8 positions in Korea. My record showed that I had served in several E8 positions; however, I don't think anyone gave a damn. In 1970, the division was authorized to promote me to E7. The Department of the army would take over this responsibility in the next physical year. Everyone on a division list for promotion to E7 would be promoted before the Department of the army taking this responsibility.

I was not on a division list for promotion. This meant several years could pass before I could be promoted. I knew of many undeserving E6s who were white who got their names on the division list through favors or just because they had the time in the army. I am sure if I was white, with my record I would have gotten on the division list.

Several weeks after being at Fort Hood, my stuff from Korea arrived— my stereo equipment and all of my baggage. My new Corvette was also ready for pick-up in St. Louis, Missouri. I took a two-week leave, picked up my stereo equipment and all of my baggage, and locked it in my assigned quarters.

I had bought my car through the post exchange, so I needed post exchange paperwork to get the car financed. I got the car financed through the credit union on post and flew to St. Louis to pick up my car. I drove to Clermont to stay for a couple of days and then drove back to Fort Hood. I had almost everything. I had a suit for every day of the week, over twenty dress shirts, and a new Corvette.

But I should have been promoted to E7. I had worked for the promotion, and now it looked like it would be several years before I got it. In May of 1970, I met Sergeant First Class Portwood. SFC Portwood was my platoon sergeant in Hawaii in 1960, more that ten years past.

I told him I did not make the division E7 list after being in an E8 position for the past year in Korea. He told me he had more than twenty four years of service and was only an E7 but was happy with his career. He said rank was not everything and that position was more important than rank.

I told him I was not happy with my current position and had requested a position as an intelligent analyst. He said that an intelligent analyst spent most of his time in the field, grading division units, and I would not be happy in that position. He said he was the assistant to III Corps and a Fort Hood career counselor and could help me become a career counselor as well. In this position, there would be little or no field duty, and I would have an office to myself, with no requirement to make formations. I would be under the supervision of the adjutant or the battalion commander. The career counselor office had air-conditioning, special furnishings—a wooden desk, a leather high-back chair, and leather office furniture. I also would have clerical support at III Corps and Fort Hood level.

About this time, I was seeing several girls: Francis from Waco, Beth from Killeen, and Robbie from Austin. Of the three, I was serious about Robbie, who was separated from her husband and had a two-year-old son, Joe. On January 28, 1971, my request to become an intelligence analyst was granted, and on February 1, I was assigned to the 163rd Military Intelligence Battalion (combat).

The battalion's mission was to test combat units and combat surveillance equipment. This was during the heart of the Vietnam War, and the unit was under extreme pressure and in the field one hundred percent of the time. In fact, the unit set up teams to rotate in and out of the field, testing units for combat readiness and combat surveillance to be used in Vietnam.

SFC Portwood had advised me correctly about field duty as an intelligent analyst. Not only that, when I was assigned, there was only one black—an EF4 assigned to my intelligence platoon, I was assigned as an assistant platoon sergeant. Most of the members of the platoon were draftees with four years of college, including the one black E4.

As assistant platoon sergeant, I had a hard time getting anything accomplished, which was a first for me. During my first month after being assigned to the 163rd MI Battalion, I made a request to attend the career counseling and recruiters' course at the USA Adjutant General School at Fort Benjamin Harrison, Indiana. I requested SFC Portwood's assistance.

For one to be selected to attend the career counseling and recruiters' course, a packet had to be submitted with a handwritten essay as enclosure #1 subject "My qualification for assignment as an Army Career Counselor/ Recruiter'

My essay read as follows: "I believe in loyalty to any unit or organization that one might be a part of. I entered the United States Army on October 12, 1959 with a tenth-grade education; my first TOE unit was Headquarters and Headquarters Battery Second Battalion Ninth Artillery, station at Schofield Barracks Hawaii. There I took and successfully completed the High School General Education Development Test (GED). I have a GT score of 115 in area aptitude. I have served in four overseas commands: Hawaii from May 1960-May 1963, Germany from October 1963—May 1966, Vietnam from November 1966—November 1967, and Korea from May 1969—April 1970. I have a total of seven years, six months overseas service. I have no bad time or court martial. I have a conduct and efficiency rating of excellent in every command that I have served."

I began this essay with the statement, "I believe in loyalty." During my early years of army life, I feel that most of the enlisted ranks were loyal to their fellow soldiers and leaders, and during those enjoyable army days, the thought of becoming a career counselor or recruiter never entered my mind. However, the past four or five years, most men in uniform only knew loyalty as a word from the dictionary. Understand me now; I say *most* men in uniform. There are still some soldiers who are loyal, and these are the ones that I would like to see stay in the army. From reading different articles on the all-volunteer army, I felt that all the things that it takes to build and maintain a good fighting team could be put back into the army.

While reading the January issue of *Army Magazine*, I read an article on discipline by retired General Hamilton H. Howze, who had been a commander for a great part of his life. He had commanded up to 10,000 men at one time. He wrote in part, "I have taught leadership extensively and written much on the subject. But I do not believe that I could (even were I 35 years younger and stronger) successfully command a company in the circumstances prevailing today, not if one defines successful command as including the capacity to take that company successfully into battle against a powerful and determined enemy." The general was speaking of that day's army and the poor discipline that existed.

I believed if I was assigned as a career counselor or recruiter, I would be able to help retain or recruit the young men who had self-discipline and that any commander could command effectively. I would be willing to go anyplace in the United States or abroad if so assigned, to contend with all the anti-war demonstrations. All the work and hours that might be involved in any type of weather to seek and find the young men who had the qualifications, the willingness, and the loyalty to become a soldier.

I wanted to become a recruiter for the longhaired hippie who did not yet know where he was going in life but had all the potential of becoming a leader anywhere, including the army. I was sure there were men in the army, as well as future soldiers, who needed and wanted good career counseling. The army had an excellent record of informing those men of the possibilities of a successful army career. I knew I could contribute a great deal to the already outstanding record. If selected for a position as a recruiter or career counselor, I would always consider the needs of the army, as well as the individuals I recruited or counseled. Once again, I was grateful to the United States Army for giving me the opportunity to request the type of duty I wanted to perform while serving the United States of America.

On June 21, 1971, I was accepted into the recruiter/career counselor program with a reporting date of July 13 to attend class number 6 of the recruiting and career counseling course at Fort Benjamin Harrison, Indiana.

On July 11, I departed Fort Hood in my new Corvette. I stopped in St. Louis and arrived in Fort Ben on the morning of the 13th and signed in and was assigned quarters. Two other black students were assigned to my quarters. There were three sleeping areas with a common kitchen, living area, and a dining area.

While at Fort Ben, I drove to Columbus in my Corvette and visited 1SG Barker. 1SG Barker was my 1SG and poker partner back in Fort Meade, when I was under flag from Vietnam. He was also responsible for my promotion to SSG E6. On another weekend at Fort Ben, I attended a jazz concert in Cleveland, Ohio.

On August 17, 1971, I graduated from the recruiter/career counselor course. My military intelligence military occupation specialty (MOS) was withdrawn as a primary MOS, and I was awarded a primary MOS of OOE40 (recruiter/career counselor).

After the recruiter/career counselor course, I took a month's leave to Florida. I drove my Corvette from Fort Ben to Florida and asked Robbie and Joe to join me. Robbie had filed for divorce, and I had thought of asking her to marry me. Robbie and Joe flew to Florida and met my family, and the three of us drove back to Texas in the two-seater Corvette. On our way back to Texas, we stopped in New Orleans to try and buy a six-pack of beer, and we were told niggers were not served there.

I was assigned as battalion career counselor for the 163rd Military Intelligence Battalion (combat) effective September 14, 1971. As career counselor, I was co-located with another career counselor. We had separate private offices. I had my own parking space, where I parked my 1970 Corvette Stingray. It was quite impressive for the men of the battalion, and I built a very good rapport that was good for first term enlistment.

More than ninety-nine percent of the enlisted men of the battalion were white. I made no formation and chose my own uniforms. Mostly, I wore a class B uniform with short sleeves during the summer months and a class A army green uniform during the winter months. I was scheduled to talk with an enlisted member about his army career about every six months and try to get a commitment for him to reenlist. I had a good record for first-term reenlistment.

By this time, I was seeing very little of Beth or Francis. However, I did run into them at the NCO club where I met both of them while working as a bouncer. I told them I was getting married, but Francis would not let go, and I had several subsequent one-night stands with her. Beth was a slim, good looking white girl who played the field, so we just became friends.

On the 28th of April 1972, Robbie and I were married, and I traded the Corvette for a mobile home. We located in Stagecoach Mobile Home Park in Killeen, close to Fort Hood. I stopped working at the NCO club and did not see Francis or Beth again.

During my assignment as the battalion career counselor for 163rd MI, I received many letters of appreciation, recognition, and/or commendation. However, I also received some misleading "enlisted efficiency reports (EERs)," the most important entry to an enlisted member's military record. From May through October 1973, I received three EERs.

On May 18, 1973, a regular report that recommended I be promoted ahead of contemporaries came.

On August 1973, I received an all-around perfect report that recommended I be promoted immediately.

October 30, 1973, upon being drafted for duty with the US. Army Recruiting Command, I received a third report that recommended I be promoted immediately and gave me an "excellent" in attitude as opposed to an "outstanding."

I was drafted for the Fourth Recruiting District, Fort Sam Houston, Texas with duty station Del Rio, Texas. After several hours on the phone, I was successful in being relieved from assignment to Del Rio and reassigned to Dallas, Texas, with duty in Killeen of the Waco Recruiting Zone. I had a reporting date of November 19, 1973.

Of about twenty recruiters assigned to the Waco recruiting zone, there was only one black recruiter. SFC Grubbs was assigned to the Temple recruiting station, and it was clear that no other black recruiters were welcome. In the 1970s, there were few black recruiters assigned to the U.S. Army Recruiting Command.

SFC Campbell was the commander of the Temple Recruiting Station, and had accepted me at the Temple Station. He said I would be assigned to the Temple substation in Killeen. At the Killeen substation, there were two recruiters—one white (SSG Corley) and one Mexican (SFC Garcia).

The first Saturday after I was assigned, SFC Campbell picked me up at the Killeen station for a trip to the Dallas recruiting main station to meet the commander and the recruiting main station sergeant major. The first thing the sergeant major said to me was, "I see you were assigned to Del Rio. How did you end up in Dallas?"

I told the sergeant major that the Del Rio area was mostly Spanish speaking, and I did not speak Spanish. His reply was, "You are the first soldier I have ever known assigned because of race. I told him I did not think race had anything to do with the assignment. It was because I did not speak Spanish.

He told me to wait outside, and the commander would see me. I waited for more than an hour and was told the commander would see me some other time. By this time, SFC Campbell had already left for Temple, and I asked Master Sergeant Butts, the Waco zone commander, if I could catch a ride with him. He said he was going back to Waco, and I could ride that far, which was about fifty miles from Killeen.

I understood that I was not welcome. I had only about five dollars and could not catch a bus to Killeen, so I accepted MSG Butts' offer, hoping that he would change his mind and have someone drive me to Killeen. There were two other recruiters, one of which was the driver. But they did not change their minds, and dropped me off on I-35 in Waco.

I was in my army uniform and was left to hitchhike home. A Mexican family picked me up. They had just enough room for me in their small car. They had their children and live chickens in a cage in the back seat. I rode with them for about thirty miles and again was dropped off along I-35 and the cut-off to Killeen. My thought was, what a way to start an assignment. But I knew that it would not get any better, and unless I made this assignment work, I would never make E7. This could very well be the end of a good career.

Chapter 22

Recruiting Duties

I would apply everything I learned at the recruiting and career counseling course at Fort Ben: 1) Know your area of assignment. 2) Develop centers of influence. 3) Look professional.

I had several things going for me. I was 6'2" tall, about 200 pounds, and made a military uniform look good. I knew many key personnel in the Fort Hood area who would help me. I was willing to work hard developing high school counselors, and I would put the time in to be successful.

MSG Butts assigned me to an area that had no support, not even a telephone, Gatesville. The area was twenty miles away from Killeen, and I was not assigned a car, as recruiters usually are. I asked what I was to do about transportation. He said I had to use my own car, and the army would reimburse me for mileage.

My wife Robbie and I had only one car, now that I had traded my Corvette for a mobile home. Robbie was a nurse and worked in Temple, more than twenty miles from Stagecoach Mobile Home Park in Killeen. But we worked it out. Robbie caught a ride with a friend, and I used the family car as my recruiting car.

Our car was a 1970 Plymouth Duster without air-conditioning. This was okay during the winter months; however, during the summer, I remember the temperatures being as high 107 degrees. Also, upon my assignment to recruiting duty, [had a low enlisted evaluation data report score—83. Recruiters who were already assigned had scores of 120 or higher.

What I was not told was that they had study material and studied as a group for the test. The owner of the mobile home park where my home was parked was born and raised in Gatesville, Texas, so I asked him to take me around the small town just north of Fort Hood and introduce me to the town's people.

He was glad to help. First, he introduced me to the city manager and asked if there was free office space for an army recruiting station. The city manager had a storage space upstairs. He cleared it out and set up a desk. I told the substation commander in Killeen that I had set up a recruiting station in Gatesville and needed a telephone put in.

Since my assignment to recruiting duty, I had already enlisted two for the army. Somehow, a work order for a telephone was approved, and I was set up to canvass the areas around and about Fort Hood. Some days, I would work from 2 a.m. to 10 p.m. I would wake up and pick up an army applicant, then drive him to Dallas for enlistment and get back home as late as 10 p.m. A normal day often would be from 6 a.m. to 6 p.m.

An applicant had to be tested to qualify for enlistment. The nearest test site was Waco, fifty miles from the substation in Killeen. An applicant was picked up at 6 a.m., and paperwork for testing had to be completed. Sometimes, there would be as many as ten applicants who would be transported in a van assigned to the substation.

Testing normally started at 9 a.m. and was over at noon. Applicants who passed the test would be scheduled for physicals and given a date to be processed at Dallas, and then driven home.

In early February 1974, I drafted a six-page letter to the commanding general at the U. S. Army Recruiting Command Fort Sheridan, Illinois. The letter explained how Master Sergeant Butts and the incoming sergeant major of the Dallas District Recruiting Command had received me when I had first requested an assignment with Dallas. The letter also explained my reassignment from duty as an army recruiter from Del Rio to the Dallas District Recruiting Command with duty at the Temple Recruiting Station.

I told him the reason for reassignment was that Del Rio was a Spanish speaking area, and I did not speak Spanish. I also informed the commander how I had been deposited along I-35, fifty miles from Killeen when I had first requested an assignment to Dallas. However, this letter was not about my early experiences with the Dallas command; it was about signing an enlisted efficiency report after successfully being assigned to the command.

I had reported for duty with the Dallas district on the November 19, 1973. It was now February 11, 1974, time for my efficiency report. For more than three months. I had made and exceeded my assigned recruiting objective, with little or no support from the command. The last straw was that Master Sergeant Butts requested I sign a blank efficiency report. I told him I would not sign the report and would write the army recruiting command at Fort Sheridan, Illinois, explaining how I was received to this district and how I was asked to sign a blank efficiency report.

I explained to MSG Butts that I would like to stay at my assigned station because I had established a good rapport with the people and the schools and knew that I could further develop the assigned area to a high-producing area. He said only that he could not understand why I did not trust him to give me a fair report, and he would see me later.

I let SFC Campbell see the drafted copy of my letter to the commanding general, knowing that the contents of the letter would be leaked to MSG Butts. On February 28, 1974, I was called to the Temple recruiting station to meet with MSG Butts. He gave me a completed copy of my enlisted efficiency report to read and sign.

The report was perfect, except the rater's comment said, "At this time I do not consider SSG Montgomery as having 1st SG potential." I did not agree with that comment, however, with the report being perfect in every other area, I did not see how it could hurt my chances of being promoted to E7. I was also given study material for my enlisted evaluation data report.

In 1973, my score was 83, and in 1974, the score was 139. I was also given a 1972 six-passenger Ford without air conditioning as a recruiting car. In July of 1974, I was awarded the army Commendation Medal. And, finally, I made the list for promotion to E7. It would take some months before I could pin on the stripes and get paid for the promotion. I felt the promotion was about five years late, thinking back to Korea, when I worked in several E8 positions—a position equal to MSG Butts', who gave me such a hard time early on in my assignment to the Dallas district. I thought back to MSGs Jones and Prior, who were black men and E8s, working as intelligence and operations sergeants, respectively, as early as 1960, when I was in Korea as only an E6. But as

SFC Portwood (a white man) said, rank isn't the only thing; position counts for something, as I learned as a career counselor with the 163rd Military Intelligence Battalion—the best position I ever had as a soldier.

During June of 1974, Thad an assigned enlistment objective of four. I enlisted 28, seven hundred percent of the assigned objective, and a Dallas record. When one thinks of this, it would seem impossible, but the record speaks for itself. To do this, it takes almost an around-the-clock effort, getting maybe two hours of sleep a night, when one considers the District Recruiting Command being 150 miles from the recruiting station. That was in June of 1974, and I would bet the record still stands, if one would take the time to research it.

During my five-year assignment with the Dallas Recruiting Command, from November 19, 1973 through October 1978, I was always in the top one percent for production. In June of 1975, I was awarded the Meritorious Service Medal—the highest medal for administrative-type duty within in the enlisted ranks.

In November 1976, I was assigned as station commander for the Killeen recruiting station, with two assigned recruiters: SFC Corley and SFC Bacon, a Medal of Honor recipient. It was through SFC Bacon that I learned friend from my unit in Vietnam, Dwight Johnson, was also a Medal of Honor recipient and had been shot and killed in his hometown of Detroit.

Dwight was the third African American recipient to be awarded the Medal of Honor. I remember the day the news was received over my unit radio. It was in late October 1967; however, the citation on file states that it was January 15, 1968. I don't know how the dates got mixed up, but I remember what I was doing when the news came over my radio.

I was preparing my track to leave LZ English, a 1st cavalry area in the Bong-Son Plains and a free-fire zone to Pleiku, the Forth Infantry Division area. The news that Johnson was shot and killed brought back every action and interaction of the Vietnam experience. The one experience in the forefront of my mind was the massacre in Pleiku, after leaving a free-fire zone in the Bong Son Plains.

There were many times I did not agree with the body count being combat kills but thought them to be collateral kills. I had to record them as combat kills and report to higher headquarters. Company A 1ˢᵗ Battalion

69th Armor had a combat kill ratio of three hundred to one. I knew Johnson and have a copy of his citation for the Medal of That he had been shot and killed in his hometown, along with the way I was received into the recruiting command, made me think the second time on how loyal I could continue to be to the U.S. Army.

On November 3, 1978, I requested to be reassigned from my position as station commander of the Killen recruiting station. I also joined a local church because I felt I had a calling in my life and could only obey this calling through the divine inspiration of the Holy Spirit.

On July 26, 1978, I wrote the Department of the Army to review my official personnel file. I received an answer on August 16. I agreed with the review; however, I could not agree on the reason conditions at the unit level put me in those positions to have a less favorable evaluation than my white peers when I was outproducing them. Sometimes, when thinking about how the "Pleiku Massacre" came about, I think it was in reaction to an African American being awarded the Medal of Honor.

As the unit operations sergeant of Company A 1st Battalion 69th Armor, I received a letter of appreciation for being the most outstanding operations sergeant for an armor unit within the Republic of Vietnam from Captain William, the commander of Company A, who was the commander at the time of the award of the "President Unit Citation"? I remember how out of control some Company A tank crews were after we departed a free-fire zone to a controlled-fire zone.

With me being an African American, I was sometimes rendered incompetent to be an operations sergeant by white tank crews, after being in the position for almost a year and during the time of heavy contact in a free fire zone.

I finally made E7, after receiving poor or lesser evaluations than my white peers over most of a five-year period —until awards and medals and/or accommodations were based on production. When recruiting became a numbers game, my evaluation could only go one way and that was up. However, I feel my promotion was about five years late in coming. After resigning my position as the Killeen station commander, I was ordered by LTC Fenn, Jr., Dallas District Recruiting Command to undergo a psychological evaluation.

"Diagnostic Impression: No mental disorder. Summary and Recommendations: SFC Montgomery scored within normal limits on all psychological tests. His current adjustment difficulties at work seem to have been brought about by a combination of factors, primarily his non-selection for promotion to E8. He feels he has been highly productive and should be elevated to positions of increased responsibility. In summary, this case can best be resolved through opening lines of communications between SFC Montgomery and his command."

During 1978—when quality points were the factor—I had the highest rating within the command. However, I was not Recruiter of the Year. District Recruiter Commander LTC Fenn, Jr. decided to give the award to a white recruiter with the highest number of enlistments, when the award was based on quality enlistment. Later during the year, I understand LTC Fenn, Jr., was relieved of his duties as the Dallas district recruiting commander for not supporting the Equal Opportunity Program.

On December 15, 1978, I transferred laterally from Dallas District Recruiting Command to Oklahoma after 15 days' leave. Before departing the Dallas recruiting command, I was told I would be a station commander—a supervisory position, not on production, and I would have army-leased housing. However, upon being reviewed by the Oklahoma commander, I was told there was no leased housing, that as an E7, I was responsible for my own housing. I would, however, be given time to locate housing for my family.

I asked the commander if he had received an enlisted efficiency report on me, and he checked with his SGM and said they had not. I asked the commander if I could call the United States Army Recruiting Command because an enlisted member was not supposed to be transferred from one command to another without an EER. And the Dallas Recruiting Command told me I would have army housing. He said I could use the phone and gave me the number of the commanding general of the recruiting command. I called and was put on hold until the commanding general picked up the phone. I told him who I was and that I was transferred without an EER and was told I would have army housing by the Dallas District Recruiting Command, but upon arriving to my new duty station, I did not have an EER, nor was there army housing for me.

He said he would get my record and have his SGM call me back within 24 hours.

The Oklahoma commander asked that I return to his office the following day for the recruiting command sergeant major's call. He gave me directions to my new assigned recruiting station and asked that I go out and introduce myself to the recruiters assigned to the station. He said they were expecting me.

I found my way to the recruiting station and found four white recruiters. A husband and wife team and two other recruiters, all staff sergeants E6s, were waiting for me. The husband and wife were the top producers. I did not like the idea of a husband and wife team working out of the same station because I felt this was a disadvantage for the other recruiters assigned to the station. I spent the day at the recruiting station to get some feel of how my new recruiters would receive me.

My money was running low. After leaving the recruiting station, I checked into a motel and made a call to my sister Gloria and asked that their company, Johnson & Montgomery, extend me a loan of $1,500 to move my family to Oklahoma City. I gave her my telephone number at the motel and asked her to call me back between 8 p.m. and 10 pm.

I waited in my room for the call but did not receive one. About 10:30 p.m., I called her back and she said that they had not had the time to talk and asked if I could call her back the next day. I told her I would.

I could not sleep, thinking what the recruiting sergeant major (SGM) would tell me the following day. I hoped he would say I could not be reassigned without receiving an EER. The following morning, I reported in at the Oklahoma recruiting command and had a cup of coffee outside of the SGMs office.

I waited for about two hours. It was a little after 10 a.m. when the SGM called me into his office to accept the call from the USA Recruiting Command SGM. The SGM first congratulated me for sustaining such an outstanding recruiting record over the past five years. He said he was sorry about what I had been put through during the past few months. He said it was the commanding general's decision that I return to the Dallas recruiting command until I received an EER, and since the last EER I received was a special one; the command could not give an adverse EER within a six-month period.

I returned to Dallas and waited all day the first day to see the commander. Again, I had to put up in a motel without any assistance or per diem from the army. I waited all day the second day without seeing the commander. On February 9, I was called aside by a GS5, Ms. Lorraine Hoover. She asked if had I received my orders. I told her I had not. She gave me a copy and told me to report in to anyone within III Corps and Fort Hood because I was being set up to be AWOL by the commander LTC Fenn.

If I had not had witnesses of the commander's actions, there was no way I could believe that an active-duty LTC could stoop so low or prove to be an outright bigot. However, during FY 1978, I received many letters of appreciation from general officers without their endorsements. Based on my accomplishments during FY 1978, I should have been named the recruiter of the year; however, this honor was given to a white recruiter with lesser accomplishments.

Why the psychological evaluation during December 1978? On the third day, the district recruiting command. GM told me to go home until I received my orders, which would be mailed to me, or I would be called to report to an assigned command.

With my orders from Ms. Hoover secured, I reported in February to III Corps headquarters to a SFC Donald W. Jauch, who told me to contact First Sergeant (1SG) Marsh. I contacted 1SG Marsh and was told he did not have any orders on me assigning me to his organization. During the first week of March, I reported to SFC Jauch again about my orders, and he again directed me to 1SG Marsh, who said he had no orders for a SFC Julius P. Montgomery. I called 1SG Marsh from MSG Graves' office about my orders in early March and again was told he had no such orders.

Several days after calling 1SG Marsh's office from MSG Graves' office, I was called at my home and ordered to report to 1SG March's office in uniform. When I reported, there were several officers awaiting a major, a captain, an SGM, and me. The major, from the III Corps judge advocate general's office, was the first to ask me where I had been for the past 32 days.

I told him I had been at home when I was not trying to find out what unit I was assigned to within III Corps Fort Hood. I told him I had visited 1SG Marsh's office and was told they did not have orders assigning me to his unit. I told him I also visited SFC Jauch at III Corps Fort Hood and had him sign a copy of orders that Ms. Hoover had given me.

Ms. Hoover had told me to get it witnessed in writing that I made an attempt to sign in at III Corps Fort Hood. I told the major that I had my orders signed by SFC Jauch and by MSG Graves of the 1st cavalry. I said I had at-tempted to sign in at III Corps and Fort Hood several times, and was told there were no orders assigning me to Fort Hood.

I told the major that, during the past few months, LTC Fenn, the Dallas recruiting command commander, had had me undergo a psychological evaluation. He had tried to process me out of his command without an EER, and then tried to set me up to be AWOL, or in this case, a deserter because it had been over 32 days since I was assigned to a unit.

I told the major I wanted to see the III corps inspecting general (IG). I gave the major a copy of my orders witnessed by MSG Graves and SFC Jauch. And he said I had his permission to see the III Corps IG. Everyone in the room except 1SG Marsh and the JAG officer left the room without a word.

The JAG officer called the III Corps IG's office and told him he had a hot case that needed immediate attention. When I got to the III IG's office, he said he thought this was a case for the Department of the army IG and that he would get the army IG on the line and let me talk to him directly.

Once on the line with the army IG, I gave him a history of my assignment under LTC Fenn. He said he would pull my record and advise me once all the details were worked out. The III Corps IG told me to go home and wait for his call and that I would have temporary duty at Fort Hood until I could be reassigned to another duty station.

I was home two days when I got the call from the III Corps IG's office. I would have temporary duty as the NCO in charge of the Fort Hood Army Community Center. The center was a central location where soldiers processed in and out of Fort Hood, had ID cards and passports made, shipped hold baggage, and were received to the post by a welcoming committee. I was to handle all perceived problems within the center and find a solution. I was not at the center long before I got my permanent change of station orders.

Chapter 23

Germany Again

On March 27, 1979, I got my orders assigning me to Germany. On May 2, I received amended orders assigning me to the 2nd Battalion 92nd Field Artillery. I got a nice letter from Command Sergeant Major Floyd English welcoming me to the unit. My port call was from Charleston, South Carolina. I would take my 1965 Chevy El Camino, drive to Charleston, process my vehicle, and catch my flight out of Charleston to Frankfurt, Germany.

I was impressed. I had never been received into a unit so nicely. In fact, the word from the Sergeant Major was, "With your cooperation, we will be able to apply a little more of the "personal into personnel." I would be in the country on May 10.

Upon my arrival, SFC Rudy Garcia received me at the Frankfurt airport in an army sedan. I was taken to the NCO bachelor quarters in Giessen, Germany. I had only my army issue of clothing in my duffle bag, and carryon baggage containing two changes of civilian clothing. The NCO bachelor quarters were located about four miles from the unit, which was a good morning run. I would have to walk or run the four miles to my office collocated with 2nd Battalion, 92nd Field Artillery my parent unit, on Rivers Barracks at Giessen, Germany until I picked up my 1965 El Camino, which would not be in port for another month.

The El Camino was some car. I had redone the body and painted it with several coats of white lacquer. It had a 350-cubic-inch engine with a full race cam and could outrun almost anything on the road. I used it to pull my 16' "bass boat." I had driven it to Clermont, and it got more looks than my 1970 Corvette that I traded on my mobile home after I got married.

I enjoyed the El Camino more than I had enjoyed the Corvette. I was looking forward to running it on the German autobahn. The car would also be a good hook for first term enlistments. As when I was a career counselor with the 163rd Military Intelligence Battalion, I had my private parking area in front of my office. I also had a private parking area in front of my office with the 92nd Field Artillery, where I would park my El Camino.

The assignment to Germany with the 92nd was ideal, with one exception —I was away from my family. My office was co-located with two other career counselors and the concern chaplain. By then, I was also an ordained lay minister, so it was ideal to be co-located with the concern chaplain. Germany had a lay pastoral program, so I was allowed to pastor a congregation at the concern chapel.

Being a career counselor and a pastor went hand in hand. I was able to counsel the soldier and invite him to church at the same time. Being a pastor also gave me other advantages: I could use army transportation, like buses and vans, and buildings. I had pastoral clerical assistance for typing and reproducing Sunday programs, and making public announcements within the Giessen army community.

Monies taken up during Sunday morning services were ours to use for whatever program I selected to sponsor within the army community. Over and above all, lay pastors in Germany were able to communicate with churches within the United States and program guest speakers from churches, seminaries, and other religious organizations.

When I got the notification that my car was in port, army transportation was provided to port for me to pick up my car. I was so excited that I fail to check the water in my radiator. There is no speed limit on the autobahn, so when Thit it, I opened the Chevy up to about ninety miles an hour. About fifty miles from port, the engine ran hot and locked up on me.

I found some water along the autobahn and filled the radiator, but the car did not cool down for an hour or more. I finally got it started and made my way to the nearest town and found a farmer who gave me enough water to fill the engine block. I made it into Giessen; however, I knew the Chevy would never be the same.

The car ran, but it leaked oil and did not have the power it had before breaking down on the autobahn. From the outside, it was still impressive, but driving it was a letdown. I was really hurt.

The reenlistment program within the 92nd was on fire, and I got some means of appreciation from Commander LTC Whitmore monthly. However, I was having problems sleeping at night. I could not put LTC Fenn, the death of Johnson, and the Vietnam War behind me.

Sunday mornings were my finest hour. The congregation at the Rivers concern was about 150 members strong. There were three other ministers: Grant, Watson, and Wilson. After service, members of the congregation would normally invite us to Sunday dinner. Once or twice a month, we would dispatch a bus from the Giessen army depot and visit other congregations within Germany. Food would be served and things conducive to good fellowship would be promoted. Guest speakers and group discussions were common.

In August 1979, when the area conference was held at the Rivers Chapel in Giessen, I was the guest speaker. My topic was "and they spoke with other tongues" Acts 2:4. The message was well received and people were overjoyed. They were dancing and praising the Lord and the Holy Spirit. After service, we had dinner in the basement near my office. We had a wonderful time.

Another advantage of being a lay pastor was, we took all of the classes of the full-time chaplains. However, I had not decided if I wanted to stay in the army past twenty years, and I had not received an EER after leaving the Dallas Recruiting Command. If I was going to be promoted to E8, I needed an EER for that period.

On August 4, 1979, I wrote the Secretary of the army and told him I had not received an EER since leaving the Dallas recruiting command. On August 21, I got a letter stating that my request would receive a complete and impartial review, and I would be advised of the final decision as expeditiously as possible.

In October 1979, I took leave from Germany for several reasons. 1) I had not received my EER from LTC Fenn, and without an EER for that period, I could not make the 1980 E8 list. If I did not make the list, for sure, I would retire. I thought I stood a better chance of retiring by making my case at Fort Hood. 2) All my monthly pay went to my wife in Texas. I had asked her to mail me a money order for $125 to arrive in Germany on the first of the month, and I was not receiving the money order on time. 3) I wanted to make sure that all of my bills were up to date before retiring from the army. That was unlikely if I was not receiving the $125 a month. 4) With all I had gone through before going to Germany, I had a good case to ask the army for a reprieve in the form of a job subsequent to retirement, or disability if a job was not forthcoming.

Before departing Germany, I requested retirement after 20 years of service and asked Chaplain Ackley and Chaplain Batluck to write a supporting letter. In October 1979, I reported on sick call at Darnall Army Hospital, Fort Hood, Texas, and was treated as an outpatient for depression. I was assigned to Operational Support Battalion 13th COSCOM, Fort Hood, Texas.

As I suspected, my personal finances at home were in disarray. I considered divorce but decided against it because I already had enough on my plate. The doctor advised me for several months during my assignment to Fort Hood that I had an outstanding record, and the army felt I should return to Germany to work in my primary MOS. However, the doctor told the army I would be admitted as an inpatient if I received orders to return to Germany.

On March 10, 1980, I was admitted to Darnall Army Community Hospital as an inpatient for depression. The Honorable Marvin Leath of the House of Representatives intervened on my behalf to have all personal belongings returned from Germany to SFC Julius Montgomery.

Chapter 24

Retirement

I retired on September 1, 1980, after twenty years of service with the U.S. Army. By this time, my family consisted of my wife of eight years, a ten-year-old stepson, my six-year-old daughter, and my four-year-old son. I also had a thirteen-year-old foster daughter.

I did not attend my retirement ceremony. I had lost all respect for what just a few years prior I would have given my life up to defend. I did feel bad not returning to Germany because it was a good assignment. Commander LTC Whitmore was fair and allowed me to run my own reenlistment program.

I had had good rapport with the chaplains and the other lay ministers. In fact, I had been offered a larger congregation at a division-sized unit several miles from Giessen. I turned it down because 1) My car was not running very well, 2) I did not think I could devote the time to a larger congregation and have a good reenlistment program, and 3) I needed to come home to see what problems my wife was having.

Another lay minister from the Church of God and Christ took the congregation and, I understand, had great success. I chose to come home and retire.

The first job I took after retirement was with Central Texas College as a learning center instructor. I was assigned to Headquarters 1st Battalion, 8th Cavalry 1st Cavalry Division. In December 1980, the Department of the Army Inspecting General's office contacted me and offered me a job as a recruiting specialist. He stated that this was the reprieve I had asked for before my retirement.

I told the IG that I had not been retired for six months—the requirement to be employed by the government following active duty. The IG office told me that that requirement would be waved, and if I wanted the job, paperwork would be forwarded to me to get a physical at Fort Hood, and I would subsequently report to Fort Jackson, South Carolina, to be sworn in as a Department of the Army GS7; and my assignment would be with the Columbia South Carolina District Recruiting Command. I accepted the job. December 18, 1980, was my last day as the learning center instructor for the 1st Battalion 8th Cavalry.

I got an outstanding letter of appreciation from Commander LTC Kendall that said, in part, that my learning center was the standard against which other learning centers at Fort Hood were measured. Upon reporting to the Fort Jackson Civil Service Office, I was told I could not be sworn in as a GS7 because I had been out of the army for only three months.

I told the officer in charge that I was told I would get a waver for the other three months. He told me that there was no waver on file, and I would have to come back the following day, after he had looked into the matter. I asked the officer if I could leave my phone number so he could call me once the problem was straightened out. I was staying with a friend in Columbia. I gave him the phone number and returned to my friend's house, about five miles away from the civil service office.

The next day, about 2 p.m., the civil service office called me and told me the waver was approved and to report to the civil service office to be sworn in.

I was driving our new car—a 1980 Mazda that my wife had talked me into buying after I started work at Fort Hood as a learning center employee. After being sworn in, I was told to report to the Columbia District Recruiting Command, to Captain Hooper. Upon reporting to Captain Hooper, I learned that I would be working out of the Greenville area, possibly assigned to Clemson or Easley.

I drove 125 miles to Greenville and was told they did not have orders assigning me to their command, and until they did, to find some place to stay and get in contact in a couple of days. I said to myself, *This is Dallas all over again.* So, I got into my car, drove to Clemson, and met a fine gentleman who was eager to talk with me. We found that we had something in common. We both had a background in military intelligence.

He was in charge of housing for Clemson University and agreed to put me up free of charge in one of the apartments on the fourth floor of the university. I said I would check with Greenville and ask if they knew anything concerning my assignment to the area. They told me they had no orders assigning me to the Greenville area.

Finally, I told them I was going to Florida for the weekend and would check with them once I was back in the area. On my return, they accused me of leaving without permission. My response was, "Permission from whom?" According to Greenville, I had not been assigned to Greenville upon my departure to Florida for the weekend. Even though I accepted the job as a recruiting specialist on January 5, 1981, I had not yet been given an area of responsibility.

On or about January 12, 1981, another recruiting specialist and I were given orders to attend a recruiting course at Fort Benjamin Harrison, Indiana. Upon returning, I was told I would be assigned to Easley Recruiting Station, Easley, South Carolina, where SSG Hyche was the station commander and would be my immediate supervisor. I did not like the idea, being supervised by an E6—someone I outranked and had many more years of experience than, but this was something I could live with. I met SGT Brown, a clerk at the Greenville headquarters, who told me it was out that the Columbia Recruiting Command's objective was to "kick me out of recruiting and to destroy my reputation as a Department of the Army civilian" because I had caused many problems for the army recruiting command during my years of active duty.

Robbie called me and asked if she could fly to Indianapolis and meet me after I graduated from recruiting school. She wanted to ride back to Greenville with me and look for a house. I told her she could fly to Indianapolis, and we would take it easy riding back to the Greenville area. After graduation, I picked Robbie up at the Indianapolis airport, and we took a slow ride to Greenville.

We made several stops at motels and ate at good restaurants. It was a good winter trip in our new Mazda. It was like a second honeymoon, something we needed after the near break-up after Germany. Upon arriving at the Greenville area headquarters, I asked for some time off to look for a place to stay. I never knew it would be such a problem.

After meeting with several real estate agencies, I realized the Piedmonts of South Carolina was a very prejudiced area, and for a black man, it would be very hard to establish the necessary rapport to be an effective recruiter. And, if what Sergeant Brown said about the recruiting command were true, it would make it hard for me because of the problems I had caused during active duty.

I was becoming somewhat worried and wondered if I had made the right decision in accepting the job. Robbie and I spent three days looking for a house we could buy; however, for two reasons, it was almost impossible to find a reasonable deal. 1) The interest rate was at 20 percent. 2) The houses the agencies wanted to sell to blacks were not acceptable.

Finally, we gave up, and one of the real estate agents found me a place to stay —with her single son, who had a spare bedroom. Robbie caught a flight out of Greenville back to Texas.

I continued to look in the paper for a house we could lease with an option to buy, and found a house advertised as an "executive special." I called and made an appointment to see the house. The agent was on Bob Jones University's Board of Directors. Bob Jones has a national reputation for not accepting blacks and I think had something to prove. The house was located in an upper middle-class neighborhood and had 3,600 square feet of living area.

I was impressed only if I could afford the house. The agent said he wanted my family to have the house and would give me the bargain of my life. He would lease the house for just $500 per month. I accepted his offer.

I called Robbie and told her I had found a house and that she should attempt to rent our mobile home. She already had someone who wanted to rent our mobile home. So, the only thing left to do was make an arrangement to move from Texas to South Carolina. The army was obligated to one move after retirement, so our move would be free.

We had three cars: a 1978 Ford double cab F-150 pickup, a 1980 Mazda, and a 1970 VW. I would have to fly to Texas and drive one of the two cars that were still in Texas and sell the stuff we could or did not want to ship. We also had a John Deer tractor with trailer that we would sell. There was other stuff that we could leave with our neighbors and pick up later.

We made the trip from Texas by way of Florida. For the most part, the children traveled in the back of the improved camper on back of our F-150 Ford pickup. I drove the pickup, and Robbie drove the VW. The trip took three days, with a one-day layover in Florida. Two days after we arrived, the moving van with our household goods arrived.

The house was located in Taylors, South Carolina, a suburb of Greenville, and about eighteen miles from Easley, South Carolina, my assigned duty station. My job was to recruit for local reserve units and for the ROTC college program at Clemson University.

Chapter 25

Civilian Recruiter
(GS7 Recruiting Specialist)

Within the Greenville area were about six active reserve units and about the same number of recruiters recruiting for those units. Making the assigned objective should not have been a problem if the recruiter was given the cooperation necessary to do the job.

I was the recruiting specialist assigned to the area. Within the recruiting command, there was one recruiting specialist to about every fifty uniformed active-duty recruiters.

Leads about persons being discharged from active duty came down through the area headquarters. If these leads were given to each assigned recruiter, including the recruiting specialist, this would account for about half of the assigned recruiter's objective. However, if the leads were given to a select recruiter, it would give an advantage to the recruiter who got the lead. It was easy to overlook one recruiter in favor of another. There were two recruiting specialists assigned to the state of South Carolina: one in Charlestown and myself. From what I understood, the recruiting specialist assigned to Charlestown had no problems making his assigned objective because 1) he was white and 2) he was able to establish rapport with his assigned recruiting area.

In the up Piedmonts of South Carolina, where an African American had a hard time establishing rapport to begin with, it was almost impossible to make an assigned objective without leads from area headquarters. During the three years that I was assigned to the Greenville area, I got no leads from area headquarters. And personnel assigned to the six reserved units did not cooperate with me.

I think everyone from the commanding general, who lived in my neighborhood, to the lowest technician assigned to the six reserve units knew me and worked to see me fail—something I had never done during 21 years of active duty.

You would think I should have given up the fight, but I would never give up. However, this assignment looked like it could be my first failure in my life. I thought of the white foreman in my hometown of Clermont, who I stood up to with my pruning knife, the big Mississippian whose ass I kicked in basic training, and the assignments I had on active duty that were above my pay grade that I was successful at. lost many hours of sleep and even had nightmares because of the obstacles placed in my path, but I hope this book can be an example to someone else pressed to fight the good fight and never give up.

From the outside looking in, one would think I had a good job. I had an assigned automobile. I could wear a suit and tie if I so chose, and for all practical purposes, I worked from 9-5, an average eight-hour day. However, within the reserve units and the ROTC program I was assigned to recruit for, almost no one would talk to me. I was the "transparent nigger" in the government car who was seen in the hill country of South Carolina wearing a tie. These towns included Walhalla, Seneca, Clemson, Pendleton, Westminster, Easley, and Pickens, South Carolina. The few African Americans I saw in these areas were mostly subservient and "knew their place." The employment in the area was logging, sawmills, and textile mills. I was employed and assigned to work this area on December 1, 1980, and was assigned my first recruiting objective in February 1981.

I resigned my position as a recruiting specialist on September 3, 1983 after the two years and ten months in the Piedmonts of South Carolina. I never made my assigned recruiting objective. While still on active duty, I had graduated from the recruiting and career counseling course on August 17, 1971. I was assigned my first objective on December 3, 1971 and my last objective on active duty in December 1979, eight years later.

I never missed an assigned objective while on active duty. In fact, I had had a lifetime recruiting average of 167 percent. But I knew every pastor, active-duty career-counselor, high school counselor, ROTC counselor, and even all the pimps and prostitutes in the area. At this point, the question was why had I not been able to meet my objective as a civilian recruiting specialist as well? The answer is simple: I was not able to establish rapport within my assigned area.

On June 15, 1983, I went to see Doctor Joseph J. Nannarello at the Department of the Army Federal Building in Greenville. Diagnosis: 1) Depressive disorder, 2) Paranoia. The recommendation was for me to take a two-month leave of absence from my job.

On June 23, 1983, Greenville area commander Captain Harold E. Neal, Jr. requested that I undergo a psychiatric evaluation again. This time, the doctor was Dr. Perry Irvine Lupo. Here is what he wrote:

"Mr. Montgomery is a 42-year-old, married black male seen for evaluation on 7-21-83 and for a follow-up visit on 8-05-83. The patient began by stating that his problems began in 1978, when he was on active duty as a recruiter in the service, when he began 'having problems with recruiting command.' He reported at that time the commander had him undergo psychiatric evaluation and that it 'found no psychiatric illness.' Apparently, from that time he was later assigned to Germany and came back to the States. He was on active duty until September 1, 1980, and since that time, there have been numerous problems, which Mr. Montgomery went into great detail about and brought a volume of information in letters that he had compiled. I reviewed these as well as the material sent to me by the civilian personnel office. Dr. Nannarello at the Veteran's Administration Outpatient Clinic in Greenville has also seen Mr. Montgomery, and I believe you have copies of these records, which I have also reviewed. Apparently, he began going to the VA in the early part of the summer of 1983 and was diagnosed by Dr. Nannarello as having Depression and Paranoia to the point he was given a two-month leave of absence from work. At the time I saw Mr. Montgomery, he had not returned to work. He reported to me that he had learned that the office and personnel in this area had already been prejudiced against him prior to his even coming to this area. He has found this area to be very prejudiced. He is unable to work with the personnel here and therefore has not been able to meet his requirements.

"I believe you are already aware of his claims about the situation here as described in Dr. Nannerello's evaluation as well as letters he has written to your various offices.

"Mental status at the time of evaluation shows the patient to be a welldeveloped, well-nourished black male who appeared his stated age. He was appropriately groomed on both occasions. He is very verbal and cooperative. Affect was not inappropriate. Thought processes were logical and goal directed. There did seem to be the evidence of paranoia, which was only in relation to the job situation, the personnel there, and this part of the country. Other than in that realm, testing appeared to be intact. Due to the paranoia, judgment and insight could be said to be impaired.

"Briefly, the patient is from Florida. He grew up in a fairly large family. There was a good deal of racial prejudice in the area he grew up in, according to him. His mother, on a number of occasions, warned him to stay out of trouble with white people. Apparently, there is a lot of competition between he and his brothers. He joined the service and apparently for a number of years did real well and became one of the top recruiters. Apparently, his problems began as he states back in 1978. 1) A friend from Vietnam who was the 3rd black to win the Medal of Honor was shot and killed in Detroit. And 2) The prejudice of LTC Fenn of the Dallas Recruiting Command. And I would judge from the volume of information from your office as well as these letters, etc., that he has compiled that this has been an ongoing problem since that time.

"He apparently draws a small amount of disability from the service as well as his retirement pay. From these two interviews with Mr. Montgomery, I would agree with Dr. Nannarello on the diagnosis of Depression, Depressive Neurosis, and Paranoia. The paranoia seems to be fairly well encapsulated and not generalized to all situations. Most of these seem to be related to the service, the civilian recruiting jobs, and this part of the country. As far as defense mechanisms, he seems to use denial, projection, a good deal of intellectualizations, and rationalizing. In my opinion, as the situation stands, and apparently has been over the four—five years, I do not feel that Mr. Montgomery is able to work in his present capacity or in other words he is disabled to work in his present capacity."

My depression was full-blown. I was seeing a doctor two times a week and was on medication, but I still had crying spells, and it was hard to get started in the morning. However, I knew [had to get started. Our children were four to seventeen. We still had two cars; we had sold the VW to one of our real estate agents, so we had the 1978 super cab pickup and the 1980 Mazda.

Our renters in Texas had moved on, so I had to go to Texas and try to sell the property or fix it up for rent. I took the pickup with my foster daughter's husband to help me move some of the things I had around the place to a friend's house. Upon arriving in Texas, I had real serious problems with headaches, numbness on one side of my body, and crying spells.

It was so bad that I checked in at the army hospital. The doctor checked my vital signs, gave me some pills, and told me to check in with my doctor when I got back to Greenville. My son-in law and I moved all of the stuff out of our shed and around the mobile home. In other words, a cement mixer, mortar box, shovels, hoes, and so on, all over to my friend's house. He ran a large home for boys.

Chapter 26

Churches Organized To Assist (Cota)

After I resigned my position as a recruiting specialist, I founded a nonprofit in Greenville South Carolina in 1984—COTA (Churches Organized to Assist). Our objective was to assist young people by having them discover successful persons within the community (we would call the discovered persons "community heroes"). The student would write about the success of one person and post their composition in a special place in the public library. Subsequently, the student would find venues where the community hero would speak. These events would be used as community fundraisers, and these funds would be used as scholarships for participating students. We would recruit churches as venues for the organization's fundraising. The program would also act as a writing program for the participating student.

While working on a COTA program and cooking dinner for the kids, I left a burner on in the kitchen with a pot of fatback that I would add to some green beans for dinner. I forgot about the pot and left for the shop that was printing booklets for the COTA program, and when I returned, the house was in flames. More than $150,000 in damages was done to the house.

I was not employed, but I was a full time student at the University of South Carolina. The COTA program was just getting started, and there was no one to take it over for me, even with a six-member board of directors. Robbie was still working, but we had no clothes except those on our backs and only a small amount of money in the bank. Our neighbors raised about a thousand dollars for us, and we moved in with friends until we could find a place we could afford. Our friends were living in government-assisted housing, and the neighbors reported us to the housing authority. So we moved before we could find a good place to live.

The apartments we moved to were called Duckett's Apartments. From the outside, things looked fine, and even on the inside, the apartment looked okay. There were only two bedrooms, and we had six in our family. At night, the apartment came alive with roaches and rats.

The problem was I was not well enough to really sell the COTA program and needed some moral support until I was well again. But I needed money to support my family. I put in an application at the Lincoln, Mercury Honda dealership and was hired, as a car salesman I was successful and the pressure that I was under seemed to dissipate. In fact, it was like a new beginning. My average income as a car salesman was about $1,500 a week plus my army retirement. I was still a student at the university, and I was not attending class. However, I had good grades and should be able to pull out of the semester with an overall grade of C to maintain my VA check if I made all the finals.

My income was good; however, I did not have the time or support for the COTA program in Greenville. So, I thought after I finished the semester at the university, sold my property, and bought a house, we would find time for COTA. I would move COTA to Clermont, Florida, find a fundraiser, and give 100 percent to COTA.

I put the property on the market for $40,000, hoping I would get at least $25,000, and I would buy or lease a place in Greenville. I got an offer for $40,000 for the property shortly after I put it on the market; however, after the buyer looked at the property and did some investigating, they offered to pay off the property and give me $5,000. I agreed.

Two years after we bought a house in Greenville, I was still selling cars. All the old problems had also returned. I was seeing a doctor at the VA two times a week for what he said was depression. In fact, he said I had symptoms of posttraumatic stress disorder (PTSD). I had uncontrollable crying spells and was unable to sleep.

I talked to most of the leading pastors in Greenville, Columbia, and a great part of South Carolina about COTA and suggested using my mobile home as a headquarters. But no one wanted to sponsor a program that was outside the norms of their church. I thought if I could get one church to sponsor the program that other churches would follow. But the answer I got was, the church membership did not want to take on the responsibility of sponsoring students that they had to teach to read and write. In other words, the church did not feel that the students had the ability to write about the community patriarchs and matriarchs of their community.

My answer to this was that the student only had to put forth an effort. In fact, COTA would help the student by giving the student a workbook and guidelines to write about the community patriarchs and matriarchs. As a child, I had very little respect for my community; as an adult, when I looked at that same community, I see greatness. Our youth need to know what our parents, grandparents, and community leaders accomplished during the 20th century.

After the close of the semester at the university, I quit my job as a car salesman in Greenville, packed my car, and moved to Clermont, Florida, with the COTA program. I had less than a hundred dollars to my name. But I had faith. My greatest accomplishment as a person was accepting Christ as the leader in my life. This did not happen until I was past thirty years old.

As a young man, for the most part, I looked upon women as sex objects and nothing more. Programs such as COTA can change the way young men and women think of their community and themselves. When I think of my life, I see many personalities. Most were no good and self-fulfilling.

As a black man, I think I have led a life that could be beneficial especially to young black youths of today. I also feel that my life has seen great hardships that could have been avoided. I think the first step of avoiding pitfalls in life is to seek out good leadership. I don't think I did that in my early years. I think I was so afraid to trust anyone because of the options given to young black men. But now I can identify both with those who made better decisions than I had and those who made worse ones. My effort by writing this program was to offer an option to those who would accept it.

After reading this book, you know a lot about me. By this time, you should know if you would consider accepting a program, I have written to better one's station in life. I am 69 years old and have done most of the things that one would think a 69-year-old black American could have done with his life in America, especially in the American South.

I am married, with four children and fourteen grandchildren. By now, you know I served in the U.S. Army and as a Department of the Army civilian together accounting for about twenty-six years. The thing about the program I am offering is that it is a family program "PG." This memoir is about my life, and the program is about what you could do to better your station in life.

Patriarchies/Matriarchies Children's Fund was founded in Austin, Texas. In 1995, COTA (Churches Organized To Assist) was our hope that churches would support a youth programs where the youth of our community could write about the success of seniors and successful members of the community.

This was a hard sell in most communities; however, we did have some success in Florida and in Texas; but not enough success, and we thought a name change would enhance the success of the program, so we changed the name to Patriarchies/Matriarchies Children's Fund, aka Hero's. The objective of the program was the same.

At this point, I think your question should be why a total autobiography to ask one to participate in a community program. I thought you should know that I am no angel. I have had some successes and some failures. However, I am still standing. I want to point out some contacts the program has had starting from as early as 1988. The program made headlines in the *Orlando Sentinel* Sunday March 20, 1988 after establishing a learning center in Clermont, Florida.

The objective of the center was to research the Lake County black community and record their contributions in the learning center. Upon arriving in Florida, it took me only a few weeks to get a building and to organize a support unit to build the program. The program was also on the Greenville evening news. However, after fourteen months in Florida, fundraising was slow, but there was hope. Several ministers from the Greenville area were willing to offer their time. But my health was not getting any better.

Chapter 27

Hospitalization

In July 1988, my wife left South Carolina with our three young children. My older son was engaged to be married to a local girl, and stayed in South Carolina with me. I was so depressed that I was almost not able to get out of bed in the morning. The only food in the house was a sack of potatoes. For about a week, I lived off boiled potatoes and did not leave the house. There was still a question about COTA, the nonprofit I had started after I resigned from The Department of The Army as a recruiting specialist. After discussing it with the boards both in Florida and South Carolina, I agreed to be hospitalized at the VA Medical Center in Augusta, Georgia.

My stepson drove me to the hospital. I was so depressed; my crying was uncontrollable. In Augusta, at the VA medical center, I was assigned to a locked ward with bipolars, schizophrenics, the criminally insane, child molesters, and some very sick people. I was locked up for about two months, and then I was assigned to a halfway ward. Afterward the halfway ward, I was sent to a PTSD ward and put on lithium. I was hospitalized from July 1988— December 2, 1988.

My wife and children were already in Texas, my house was going into foreclosure, and I was looking for a buyer for the house. My neighbor knew the parents of Calvin Garnett, a basketball superstar (who was still in high school but would go from high school to professional basketball and become a instance multimillionaire). The Garnetts were looking for a house in my neighborhood, and agreed to buy mine. I was given time off from the PTSD ward in Augusta to travel to Greenville to close the deal on my house with the Garnetts and save the house from foreclosure and give me some instance cash to travel to Texas after I was discharged from the hospital.

On August 19, 1988, I wrote to Vice President George Bush after he accepted the Republican Party nomination for the office of president of the United States. The letter to the vice president explained in detail the problems I had from 1979-1988. I wrote again on November 5, 1988; however, he had already addressed my August 19 letter through Dr. Mark W. Wolcott.

Dr. Wolcott's letter read: "Your letter of August 19, 1988, addressed to Vice President George Bush, has been referred to our office for reply. Your letter clearly describes your hazardous military service and the psychological and personal difficulties you have experienced since that time.

"We are aware that you are currently in treatment at the Augusta Veterans Administration Medical Center and have spoken with your staff physician, Dr. Amarasinghe. We are encouraged by the progress you are making and urge you to continue to work with your therapists during this hospitalization and, after you are discharged, in outpatient care."

I was discharged to outpatient care in December 1988. My crying spells were now controlled through prescribed medication and therapy. After being discharged from the hospital, I moved to Austin to be close to my family. My wife had said she could not put up with my depression and wanted me to find a place of my own. I checked into a motel and discussed a possible separation. I told her I would be medically retired with an income in an amount that would support our family. There were now four children. My last son was born June 16, 1982, shortly after moving to South Carolina. I was medically retired in January 1989 with 100 percent disability. My medical retirement, social security and army retirement was close to $6K a month— more than enough to support my family. In February of 1989, I was reunited with my family in Austin, Texas.

Hoping to keep COTA vibrant, on March 5, 1991, I introduced the program to the president of Prairie View A&KM University as a possible tool for students to interact and identify patriarchs and matriarchs who had made local and national contributions. The university suggested that I invite other colleges into the program and write a grant to implement the program.

During the 1994 and 1995 school year, we established a club in Austin on the campus of Gordon A. Bailey Middle School with more than 25 members. The club members interacted with local military organizations, including members of the National Medal of Honor Society, Lyndon B. Johnson Library, Congressman Lloyd Doggett, and Colonel Carmine A. Vito, USAF Ret. and the first to fly a U2 spy plane over the Soviet Union.

On February 7, 1998, the Hero's Club unveiled "The Lyndon B. Johnson Patriarch Poster" at Givens Recreation Center. On October 30, 1999, those on the poster as community "heroes" were honored at Mt. Olive Baptist Church, as an "Affirmation of 20th Century Heroes." The guest speaker was Mr. Harry J. Middleton, author of *The White House Years*. He was the former speechwriter for President Lyndon B. Johnson and director of the LBJ Library and Museum.

I have needed help throughout my life, and for the most part, I received that help in one form or another. Being a black kid, things did not come easy. Being a black man, at times life seemed impossible, but I kept asking for help. Several times, I asked the president of the United States for help, and then the vice president. After 26 years of federal service, my help came in the form of 100 percent medical retirement.

APPENDIX

MEMORIAL OF DWIGHT H. JOHNSON

The first public program Hero's did in Texas was Memorial Day, May 29, 1995—a memorial service for Specialist 5 Dwight H. Johnson, a black Medal of Honor recipient. First, we called Dwight's hometown, Detroit, Michigan, and asked that the mayor do a proclamation. The answer was they would, and we offered to present a plaque to the mayor honoring Dwight. They said they were not really into medals of honor and did not know if the mayor would have the time to accept the plaque on the city's behalf. I flew to Detroit and was not able to get an appointment with the mayor. The proclamation was given to me in the hallway of city hall. I still have the plaque in the hope that at some future date, the sitting mayor will be honored to accept the Dwight H. Johnson Memorial Plaque.

Following is the program from the Dwight H. Johnson Memorial Service:

Silent Prayer……..………..……………………………….Congregation

Prelude…………………………………………………………Organist

Posting of the Colors…………............………… Alex Morales (Army Ret.)

Reading of the Scriptures…………..……Major Gary Offineer (Army Ret.)

Invocation……………………………Reverend Sterling Lands II, D.D.

Musical Selections………………………………………….……Choir

Eulogy: A Time to Mend ……………………………….…...Reverend J. Paul Montgomery, the Decease's Combat Unit

A Hero's Reflection……………..………………………….MSG Roy Benavidez (Army Ret.), Medal of Honor Recipient Presentation of the Memorial Plaque. MSG Roy Benavidez (Army Ret.) and Reverend Raphael Smith, D.D.

Recessional: "Battle Hymn of the Republic"……………….Congregation

Postlude…………..…………………………………………….Organist

The Eulogy: "A Time to Mend?"……………………….....Rev. J. Paul Montgomery (member of the deceased's combat unit)

> To mend: To set something right which has been wrong.
> Text: Ecclesiastes 3, Romans 12, Eccl. 4-9:
> "A time to weep, and a time to laugh;
> A time to grieve and a time to dance;
> A time for scattering stones, and a time for gathering stones together;
> A time to embrace and a time to refrain from embracing
> A time to find; and a time to lose;
> A time for keeping, and a time for throwing away;
> A time to tear, and a time to repair;
> A time to be quiet, and a time to speak up;
> A time for loving, and a time for hating;
> A time for war, and a time for peace;

"What does one get by doing the right thing at the right time? Romans 12:1 says that we should present our bodies as a living sacrifice, to be used by God, and we should not look for a great return. To present one's body as a living sacrifice is the right thing to do.

"Does not a soldier do just that? He presents his body as a living sacrifice, for the betterment of his country, and for the most part, he asks little in return. The Book of Ecclesiastes tells us our greatest return from God is through our works, for our works and abilities are God's gifts to us.

"Today we are here to honor our fallen heroes—those who, in fact, presented themselves as living sacrifices. Those who did great works, and for most part, did so because they too felt it was the right thing to do.

"In particular, today, we want to honor heroes who have gone above and beyond the call of duty—Medal of Honor recipients. The Medal of Honor was first presented in 1863, during the Civil War. Sixteen free blacks were recipients of the highest honor during that war. After the Civil War (during the 20th Century), only four blacks to my knowledge received this highest honor. We will honor one of these four here today. We have tried to have representation here today across the racial spectrum of America, for all races of Americans fought together, and many died together.

"I am reminded today of a warm August morning in Fort Sill, Oklahoma. I was a 21-year-old soldier. My battalion was in training for an overseas assignment to Germany. Preparations included our becoming refamiliarized with our personal weapons. After a march of about ten miles to the rifle range, we found the range in a bad state of repair. After removing the covers from the prefabricated foxholes, we found webs! Within these webs were deadly black widows, hundreds of them, as if they had taken over the range due to its poor state of repair, or because the range had not been used for such a long time.

"In these webs, we also saw the skeletons of various insects. The black widows had sucked the life out of the insects and left only skeletons hanging in their places. On that warm summer morning at Fort Sill, Oklahoma, we had to call off target practice and call on the post engineers to come out and exterminate the black widows within those deadly webs.

"In many cases, when soldiers have returned from war, they come from having presented their body as living sacrifices. They come home and find that they, too, are caught up in deadly webs. While in this deadly entanglement, the innermost parts of their beings are sucked until only a skeleton remains in place. They become numb, with little or no feeling. They come to have little or no concern for self or family.

They become drug or alcohol dependent. They become a nuisance to our fast-paced American society. And, too often, those who have offered their bodies as living sacrifices are pushed to the point of taking their own lives. This seems like a better reward, after having offered themselves so completely as living sacrifices.

"America, we can do better, and must do better. For America, if you look around, you can see the fruit of their work and their sacrifice. It is called freedom. It is schools and universities. It is the home in the suburbs. It is called "The American Dream."

"Verse 16 of Ecclesiastes 3 reads, 'and moreover, I saw under the sun that in the place of justice, that wickedness was there; and in the place of righteousness, that inequity was there.' I submit that the government and the churches have shown little compassion for soldiers who have gone to distant lands to sacrifice themselves with the best of interests of the church and government in mind. Today, we can also say that the compassion which has been shown has come too late for many, for those who have been left as skeletons hanging in the black widow's webs, or those who have been pushed to the point of suicide.

"Ecclesiastes 3:22 reads, 'Wherefore, I perceive that there is nothing better than that a man should rejoice in his own works; for that is his portion.' If you find it possible to consider the soldier today, I pray that you would understand the work these soldiers wrought through blood, sweat, and tears, and that you would allow the soldiers or their loved ones to have their portion. They have earned it, and it is their gift from God. The scripture asks, 'for who shall bring them to see what shall be after them?' We, as men and as women, should enjoy whatever gift God has given us. This is all that we have.

"The Bible tells us that God gave us ability, in other words, our works, and that there is no greater enjoyment. In Romans 12:6, we read, 'Having then gifts differing according to the grace that is given to us, prophecy according to the proportion of faith.' In other words, let each of us be compassionate toward the rest, based on whatever gift God has given to us. Consider what part your works play in our communities, and consider also how another helps you. It is time for mending in every facet of our society. We can only mend by working together, and helping one another.

"SP5 Dwight H. Johnson had many talents. He was an outstanding soldier. He was agile. He used his agility to defend and rescue fellow soldiers. He was a quick thinker. He used this skill to overcome almost insurmountable odds and bring a dire situation under control. He was caring. He used this gift to carry others to safety in most dangerous conditions. Now, we remember and honor him. He is an example to all. "With this example before us, we should start a new day. We should give freely of ourselves as God has given to us freely our different gifts. With our gifts, we should mend those things that we find broken within our society, and through this giving of ourselves, we will enjoy the gifts from God, who made the heavens and earth."

****

HERO'S IN SCHOOLS

—Patriarchies/Matriar' Children's Fund (Akahero's)

During the 2001-2002 school year, the program was offered to the Austin Independent School District in Austin, Texas, as an after-school program. The program was short of personnel and was only able to be placed in one school—Kealing Middle School. Quick facts about the program: 1) Confidence builder 2) Provides instructor for program 3) Serves grades 6-12, 4) ten students per class 5) 30–60-minute sessions 6) Suited for 4-, 6-, or 8-week session 7) Ideal for a classroom 8) $7.50 per session per student.9) Description: This program is about finding heroes within your own community and finding ways to interact with each hero in a positive environment. 10) Objectives/Academic Area Emphasized: Building confidence. 11) References: Available Upon Request. 12) Previous School District Experiences: Gordon A. Bailey Middle School during the 1994—1995 school year.

The students interacted with the following community heroes: Harry J. Middleton (Director LBJ Library), Mrs. Robbie Alexander (Matriarch of Mt. Olive Baptist Church), and Mr. Chester Watson (Patriarch of Mt. Olive Baptist Church). Finding and recognizing our patriarchs and matriarchs is the first step in building a support system between our communities. In other words, colleges, universities, government, nonprofit organizations, and the corporate community must be involved in establishing a strong support system for our community youths, grades 1-12.

Other recognition programs to follow will be a program to recognize siblings of our patriarchs and matriarchs. These siblings may be recruited from corporate, labor, government, entertainment, sports, and other communities who agree to support our patriarchs and matriarchs programs.

The youth of our communities in grade 1-12 will now come together using the patriarch and matriarch and siblings to construct an adopted community family tree.

This family tree, made up from a wide spectrum of our demographics, including our government, sports, corporate, labor, and other communities, will work together to ensure our children the best possible chance of being all they can be.

Be a part of this initiative by signing up and supporting Patriarchies/ Matriarchies Children Fund, Inc., aka Hero's.

The following list of names shows some of the early community personnel who have asked to sign up to being community heroes. Most have biographies filed in the local library:

1) The Honorable Wilhelmina Ruth Fitzgerald Delco—Former Texas State Representative

2) Former Attorney General Dan Morales—Former State Attorney General

3) Former Councilman Willie Lewis— Former City Councilman

4) Former Chief Michael C. McDonald—Former Asst. Chief of Police

5) Former Mayor Gustavo L. Garcia—Former Mayor

6) Mr. Charles W. Gates—Director of Aviation

7) Former Sheriff Margo L. Frasier—Former County Sheriff

8) Judge Brenda Kennedy—Judge

9) Representative Dawnna Dukes—Texas State Representative

10) Senator Rodney Ellis—State Senate

11) Lt. Gen John Q. Taylor King, Sr., Ph.D.—Chancellor and President Emeritus of Huston Tillotson University

12) The late Rev. Raphael C. Smith, DD—Former Pastor Mt. Olive Baptist Church

13) Elder Sylvester Copeland—Former Pastor P.E.H.C. Copperas Cove, Texas

14) Pastor Kennedy Young—Pastor Olivet Baptist Church

15) Dr. Grant Coffman—Founder Olivet Bible institute

16) Mrs. Fairy Chism Barlow— Olivet Baptist Church

17) Mrs. Betty Meshack Mann— Olivet Baptist Church

18) Pastor J. Townsend —Peaceful St. James Baptist Church

19) Mrs. J. Townsend — Peaceful St. James Baptist Church

20) Mrs. Brenda Johnson—Olivet Baptist Church

21) Mr. Chester Watson—Mt. Olive Baptist Church

22) Mrs. Robbie Alexander—Mt. Olive Baptist Church

23) Mr. Harry J. Middleton—Former Director L.B.J. Library

When a person agrees to be a hero of Patriarchs/Matriarchs Children's Fund, a book, preferably a biography or autobiography of the Twentieth Century will be placed in a special place in the library in the name of the "community hero/matriarch or patriarch." These books will become topic of discussions in the "heroes book club" on Saturday mornings.

Our kids need help to be all they can be. This especially holds true for black kids. I hope this program attracts the attention of all our community.

J. Paul Montgomery's birthplace

The Montgomery's first rented house

J. Paul Montgomery as a young man

J. Paul Montgomery's nuclear family

Big Mama

J. Paul Montgomery's parents

8-inch Howitzer

8-inch gun emplacement in demilitarized zone in Korea

M48A3 tank used in Vietnam

Command post armored personnel carrier

J. Paul Montgomery at recruiting conference

J. Paul Montgomery with wife and children

Honor guard at Dwight H. Johnson's memorial

*Reverend Raphael Smith and Roy Benavidez
At Dwight H. Johnson's memorial*

ABOUT THE AUTHOR

J. Paul Montgomery was born in Clermont, Florida, to a large family that worked the orange groves. His vision of leaving his small town and becoming an airplane pilot led him to join the U.S. Army to make a better life for himself. After twenty-one years in the army and five years as a civilian recruiter, Montgomery became an ordained reverend and founded the nonprofit Churches Organized to Assist (later renamed to Patriarchies/Matriarchies Children's Fund, AKA Hero's) to expose black youth to community heroes and provide positive role models for them. As a disabled veteran, Montgomery is now retired. Married, with four children and fourteen grandchildren, he lives in Austin, Texas, with his wife Robbie.

www.ingramcontent.com/pod-product-compliance
Lightning Source LLC
LaVergne TN
LVHW010203070526
838199LV00062B/4476